TRAVEL, COMMUNICATION AND GEOGRAPHY IN LATE ANTIQUITY

Travel, Communication and Geography in Late Antiquity

Sacred and Profane

Edited by
LINDA ELLIS and FRANK L. KIDNER
San Francisco State University, California, USA

ASHGATE

Published by
Ashgate Publishing Limited
Gower House
Croft Road
Aldershot
Hants GU11 3HR
England

Ashgate Publishing Company
Suite 420
101 Cherry Street
Burlington
VT 05401-4405
USA

Ashgate website: http://www.ashgate.com

British Library Cataloguing in Publication Data
Travel, communication and geography in late antiquity : sacred and profane
    1.Travelers – Rome – History – To 1500 – Congresses 2.Communication – Rome –
    History – To 1500 – Congresses 3.Voyages and travels – Religious aspects – Christianity
    – Congresses 4.Christian pilgrims and pilgrimages – Social aspects – Rome – Congresses
    5.Christians – Rome – Correspondence – Congresses 6.Rome – Intellectual life –
    Congresses 7.Rome – Social conditions – Congresses 8.Rome – Historical geography –
    Congresses
    I. Ellis, Linda II. Kidner, Frank L.
    913.7'046

Library of Congress Cataloging-in-Publication Data
Travel, communication and geography in late antiquity : sacred and profane / edited by
    Linda Ellis and Frank L. Kidner
        p. cm.
        "The papers presented in this volume resulted from the fourth biennial conference on
    Shifting Frontiers in Late Antiquity, 'Travel, Communication, and Geography in Late
    Antiquity,' sponsored by San Francisco State University, March 8-11, 2001" –Preface.
        Includes bibliographical references and index.
        ISBN 0-7546-3535-X (hardback : alk. paper)
    1. Christian pilgrims and pilgrimages—Rome—Congresses. 2. Travel—Rome—
    Congresses. 3. Communication—Religious aspects—Christianity—History—Congresses
    4. Communication—Rome—Congresses. I.Ellis, Linda. II. Kidner, Frank L. III. San
    Francisco State University. IV. Biennial Conference on Shifting Frontiers in Late
    Antiquity (4th : 2001 : San Francisco State University)

    BV5067.T73 2004
    913—dc22

                                                                              2003060078
ISBN 0 7546 3535 X

Printed and bound in Great Britain by MPG Books Ltd, Bodmin, Cornwall

Contents

List of Figures

List of Contributors

Scott Bradbury
Department of Classical Languages
and Literatures
Smith College, Northampton, Mass.,
USA

Daniel Caner
Department of History
University of Connecticut, Storrs,
USA

Gillian Clark
Department of Classics
University of Bristol, UK

J. F. Drinkwater
Department of History
University of Nottingham, UK

Maribel Dietz
Department of History
Louisiana State University,
Baton Rouge, USA

Hugh Elton
Director, British Institute of
Archaeology at Ankara, Turkey

Cam Grey
Department of History
University of Chicago, USA

Ray Laurence
Director, Centre for Roman Studies
University of Reading, UK

Noel Lenski
Department of Classics
University of Colorado at Boulder,
USA

J. H. W. G. Liebeschuetz
Department of Classical and
Archaeological Studies
University of Nottingham, UK

Michele R. Salzman
Department of History
University of California, Riverside,
USA

Claire Sotinel
Ausonius Institut de Recherche sur
l'Antiquité et le Moyen-Age
University of Bordeaux, France

Edward Watts
Department of History
Indiana University, Bloomington,
USA

Preface

The papers presented in this volume resulted from the fourth biennial conference on Shifting Frontiers in Late Antiquity, 'Travel, Communication, and Geography in Late Antiquity', sponsored by San Francisco State University, March 8-11, 2001.

All abstracts submitted for conference participation were reviewed by the Editorial Board for the Society for Late Antiquity. Members of the board are: Gillian Clark (University of Bristol); John Drinkwater (University of Nottingham); Hugh Elton (British Institute of Archaeology at Ankara); Linda Jones Hall (St. Mary's College of Maryland); Jacqueline Long (Loyola University, Chicago); Ralph Mathisen (University of South Carolina); and Hagith S. Sivan (University of Kansas). The volume editors, who were also the conference organizers, wish the thank the board members for their considerable time and efforts not only for reviewing abstracts, but also for selecting papers and refining the content of this volume. We would like to thank John Drinkwater for agreeing to write an introduction on substantially short notice. Acknowledgement is also due to the anonymous reviewer, selected by Ashgate Publishing, for insightful commentary on the manuscript.

The editors also wish to acknowledge the following administrative offices and academic units at San Francisco State University whose generous funding made possible the sponsorship of this conference: Office of the Vice President and Provost; Office of the Dean, College of Behavioral and Social Sciences; Office of the Dean, College of Humanities; Department of History; and the Department of Classics. Gillian Clark gratefully acknowledges the support of the British Academy and the University of Bristol.

The editors could not have brought many aspects of this project to timely completion without the invaluable work of Christine Abadilla Fogarty, of the Museum Studies Program at San Francisco State University, who coordinated the conference registration logistics, designed and formatted the conference program, and compiled and formatted the entire manuscript for the publication of this volume. The photograph for the book cover was provided by Frank L. Kidner. Finally, we would like to thank the San Francisco Cable Car Museum for hosting *gratis* our conference reception.

Editors' Introduction

In recent years historians have increasingly insisted that Late Antiquity (c. 260 to c. 640) can no longer be viewed as a period of 'decline and fall' sandwiched between the Classical World and the Middle Ages. It was an age with its own distinctive political institutions, social structures, and economic, religious, and cultural life. Two of its central features were the construction after 260 of a centralized and increasingly intrusive late Roman state and the establishment of Christianity as the official religion of this state during the fourth century. Both State and Church rested on universalizing ideologies manifested in the first instance by the Imperial cult and in the second by the Biblical command to 'make disciples of all nations...'. The concrete institutionalization of these ideologies resulted in, among other things, a marked increase in long distance travel and the creation of new large-scale communication networks during the late antique period. Roads and sea lanes in Late Antiquity were crowded with travelers and news bearers of all sorts: military units, students, laborers, ecclesiastical couriers, private letter carriers, out-of-favor members of the Imperial family, monastics, and Christian pilgrims. The papers in this collection examine both the reasons for and the ramifications of this upsurge in travel and communication across the Empire.

The editors of this volume see geography, travel, and communication as interlocking aspects of one type of human experience and activity. In Late Antiquity, travel meant confrontation with land and sea. And land and sea often set limits to the times and places of travel. But geography is not only a physical fact, it is also a cultural construct and as such it can be imagined in different ways for a variety of purposes. For example, geography can be conceptualized as a 'sacred landscape' in order to address basic religious problems.

Travel and communication are also linked in complex ways. The link is obvious in cases where travelers carry letters or gifts from a sender to a recipient. But the link is also there when travel becomes a means by which people communicate something about their social selves and their values. In this case travel serves as an enacted metaphor for other things of importance. Thus, like geography, travel can be constructed culturally. Finally, the locus of travel, travel routes, can serve as the place where messages can be communicated to people by those either possessing or claiming authority in the world.

But what of those who could not or would not travel? In Late Antiquity, the next best thing was to send a letter. Like travel, letters were put to a wide variety of uses and served many purposes. Letters could be used to create networks that fostered the political and social ambitions of provincial elites engaged in the delicate to and fro of negotiation with the centralized authoritarian state. Letters could also serve to articulate, codify, and broadcast the social identity of those elites in a time of rapid social and religious change. They could also be used as vehicles that served as autobiographical statements aimed at contemporaries and posterity.

All of these aspects of geography, travel, and communication were at work in Late Antiquity and all are explored in the essays that follow. Together they constitute a rich collection of innovative scholarship on these aspects of Late Antiquity. In collecting and organizing the essays for this volume, we share the position, expressed by several participants in the Merida Conference on *East and West: Modes of Communication*, and summarized by Thomas Noble that 'Large entities, political, social or economic ones, can always be assembled from the tesserae of small spaces. But the tesserae alone are tangibly real and the large picture is an illusion, a suggestion of what reality might be like.'[1] Each of our essays sheds new light on aspects of the notable increase in travel and communication across the Late Roman world and thereby helps in the historical reconstruction of the larger wholes.

---

[1]Evangelos Chrysos and Ian Wood (eds.), *East and West: Modes of Communication. Proceedings of the First Plenary Conference at Merida* (Leiden: Brill, 1999) 277.

Introduction

And Up and Down the People Go

J. F. Drinkwater

It is not the aim of this collection of papers to offer a comprehensive treatment of travel and communication in Late Antiquity. Such a study would be necessarily long and, in places, potentially tedious, as all aspects of the topic were identified and pursued in depth. Here, rather, exempt from such obligations, we find a group of scholars able immediately to come to grips with what they see as characterizing the age in terms of the movement of people and information. They deal with aspects that especially interest them and which are the objects of their current research; and they are not afraid to propose novel, even controversial, and so stimulating views. Their contributions also allow them to signal what bigger ideas may be in the wind—in particular, it would seem, given the content of Part III of the volume, reconsideration and reinterpretation of what should be understood by *peregrinatio*, 'pilgrimage'.

The editors have given the papers a clear and logical order. However, as I have just indicated, in this Introduction I will not keep to this order and will not therefore produce a mechanical summary of its content. My intention is, instead, to give a quick impression of the volume, to establish some less obvious links and to make a few suggestions of my own, derived from what is said here. In this respect, I first have to say that for me the most striking aside of the volume—an observation that I have now pondered many times—occurs in Caner's study of the attractiveness of Sinai to monks and pious visitors. Clark later talks of 'spiritual tourists'. Caner touches on the damaging effect of such spiritual tourism on the society and economy of the indigenous pagan nomadic population of the region. This caused the 'natives' to attack the incomers, and the incomers to struggle to devise an intellectual strategy to help them make sense of such attacks and their dreadful consequences in the context of their faith in a beneficent Divine Providence. There is still a tendency for modern historians of Late Antiquity to join the 'winning side', i.e., to consider events from the perspective of the Christians, which in this case means from that of the pilgrims. However, in this instance I cannot help but feel that the 'natives' had a good deal of right on their side. It must have been extremely unpleasant to see one's ancestral land turned into what, to deploy an anachronism, might be termed a Christian theme-park, 'The Mount Sinai Experience'. I wonder what a study of this development from the Saracens' point of view might yield.

Throughout the volume there runs the assumption that travel and communication were more frequent under the Late Empire than in any preceding period of Classical Antiquity. Such a view has a long and distinguished pedigree. It was expressed very elegantly, for example, by John Matthews in his description of the activity generated by an increasingly complex imperial administrative system, and the demands made on rulers to appear closer to their subjects: 'By the increase in the "incidence" of government, by the multiplication of the imperial office, and by their own willingness to travel the frontiers of the empire ... the late emperors offered to their subjects that personal concern and "presence" ... to which panegyrists of the early fourth century attached particular importance' (*The Roman Empire of Ammianus*, 1989, 254). Here the point is made explicitly by Bradbury in respect of the pagan provincial aristocracy of the Greek East, striving to preserve its position in a region unbalanced by the creation of an imperial capital at Constantinople. Alongside politico-military and civil movement was, of course, that involving the Church, as bishops strove to manage its increasingly complex affairs between themselves or were summoned by emperors to synods and councils, and as less senior Christians left home in an effort to distance themselves from their ordinary lives and to draw nearer to God: so we return to *peregrinatio*. The impression of increased and, as it would seem, 'anxious' movement in this period is surely correct. However, my feeling is that it would be gratifying to see it methodically tested and nuanced with, say, direct attention being given to establishing the likely level of travel and communication during the High Empire as a reliable measure of comparison, and with closer consideration of likely contemporary irregularities, and perhaps even voids, in such activities. In short, was this increase in travel and communication a general phenomenon and, if not, why not, and with what result? For example, the conditions reconstructed by Watts in respect of travel for academic purposes in the East could hardly have been replicated in full in the West, especially in Britain. Here, as far as we know, there was not even one school of rhetoric to keep local students and teachers on the island, to attract others from outside and, generally, to keep the place firmly within the sphere of Greco-Roman life. Britain's lack of links with the wider Empire must surely have contributed to its withdrawal from imperial life in the fifth century and its subsequent adoption of basically Germanic culture and language.

For people to travel and communicate there must exist the means of travel and communication. In Antiquity, this meant routes by land or sea. Mention of sea-travel occurs where one might expect it, for example in Watts' reference to voyages between Alexandria and mainland Greece. However, the main impression given by contributors such as Bradbury, Sotinel and, especially, Elton (who demonstrates closely how appreciation of the Cilician road-network allows reconstruction of otherwise unknown details of major military campaigns in the province) is of the continuing overriding importance of travel by land. Late Antiquity was not a society with salt in its veins, poised to venture into the Atlantic. But its commitment to roads remained strong. Laurence shows, from the study of milestones, how long-lived Roman main roads were, thanks to constant maintenance. In Italy, indeed, such regard and maintenance may even be traced from the imperial into the post-imperial period, thanks to rulers, both emperors and kings, who realized that such activity projected a comforting image of the continuation of traditional order, particularly in times of political change. Laurence also stresses the role of milestones as the media of this propaganda—a means of communication in their own right, like coins, though in their case the user had to come to them, rather than they to the user. So, returning to the short quotation from Tennyson's *Lady of Shalott* which forms the title of this Introduction, 'Up and down the people go', it takes little to imagine what a modern traffic census might have detected on late imperial roads: emperors (ever on move), armies, administrators, envoys, ecclesiastics, academics (students and faculty), landowners, traders, pilgrims, and invaders. A number of these categories are picked up by contributors; some are noticed and discussed, some just noticed. Some, however, it has to be said, are ignored (Elton refers to Persian attacks, but elsewhere there is no real treatment of barbarian invaders); and yet— which again points up the strength and joy of a volume such as this—some are dealt with who are not on the list. Thus, from social extremes, we find Grey's western agricultural workers (possibly skilled craftsmen, but hardly the movers and shakers for whom Laurence's milestones were intended), and Lenski's proposed eastern refugee empresses (movers and shakers indeed, but now fleeing imperial power-centers that had become too dangerous for them). (It should be noted that both Grey and Lenski dramatically point up something of the flexibility of late Roman society, in demonstrating the opportunities for change and advancement—or, at least, survival—that could be available to the lower classes and to wealthy women. Opportunities for women are also noted by Dietz.

Also somewhat surprising is contributors' identification of a certain dislike of travel even (perhaps especially) on the part those who were not threatened and had the means to afford the best conveyances and accommodation: Bradbury's Libanius, Salzman's Symmachus and Clark's Augustine. (Indeed, after reading Salzman on Symmachus' complaints in this respect, one is bound to think that his is a classic case of 'travel narrowing the mind'.) On the other hand, which perhaps ought to have been taken more into account in this, the picture may be distorted by the conventions of ancient rhetoric and aristocratic mores. Salzman notes that Symmachus must have traveled farther than his letters indicate, if only to manage his extensive estates. We may, therefore, simply be in the presence of genteel grumbling intended to demonstrate respect for aristocratic *otium*, and so producing a (perhaps nominal) disdain for stresses and strains of travel necessary for *negotium*, whether on private or on public business. Whatever, the new interpretation of pilgrimage, touched on above, seems connected in some way to professed dislike of travel. The argument seems to be that we must eschew anachronism, and not regard late antique pilgrimage as being much the same as its late-medieval successor—not familiar, cosy, 'Chaucerian', but something much more novel, and much harsher, allowing it to be exploited for ascetic purposes. This is argued strongly by Dietz, who sees pilgrimage as originating in a sort of itinerant monasticism, with the journey mattering more than the destination. It is also taken up by Clark in her study of the use of *peregrinus* and its derivatives by St. Augustine. Examining the Classical meaning of the word, and its reinforcement by later Neoplatonist writers, she shows how *peregrinatio* may be understood as characterizing the person who undertook it as being a stranger in a strange land. Augustine's vocabulary was strongly affected by both Classical and Neoplatonist traditions, so in his texts 'pilgrimage' can be interpreted either in the standard way or, much more darkly, as a going away, an undertaking of a sojourn in an alien place. This sojourn is necessary, stimulating and illuminating, but essentially uncomfortable and thankfully only temporary. The idea is applicable, as in Augustine's own career, to real travel, but may also be used metaphorically, of a life or of a religious or intellectual formation spent—whether travelling or not—distant from God. The Church, too, may in this way be seen as a pilgrim adrift in the sublunary world. The concept and consequences of the harshness of travel are, it seems to me, also picked up to some degree by Lenski, whose four imperial ladies (Helena, Eutropia, Aelia Eudocia and Eudocia, wife of Huneric) move only because they have to. That they end up in the Holy Land is secondary: again, distance matters more than destination. However, ironically, one of the major results of their travelling and of their reconstruction of their social position and their identities was yet another Christian theme-park, this time 'the Jerusalem Experience', the development of which (Dietz's monasteries and *xenodocia*) made travel somewhat easier for others and so must have helped to institutionalize ascetic pilgrimage. Very similar hardship is also central to Caner's argument: the travails and dangers of Sinai pilgrimage are unavoidable, and must be borne to gain God's grace.

Very different from the preceding is, at the heart of the book, the section dedicated to epistolary networks. Letter-writing was, of course, of great importance to late antique culture and since the publication of Samuel Dill's *Roman Society in the Last Century of the Western Empire* (1905) historians have given due consideration to its products. In particular, it is now recognized that the exquisite triviality of many of these fulfilled an essential social function—that of advertising both writer and recipient as the 'right' people and, through an epistolary 'old boys' net', ensuring that the 'right people' stayed in control. As Salzman puts it, 'The representation of self was a key motivation'. Bradbury touches on the dire consequences of failing to gain entry into or falling out of this magic circle, in noticing how difficult it was for 'poor boys' to obtain posts in the imperial administration. (All this may strike us as odd but, in terms of communication, when first drafting these words I found myself musing on the cultural and social significance of modern university-teachers' insisting on students' writing grammatically, and spelling and punctuating correctly.) Yet clearly there must have been more to these letters than their being just Dill's elaborate 'visiting cards' (1905, 153). They could and did contain matters of substance: as Bradbury and Grey show, letters of recommendation could not have been more important to the people who carried them, from young nobles to a range of agricultural workers. However, I have always felt that even this can be only part of the story. There must always have been 'real' news—military, political, fiscal, economic—which the political nation of the Empire needed to know. How did it circulate? Presumably by word of mouth, carried by the bearers of 'ordinary' letters, but surely also in secret correspondence, which has not survived. Hints of the existence of lost 'shadow' letter collections are to be found in the sources, for example in Ammianus' account (20.8.2-18) of Julian's two letters defending to Constantius II, defending his usurpation, one public and fairly reasonable and conciliatory, the other confidential and 'written in a more reproachful and bitter tone'. I feel that we may see the same suggested by Liebeschuetz's study of the correspondence of bishop Ambrose of Milan.

Liebeschuetz argues that Ambrose's should not be seen as just another fourth-century letter-collection. Rather, it was consciously modelled on that of Pliny the Younger; and, more, in preparing his Book 10, Ambrose took the idea of imperial correspondence much further than his model. This is because Ambrose's Book 10 comprises not so much letters as 'a series of dossiers', recording real events (e.g., the dispute over the Altar of Victory and the confrontation with well connected Arians in Milan) and attempting to shape future interpretation of these events for the benefit of the Church and of Ambrose's own reputation (the latter, as it turned out, very successfully). In other words, to use that ugly but powerful and extremely useful modern term, Ambrose intended to give this information the right 'spin'. However, my point here is that much of the material upon which the 'dossiers' were based must have been put into circulation earlier, contemporary with the events with which they deal, as authentic 'news'. What Liebeschuetz implies therefore fits in very nicely with Sotinel's observations on information 'as an indispensable tool for exercising power and control'. She demonstrates the importance of various types of ecclesiastical news, and how this news was carried to and from Rome to emperors in the east-along official routes rather different from those used by ordinary traders and pilgrims. Sotinel indeed suggests that such was the significance of this information that the imperial authorities may have insisted on routing it through Ravenna to give themselves greater power in controlling its dissemination. Overall, there is the hope that the treatment of Church news, because this news was regarded as being in some way different from secular news, may allow us to see how important 'real' intelligence may have been circulated.

PART ONE
ASPECTS OF SECULAR TRAVEL
IN LATE ANTIQUITY

Part One

Aspects of Secular Travel in Late Antiquity

Introduction

The four papers grouped in this section call attention to the many factors that shaped non-religious travel in the late antique world. Elton reminds us of the basic constraints that geography placed on state and military travel in this period. Watts discusses the way educational centers rose and fell during Late Antiquity and presents travel in terms of the relation of centers to peripheries, issues of interest in current scholarly discussion of the late antique world and its transformation. Cam Grey discusses evidence for the movement of rural laborers from one landlord's estate to another. Analysis of this kind of travel contributes to the ongoing reassessment of the juridical and economic status of the colonate in the Late Empire and the disparities between legal representations of the group and their actual condition 'on the ground'. Some of Grey's rural laborers traveled from estate to estate on roads. These roads are the subject of the last paper in this section. In it Ray Laurence discusses the multiple functions of milestones along the late antique road system. They not only measured distance for the traveler but also communicated a variety of state-sponsored messages to those who moved along the road system. Laurence thus call attention to an underutilized form of evidence drawn from late antique material culture that can help us to understand change in the political world. Laurence also emphasizes the communicative aspects of the milestone system and thus points to the second section of papers in this collection.

Chapter 1

Cilicia, Geography, and the Late Roman Empire

Hugh Elton

This paper shows how geography affected warfare in a predictable way in Cilicia, today the part of Turkey north of Cyprus. In the period covered here, the third to seventh centuries AD, two types of campaigns can be distinguished, those fought between two field armies in the plains and those between a field army and small forces defending positions in the mountains. These types of campaigns, rather than the nature of the opponents, i.e., Romans against Sassanids or Romans against Romans, determined the location of engagements. A subcategory of operations not considered is Roman actions against raiders, such as the Goths, Isaurians or Huns who plundered the region occasionally.[1]

Cilicia was surrounded by the Taurus and Amanus Mountains and access was confined to a few passes.[2] Interestingly, mountain passes were not good military barriers since the constricted space made deployment and maneuver difficult. Thus fighting in the pass itself was usually only carried out by heavily outnumbered forces who also ran the risk of being trapped by outflanking forces.[3] The classic example of this is the outflanking of the Spartan Leonidas at Thermopylae in 480 BC, but it is worth noting that Gauls broke through here against the Phocians in 289 BC, and that Cato turned Antiochus III's flank at the same pass in 191 BC.[4] Even knowledge that a pass could be outflanked did not stop it happening. Other routes existed across the Taurus Mountains besides those discussed here, but these were tracks unsuitable for the passage of large armies, though often passable for raiders and flanking forces.

---

[1] Shaw, B.D., 'Bandit Highlands and Lowland Peace: the Mountains of Cilicia-Isauria', *Journal of the Economic and Social History of the Orient* 33 (1990), 199-233, 237-270; Syme, R., 'The Subjugation of Mountain Zones', *Roman Papers* 5 (Oxford, 1988), 648-660.

[2] For an introduction to the geography of the region, Admiralty Handbook, Naval Intelligence Division, *Turkey*, 2 volumes (London, 1942-1943); Mutafian, C., *La Cilicie au carrefour des empires* (Paris, 1988), 2 vols.; Hild, F. and Hellenkemper, H., *Tabula Imperii Byzantini V: Kilikien und Isaurien* (Vienna, 1990).

[3] Clausewitz, C. Von, *On War*, ed. Howard, M. and Paret, P., (Princeton, 1976), 6.15-17, 7.11.

[4] Herodotus 7.213-218; Pausanias 10.22; Plutarch, *Cato* 13.

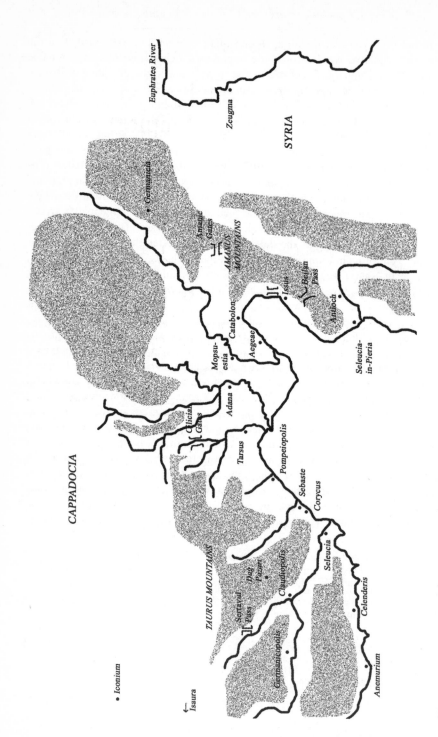

Figure 1.1 Cicilia in Late Antiquity. Courtesy Hugh Elton

In the first type of campaign, those fought between two field armies in the plains, the objective was to force the opponent's field army into an untenable position. These campaigns occurred between rival imperial candidates in Roman civil wars and in campaigns between Rome and Sassanid Persia. The campaigns were confined to major roads, usually the great military highway which ran through Cilicia and linked Constantinople to Antioch. The armies which fought these campaigns were large, often more than 30,000 strong, and were accompanied by enormous baggage trains with thousands of wagons and pack animals. Julian's army in Persia in 363 was four miles long on the march. The wheeled transport accompanying such armies, whether Roman or Sassanid, could rarely stray from major roads. Similarly, supplying these forces when they were on major roads was much easier.[5] In the second type of campaign, smaller armies attempted to besiege the enemy in their mountainous bases. To be besieged was never the primary strategy of the defenders, but was often the result of failure in an earlier battle fought along major roads in the lowlands. These campaigns only took place in Isauria, the mountainous western part of the region. They did not occur in the eastern lowlands of Cilicia or in the poorly urbanized eastern Taurus or Amanus. These principles together with an understanding of Cilician geography can be used to attempt to fill some gaps in the historical record.

The Sassanid Persian invasion of 260 shows some constraints that geography placed on the movement of armies, even without the presence of an opposing force. After a battle somewhere between Edessa and Carrhae, the Roman Emperor Valerian was captured and Sassanid armies drove west.[6] Much of our knowledge of this campaign comes from the Naqsh-I Rustam inscription erected by the Sassanid king Sapor, but the inscription says nothing about the route taken between the capture of Valerian and the Sassanid arrival in Cilicia.[7] Large armies could take two routes between Syria and Cilicia, both of which involved crossing the Amanus Mountains. The usual route was the military road, also used by pilgrims to the Holy Land.[8] One was in the south at the Syrian Gates, the modern Beilan Pass (750m).[9] The other, far less traveled, was in the central Amanus, crossing at the Amanic Gates, near the modern Hasanbeyli Pass (1150m), though several smaller passes existed in the vicinity. Since Roman sources

---

[5] Elton, H.W., *Warfare in Roman Europe* (Oxford, 1996), 236-239, 244-245; Ammianus Marcellinus, ed. Seyfarth, W., (Leipzig, 1978), 25.5.6.

[6] Dodgeon, M.H. and Lieu, S.N.C., *The Roman Eastern Frontier and the Persian Wars, AD 226-363* (London, 1991), 57-67.

[7] Maricq, A., 'Res Gestae Divi Saporis', *Syria* 35 (1958), 295-360; Kettenhofen, E., *Die römisch-persischen Kriege des 3. Jhrhdrts. n. Chr.* (Wiesbaden, 1982); Sprengling, M., *Third-Century Iran, Sapor and Kartir* (Chicago, 1953).

[8] French, D., *The Pilgrim's Road*, BAR S105 (Oxford, 1981); Mitchell, S., *Anatolia* (Oxford, 1993), 1.124-136; Hammond, N.G.L., 'One or Two Passes at the Cilicia-Syria Border?', *Ancient World* 25 (1994), 15-26.

[9] North of the Beilan Pass was a second set of Cilician Gates at Issus; when Niger's army attempted to block these in 193, they were outflanked, Dio 75.7.1-8.

(though, interestingly, not Sapor's inscription) record the capture of Antioch, the Sassanids can be assumed to have entered Cilicia via the Beilan Pass.[10]

Once across the mountains, Persian forces proceeded to sack the lowlands thoroughly, ravaging sixteen of the seventeen bishoprics in the province of Cilicia. But in the uplands of Isauria, Sassanid forces reached only the coastal cities of Celenderis, Anemurium, Selinus, Myus, Antioch-ad-Cragum, Domitiopolis and Seleucia.[11] The difficulties of access along the coastal road would suggest that only a part of the Sassanid army was involved in this part of the campaign. The major cities of the Calycadnus Valley, Claudiopolis and Germanicopolis, were not directly affected by the Persians, possibly because it was easier for the Romans to defend the mountains.

Sapor's troops then left Cilicia, advancing across the Taurus to Cappadocia. There were two routes across the Taurus, though the road north of Tarsus, the Cilician Gates (Gülek Bogazi), was the only practical route for a large army.[12] The second route across the Taurus followed the Calycadnus Valley from Seleucia to Claudiopolis, then ran on to Iconium. The ancient route is uncertain. It may have followed the modern road, leading to the Sertavul Pass, or it may have run a little farther east, via Dagpazari. This pass was not suitable for wagons and saw little non-local use in antiquity.[13] Part of the answer may be the relative heights of the passes. The Cilician Gates were only 1050m, the Sertavul Pass 1610m. Moreover, crossing the Cilician Gates involved spending less time in the mountains, whereas the Calycadnus Valley involved long and difficult mountainous marches. Since Claudiopolis was not sacked, Sapor can be assumed to have taken the Cilician Gates on his march to Cappadocia.

For most of this campaign, the Sassanids faced little opposition. But when a Roman army arrived, then the pattern of operations changed. One of Valerian's generals, Ballista, campaigned along the southern coast of Cilicia. He relieved the besieged Pompeiopolis (possibly not listed in Sapor's inscription and perhaps never sacked), and then won a victory at Corycus and Sebaste in which 3000 Persians were killed.[14] It is possible that Ballista arrived in the region by sea.

---

[10] Downey, G., *A History of Antioch in Syria* (Princeton, 1961), 587-595.

[11] The Isaurian city of Domitiopolis is sometimes described as an inland site, though the evidence for this is very weak, see Elton, H., 'Where was Domitiopolis?' (forthcoming).

[12] Cilician gates, Mutafian, *Cilicie*, 231-251; Hild, F., *Das byzantinischen Strassensystem in Kappadokien* (Vienna, 1977), 57-58; Williams, F., 'Xenophon's Dana and the Passage of Cyrus' Army over the Taurus Mountains', *Historia* 45 (1996), 284-314, esp. 308-312 on minor routes across the Taurus.

[13] Frederick Barbarossa did cross the Taurus via the Calycadnus valley in 1190, the only major ancient or medieval force known to have done so. After capturing Iconium, Frederick had a choice between continuing to fight his way through Seljuk territory to cross at the Cilician Gates, or to take the Calycadnus crossing immediately. Ansbert described the army as 'laboring on a difficult road and on rocky cliffs hardly accessible to isolated ibexes and to birds, besides the heat of the sun and the boiling humidity', *Historia de Expeditione Frederici Imperatoris*, ed. Chroust, A., *Quellen zur Geschichte der Kreuzzügges Kaiser Frederick I* (Berlin, 1928), 90-91.

[14] Syncellus, *Chronographia*, ed. Mosshammer, A.A., (Leipzig, 1984), 466.

Roman soldiers were used to sailing into Cilicia, though usually to Aegeae, where many troops were disembarked for eastern campaigns (though Seleucia in Pieria in Syria was also used). Aegeae's importance is nicely shown by the tombstone of Vivius Batao, a soldier of Legio II Parthica who died at Aegeae in 215. He was buried at Catabolon, but not commemorated until his unit reached Apamea in Syria.[15] The absence of a Roman field army to oppose Sapor allowed military operations to take place throughout the lowlands. However, with the exception of the attacks on the Isaurian coastal cities (perhaps the action of a detached group), the Persians avoided fighting in the mountains.

The Roman civil wars of 276 and 313, both involved large Roman field armies on the military road. In 276, Florianus marched south from Bithynia while Probus marched west from Syria. Florianus would have crossed the Taurus at the Cilician Gates, Probus would have crossed the Amanus at the Beilan Pass. When they met east of Tarsus, some inconclusive skirmishing followed. Florianus was then abandoned by his army, captured and executed.[16] The same pattern can be seen in 313 after Licinius defeated Maximinus Daia at Adrianople. Maximinus fled east with so few troops that he was forced to make a stand in the Cilician Gates rather than fighting in the plain. When Licinius' men outflanked the Gates, Maximinus retreated to Tarsus. Again too short of resources for a field battle, he was forced to undergo a siege, though soon committed suicide.[17] In both cases, the action was confined to major roads. Maximinus might have been better off retreating to the mountains, but without local support, he would have been unable to supply his troops for long.

Three wars of the late fifth century involved field armies campaigning in the Isaurian Mountains. These were the wars between Basiliscus and Zeno (475-76), between Zeno and Leontius (484-88) and between Anastasius and Longinus (491-97). In the first of these cases, when Basiliscus seized power in Constantinople, the emperor Zeno fled with a few followers to Isauria. He was besieged at Sbide, a small mountain city north of Germanicopolis, only 10km from Zenonopolis where he was probably born. Zeno was able to persuade Basiliscus' generals to return their allegiance to him and by 476 was back in power in Constantinople.[18] In the second case, Leontius declared himself emperor at Tarsus on 19 July 484 and then moved on to Antioch in Syria. Zeno sent John the Scythian against him with a combined army and fleet. These forces rapidly defeated Leontius' field army at Antioch in September. Leontius then retreated into the Isaurian Mountains where

---

[15] Balty, J.C. and Van Rengen, W., *Apamea in Syria: the winter quarters of Legio II Parthica* (Brussels, 1993) #2 = *l'Année Epigraphique* 1993.1572; Van Berchem, D., 'Le port de Séleucie de Piérie et l'infrastructure logistique des guerres parthiques', *Bonner Jahrbücher* 185 (1985), 47-87.

[16] Zosimus, *Historiae*, ed., Mendelssohn, L., (Leipzig, 1887), 1.64.

[17] Barnes, T.D., *Constantine and Eusebius* (Cambridge, MA, 1981), 62-63; Lactantius, *D MP* 46-49.

[18] Theophanes, *Chronographia*, ed., de Boor, C., (Leipzig, 1883), *AM* 5967; Elton, H.W., 'Illus and the Imperial Aristocracy under Zeno', *Byzantion* 70 (2000), 393-407.

he was besieged in the fastness of Papirius for four years. The fortress finally fell to John through treachery in 488.[19] Lastly, Longinus of Cardala rebelled against Zeno's successor, Anastasius, in 491 and assembled an army which he led to destruction at Cotyaeum in Phrygia in 492. After the battle of Cotyaeum, the Roman forces, again under John the Scythian, pursued the rebels into the mountains. One Roman force captured Claudiopolis, but was then cut off and besieged there until another Roman force could relieve them.[20] Other Isaurians continued to hold out in the mountains, bringing in food from the ports along the coast. It was not until 497 that John the Scythian was able to capture and execute the remaining rebel leaders.[21] In all three cases, the forces trapped in the mountains did not start the wars intending to fight there—for Zeno it was a refuge after losing his throne in a coup, for Leontius and Longinus, a refuge after defeat in a field battle. These victories did not finish the conflicts, but instead only moved it to another phase, that of a long siege in the rebels' homelands. The length of these wars suggests the logistical difficulties faced by large armies in the mountains. Roman siege technology was sufficiently advanced to capture well-defended cities in a matter of weeks in the plains, but capturing mountain fortresses was a different matter, with the remoteness of many of these sites making it difficult to provide logistical support.[22]

The course of these fifth-century wars was similar to the first of the two seventh-century campaigns fought by the Romans against the Sassanids. When the Sassanids invaded in 613, they defeated a Roman field army at Antioch. The Romans then retreated into Cilicia. Since the next battle was fought at Alexandria-ad-Issum, the retreat route was probably over the Beilan Pass. Even in this situation, the Romans did not try to hold the pass. With the defeat of the Romans at Alexandria, the Sassanids occupied Tarsus and the rest of lowland Cilicia.[23] Like the imperial armies of the fifth century, and unlike Sapor's attack of 260, the Sassanids were attempting to occupy the region. In 615, a new Roman mint and arms factory were established at Seleucia, to support the imperial field armies defending Isauria and western Cilicia. It was not until 617 that the mint at Seleucia stopped producing coins, presumably when the Sassanids captured the city. Then in 617/618, a new mint appeared at the city of Isaura, farther inland. The production dates and similarity of the coin designs suggest that the same workmen were present at both mints, or that is, the Isauran mint was the relocated

---

[19] Malalas, *Chronicon*, ed., Dindorf, L., *CSHB* 15 (Bonn, 1831), 389.

[20] Theophanes, *AM* 5986.

[21] Theophanes, *AM* 5988; Marcellinus Comes, ed., Mommsen, T., *MGH AA* 11 (Berlin, 1894), sa 497; Theodore Anagnostes, Theodore Anagnostes, *HE* ed., Hansen, G.C., (Berlin, 1971), 449 (126.21-23).

[22] Elton, *Warfare* 257-263.

[23] Howard-Johnston, J.D., 'Heraclius' Persian Campaigns and the Revival of the Eastern Roman Empire', *War in History* 6 (1999), 1-44; Howard-Johnston, J.D., 'The Official History of Heraclius' Campaigns', Dabrowa, E., ed., *The Roman and Byzantine Army in the East* (Cracow, 1994), 57-87; Foss, C., 'The Persians in Asia Minor and the End of Antiquity', *English Historical Review* 90 (1975), 721-747.

Seleucia mint. The closure of the mint at Isaura in 618 indicates complete Persian domination of the uplands. Like the fifth-century wars, it was a long drawn out process, not a swift conquest, the result of the Romans being supported by the population of the region.[24] A further difference from the 260 raid was the Sassanids' ability to invade Cyprus in 619. With an occupation of the lowlands since 613, the Persians had an opportunity to develop some naval power in the Mediterranean.[25]

In the last example, the Roman counteroffensive of 626 brought about a reversion to the pattern of Roman civil wars. With Constantinople under siege and much of Anatolia still occupied by the Sassanids, Heraclius launched a major counterattack against Persia from Armenia. He probed south to the Euphrates and Samosata, then withdrew west, followed by Persian forces under Shahrbaraz. Coming from farther north than the other armies discussed, Heraclius entered Cilicia via Germanicia, probably crossing at the Amanic Gates. Once the armies faced each other in the Cilician lowlands, the pattern was the same as with Flavianus and Probus in 276. Heraclius marched across upper Cilicia and joined the military road, probably around Mopsuestia. He then continued west to Adana, where he fought an inconclusive battle against Shahrbaraz. After this, he retreated north to Cappadocia, presumably crossing at the Cilician Gates.[26] The involvement of these large armies again produced campaigns on predictable routes.

This paper has attempted to show that the processes of moving large numbers of men, animals and wagons for military purposes were heavily influenced by the landscape. The influence was so strong, I have argued that, even when the sources do not tell us which routes were taken across the mountains, we can make confident guesses. However, the presence of a road or communication route did not mean that armies would use them. Roman itineraries do list both the upper Calycadnus Valley and the Cilician Gates as Taurus crossings but they give no sense of which was the most frequently used route.

---

[24] Zacos, G. and Veglery, A., *Byzantine Lead Seals* (Basel, 1972-1985), #1136; Grierson, P., *Catalogue of the Byzantine Coins in the Dumbarton Oaks Collection and in the Whittemore Collection*, vol. 2 (Washington, 1966), 39, 327-331; Foss, 'Persians', 729-730; Grierson, P., 'The Isaurian Coins of Heraclius', *Numismatic Chronicle* (1951), 56-57; Donald, P. and Whitting, P., 'A VIIth Century Hoard from Cyprus', *Numismatic Circular* 75 (1967), 162-165, 204.

[25] Sophronius, *Life of John the Almsgiver* 13, Delehaye, H., 'Une vie inédite de Saint Jean l'Aumonier', *Analecta Bollandiana* 45 (1927), 5-74; cf Calocaerus campaign, Theophanes, *AM* 5825 = Jerome, *Chron.* sa 334, ed., Burgess, R.W., *Studies in Eusebian and post-Eusebian Chronology* (Stuttgart, 1999), 215-217.

[26] Theophanes, *AM* 6116; Foss, 'Persians', 726-7 and n 3.

Chapter 2

Student Travel to Intellectual Centers: What Was the Attraction?

Edward Watts

The *Theophrastus*, a dialog written by Aeneas of Gaza, begins with the chance meeting of two former schoolmates, Euxitheos and Aegyptus, at the port of Alexandria.[1] Both men studied philosophy together in Alexandria before Euxitheos decided to return to his native Syria. In spite of his connection to the city, Euxitheos' return to Alexandria had not been planned. He had only put in at the port because a storm had blown him off-course during a voyage from Syria to Athens. The purpose of his journey was to undertake high-level philosophical study. Though Euxitheos had received philosophical training before, he felt that his education was incomplete. In his mind, he could only be fully formed as a philosopher if he completed his training in Athens. To Euxitheos, and presumably a part of Aeneas' audience as well, Athens represented the foremost intellectual center in the Eastern Mediterranean. It was simply the best place to become thoroughly immersed in the ideas of both ancient and contemporary thinkers.[2] For intellectuals like Euxitheos, a trip to the schools of Athens was an essential part of philosophical education.

The sort of journey that Euxitheos aimed to undertake was common in Late Antiquity. Then, as now, the reputation of renowned educational centers caused many students to undertake long voyages so that they could attend the best known schools. To see this, one need only recall the fascination young Libanius had with the schools of Athens. When Libanius was still a youth, Iasion, a Cappadocian friend, regaled him with tales of Athenian teachers, their rhetorical competitions, and their schools.[3] These stories made Libanius long for the time when he too

---

[1] The standard edition of the *Theophrastus* is that of M. Colonna (1958), *Teofrasto*, Napoli: Salvatore Iodice. Euxitheos' arrival in Alexandria and his encounter with Aegyptus unfold on pp. 1-3 of Colonna's text.

[2] This is the sentiment that Euxitheos is made to express on p. 3.10-14.

[3] Libanius, *Oration* 1.11.

would be able to go to Athens and study.[4] Looking back on that time in his life, Libanius later wrote 'I think that, as Odysseus did, I would have looked past marriage with a goddess to see the smoke of Athens'.[5] These visions that gripped Libanius in childhood held him through adolescence and, when he reached the age of 22, they pushed him to undertake the journey to Athens. Like Euxitheos, Libanius was unable to resist the allure of the Athenian schools.

In the same way that younger students could not wait to travel and become a part of the culture of a famous intellectual center, older graduates of prominent schools traveled to remain a part of this culture. One example of such a man was Diogenes of Oinoanda. Though he is not, strictly speaking a late antique figure,[6] Diogenes provides the most tangible evidence of the connection former students continued to have with intellectual centers. Diogenes was responsible for the carving of a massive Epicurean text upon the wall of, ironically enough, a Stoa in his Lycian city.[7] On this monument, Diogenes makes it clear that he considered himself a member of an Epicurean community that was centered upon schools in Athens and Rhodes. Even in his old age, Diogenes indicates that he was a frequent visitor to these centers. Diogenes spent the winter with his philosophical companions in Rhodes and, in the spring, made trips to see other Epicureans in Athens and other cities on the Greek mainland.[8] In the early second century, the Epicurean communities of the Aegean region had a quite contentious rivalry with the Stoic schools in the region. Though sources preserve the tone of this rivalry better than they convey the specifics disputes that characterized it, it is known that Epicureans battled Stoics about a host of issues. These ranged from doctrinal disagreements to which school could claim a better poet.[9] As a faithful member of

---

[4] Later in *Or.* 1.11, Libanius remarked: 'From these stories a certain desire for that country (Athens) seized my soul.'

[5] *Or.* 1.12.

[6] The arguments put forth by M. F. Smith (1996), (*The Philosophical Inscription of Diogenes of Oinoanda*, Wien: Verlag der Osterreichischen Akademie der Wissenschaften, pp. 38-9) demonstrate that Diogenes erected it in c. 120 AD.

[7] The pieces of Diogenes' inscription have been collected and translated by M. F. Smith (1996) in the work cited above.

[8] For these journeys see fragments 62 and 63.

[9] The contest between the schools is most clearly seen in the dedicatory inscription carved to honor the poet Heraclitus (*TAM* II.910). This poet was honored as a 'Homer in the field of medical poetry' by the Epicurean community of Athens. Not coincidentally, the medical poet Sarapion had the phrase 'poet ... and Stoic philosopher' inscribed on his funerary monument in Athens. His contemporaries also marked him as a stylist on par with Homer and Hesiod (Plutarch, *De Pythiae oraculis*, 396 F). Clearly Diogenes' Epicurean school was looking for a medical poet of their own who could compare to that found by their Stoic rivals. For more on this controversy see J. Oliver (1976), 'The Empress Plotina and the Sacred Thymelic Synod', *Historia* 24, pp. 125-8.

this intellectual community, Diogenes knew of these quarrels and his inscription proudly echoed the Epicurean criticisms of Stoics he had heard about in his travels.[10]

Travel enabled Libanius to become a part of the intellectual life surrounding a major educational center and it helped Diogenes to maintain ties to the schools where he studied. Voyages to school then played an important role both in introducing students to intellectual centers and in keeping them attached to these centers after they left. It is understandable that intellectual centers had a certain appeal. However, in Antiquity, as today, schools and places of study became both fashionable and unfashionable with the passage of time. This was usually a long process of development. When an intellectual center became a destination for student travelers, it was usually at or near its height of popularity. Hence, while individual stories like those of Libanius or Diogenes show the city already well-established as a destination for student travelers, they do little to explain why it first became a major destination for students from abroad. They also do little to show why travelers eventually ceased to travel to it.

Because so much individual choice was involved in the decision to travel to school, the reasons individual foreign students traveled to the major schools of the late antique world are, to some extent, an impossible thing to explain. However, alongside the multitude of stories told by individual student travelers, surviving sources do provide a type of evidence that allows us to explain their trips on something more than a case by case basis. In Late Antiquity there are a number of occasions when clusters of students from one region of the empire became attracted to one specific intellectual center at the same time. These clusters of students developed rather quickly, continued for a few decades, and then, eventually, disappeared after a few generations of students from that region passed through that city. There are a number of examples like this. It seems, for instance, that clusters of Cappadocians were drawn to the school of their countryman Julianus and his successor Prohaeresius in Athens in the fourth century.[11] So, too, a number of Gazans may have converged upon Alexandria in

---

[10] Though the Stoics are not the only victims of his polemics, they are the most prominently featured. Among the Stoic doctrines that Diogenes mentions and criticizes were the view that visions are illusions of the mind (fr. 10) and their view of causation (fr. 33).

[11] One gets a sense of the attraction this school had for Cappadocians in the mid-fourth century from the letters of Gregory Nazianzen. His writings tell of four Cappadocians (himself, Basil of Caesarea, Eustochius, and Stagiros) who studied in Athens during the later years of Prohaeresius' career. Given his predecessor Julianus' ties to the region, it would be surprising if Prohaeresius did not draw students from there. Though he is purposefully vague about the geographic origins of Prohaeresius' students, Eunapius seems to confirm that Prohaeresius enjoyed a strong recruiting presence in all of the regions around Cappadocia. Eunapius states that Prohaeresius drew students from Pontus, Caria, Lycia, Lydia, and the regions around those provinces (*Vitae Sophistarum* 487). Cappadocia surely fits this description.

the later decades of the fifth century.[12]   Nevertheless, the best attested and most clearly documented student migration is that of Alexandrian pagans who journeyed to the Athenian Neoplatonic school of Plutarch, Syrianus and Proclus in the fifth century.   The collection of evidence relating to these students and their voyages makes it possible to explain both how intellectual centers attracted such a large number of students from one region and why these students ultimately stopped making such trips.

The migrations of Alexandrian philosophy students to Plutarch's school seem to have begun around 400 when Syrianus, a member of a well-connected Alexandrian family, journeyed to Athens to study under Plutarch.[13]   Not many years later he was followed by his countryman Hierocles.   Given our modern understanding of Alexandrian intellectual life at this time, one may be surprised to find two Alexandrian students leaving to study abroad at a time when Hypatia was at the height of her powers.   In the seventh book of Hierocles' *On Providence* the author gives a subtle yet unambiguous clue as to why he chose to travel to Plutarch's school at that time.   He describes:

> The doctrine professed by Ammonius, Plotinus, and Origen as well as Porphyry and Iamblichus.   They and their successors are all a part of a holy race.   This is true into the time of Plutarch, the one who was (my) master and taught (me) these doctrines.   All of these men were in agreement with the philosophy of Plato and celebrated the doctrines in a pure state.[14]

---

[12] Two Gazans who studied in Alexandria in the later decades of the fifth century are known to us.   Beyond these two men (Aeneas of Gaza and Zacharias Scholasticus), however, there are a number of indications that Gazan intellectual life in the late fifth and early sixth centuries was strongly tied to the community of scholars in Alexandria.   One of the highpoints of Procopius of Gaza's career was the rhetorical crown he won in Alexandria (Procopius, *Ep.* 48, 96) and, while there, he also met a Gazan named Diodorus. In addition, both Aeneas and Zacharias wrote dialogs (the *Theophrastus* and *Ammonius,* respectively) that were set in Alexandria, featured Alexandrian characters, and dealt with philosophical ideas that were hotly contested in Alexandrian schools at that time. Furthermore, Alexandrian figures like Gessius appear consistently in their correspondence (e.g. Aeneas, *Ep.* 19-20, Procopius, *Ep.* 16, 102, 125, 164).   Though student travel between Gaza and Alexandria is not particularly prominent in our sources, the intimate connections between the intellectual communities of the two cities strongly suggests that Aeneas and Zacharias were not the only two Gazans to travel to Alexandria at that time.

[13] Syrianus' arrival in Athens must have occurred c. 400 because, by the time Synesius writes *Ep.* 136 in c. 410, it seems likely that Syrianus had already been installed in a high position in Plutarch's school.   This is based upon the chronology put forth by Alan Cameron and J. Long (1993), *Barbarians and politics at the court of Arcadius*, Berkeley: University of California Press, pp. 409-11.

[14] Photius, *Bibliotheke*, 214.173a.   It is notable in this context that Damascius styles Hypatia a 'mathematician' instead of a 'philosopher' in *Vita Isidori*, fr. 106 A (ed. P. Athanassiadi in *Damascius: The Philosophical History*, Athens: Apamea, 1999).   This is Epit. 164 in the edition of C. Zintzen (*Vitae Isidori Reliquiae*, Hildsheim: Georg Olms,

Hypatia and her followers are noticeably absent from Hierocles' divine race. The reason for this is clear. The type of philosophy that she taught was doctrinally distinct from that of Iamblichus.[15] To men like Hierocles, such neglect of the chain of Platonic interpretation marked her teaching as impure and unworthy of consideration by true philosophical initiates.[16]

Hierocles was not the only Alexandrian who left home because he found the doctrines taught by Alexandrian teachers impure. Almost two decades later, Proclus made the same trip from Alexandria to the school of Plutarch for a similar reason. In his biography of Proclus, Marinus says:

> After passing his time with philosophers in Alexandria and enjoying their company in so far as they were able, Proclus looked down upon the teachers there when, in a common reading of a text, it seemed to him that they no longer bore true to the intention of the philosopher in their interpretations ... (in consequence) Proclus went forth to Athens ... so that the pure, unadulterated teaching of Plato would be saved.[17]

Proclus did not leave for Athens because of a lack of skill among Alexandrian philosophers. He left because they were unwilling or unable to teach the true meanings of the texts. Proclus knew that what he considered the true, pure teaching of Plato was preserved only with Plutarch in Athens.

Plutarch's school also benefited from the great reputation its master enjoyed. Hierocles, for example, placed Plutarch among the most influential thinkers of history. Proclus shared this sentiment. He even urged one of his students to come to Athens and work at the Neoplatonic school out of respect for the memories of Plato, Iamblichus, and Plutarch.[18] In the eyes of his followers, Plutarch enjoyed

---

1967). Because the text of Athanassiadi is not yet as widely available as that of Zintzen, both editions will be cited together in this study.

[15] Owing to the complete absence of philosophical writings by Hypatia, one can only judge her interest in the ideas of Iamblichus from the works of her student Synesius. It is telling then that Synesius' works are completely lacking any mention of Iamblichus or his ideas. His citations include 126 from Plato, 20 from Aristotle, 9 from Plotinus, 3 from Porphyry, and none from Iamblichus (see A. Fitzgerald (1926), *The Letters of Synesius*, Oxford: Oxford University Press, p. 16). This is, of course, quite distinct from the overt link between Plutarch and Iamblichus made by Hierocles.

[16] The concern for Neoplatonic orthodoxy that Hierocles shows in *On Providence* is not unique. The best illustration of the trend is found in Damascius' discussion of Dominus. Damascius says that he was a competent mathematician who 'distorted many of Plato's doctrines. However this was completely undone by Proclus who wrote against him a whole treatise "purificatory of Plato's doctrines", for so it is entitled.' (*Vit. Is.*, Athanassiadi, fr. 89A; Zintzen Epit. 134, fr. 218). The concept of Neoplatonic 'heresy' is further discussed by P. Athanassiadi (1999), p. 223 n. 237.

[17] Marinus, *Vita Proculi*, 10.

[18] *Vit. Is.* Ath. 98C, Z. Epit. 150.

the company of some quite distinguished peers.   Some of this reverence undoubtedly arose from the close contact these students had with their teacher, but there is little doubt that Plutarch's reputation as a scholar was known to all of them before they arrived in Athens. It must have helped draw Alexandrians to his school. Indeed, it is a testimony to Plutarch's ability to attract such students to Athens that Synesius thought it fit to level the notable slander that the Athenian successfully recruited students only because he bribed them with pots of honey.[19] This bitter attack on Plutarch by one of Hypatia's most loyal students indicates that the migration of Alexandrian students to Athens had become a real concern for those affiliated with Hypatia's school.

After their time in Athens, this first generation of Alexandrian Plutarchans followed two different paths. Hierocles returned to Alexandria and began teaching there. Syrianus and Proclus remained in Athens. Both men were destined to succeed their master as the head of the school. Each of these paths is significant. First, by returning to Alexandria and teaching as he did, Hierocles brought the ideas of Plutarch to Alexandria. His school gave Alexandrian youths a place to study these doctrines without leaving home. It also introduced the teachings of Plutarch more fully into Alexandrian intellectual life.   When compared to the Athenian school of Plutarch, however, Hierocles' institution was something of a second rate operation. Only two of Hierocles' students are known (and that is only if one includes Aeneas of Gaza among them) and they are as notable for their asceticism as for the quality of their thought.[20] Hierocles certainly had more than just these few students, but our lack of information about his school is probably due to more than just the accidents of historical preservation.   When Hierocles opened his school, Plutarch, his teacher, and Syrianus, a student judged by Plutarch as superior to Hierocles, both remained in Athens teaching the same doctrines that he did.[21] Although Hierocles was the

---

[19] In *Ep.* 136, Synesius writes 'Now, in our age, Egypt has received and cherishes the fruitful wisdom of Hypatia. Athens was long ago the home city of the wise: but now beekeepers alone bring it honor. Such is the case with that pair of Plutarchan sophists who draw the young to their lecture room not by the fame of their eloquence but by jars [of honey] from Hymettus.' Given the time and place of this letter's composition, Synesius here must be referring to Plutarch and one of his deputies. By highlighting the difference between the teaching of Hypatia and that of Plutarch, Synesius is making a statement similar to that of Hierocles. His teacher is correct while her rival is corrupt (though, in this case, his corruption is of a financial and not a philosophical sort).

[20] Hierocles' best known student, Theosebius, appears in the *Vit. Is.* (Ath. 45A, B; 46 B, D, E; Z. Epit. 54, 56, 58, 59, fr. 106, 109, 110). The prominence of Hierocles in the early passages of the *Theophrastus* suggests that Aeneas may have been a student (for example, 2.8ff). P. Athanassiadi (1999), p. 153, n. 128 speculates that Aegyptus in the *Theophrastus* may have been based upon a real character. If so, he too was a student of Hierocles.

[21] Syrianus' selection as successor designate indicates that he was judged by Plutarch to be his most promising pupil.

local source for this sort of teaching, his presence in Alexandria probably also served to attract more students to Athens. With the Athenian school the more prestigious of the two institutions, many serious students of Neoplatonism would have chosen to bypass the Alexandrian school of Hierocles and go straight to the more highly regarded school in Athens.

Despite the foundation of Hierocles' school, Athens remained the intellectual center of this brand of thought. Syrianus, and later Proclus, benefited greatly from this. Both men seem to have used the reputation that Plutarch's school had enjoyed in Alexandria to attract an even greater number of accomplished students from that city. Syrianus headed the school for approximately seven years and, in that time, he is known to have drawn three Alexandrian students.[22] Proclus, who headed the school for much longer, attracted another stream of students from Alexandria. Among those known to us are Ammonius, Heliodorus, Zeno, Isidore, and Asclepiodotus. More interesting still, at least some of these students came to Athens already equipped with basic philosophical training. Isidore, for example, came to Athens only after extensive training under two Alexandrian teachers.[23] For students like him, the Athenian school must have been something like a prestigious graduate school. Nevertheless, whether a student had previous training or not, Athens remained the intellectual center to which ambitious and skilled Alexandrian intellectuals journeyed to receive the highest level philosophical training.

The school also benefited from the Alexandrian political and social connections Syrianus and Proclus maintained. Both men were known as intelligent and influential men within Alexandria the community. An Alexandrian himself, Syrianus enjoyed a close relationship with some of the important pagan families in the city.[24] As philosophy became more of a hereditary pursuit in the fifth century, these personal connections inevitably helped to attract students.[25] It

---

[22] These were Hermeias, Gregory, and Ulpian. As one would expect, the sources preserve the names of only the most notable students. There were likely more than three who came at this time.

[23] It seems from the *Vit. Is.* (Ath. 71B; Z. fr. 160, 162, 267) that Isidore was trained in philosophy by Heraiscus and Asclepiades in Alexandria before going to the Athenian school of Proclus.

[24] Syrianus was related to the grammarian Ammonianus (*Vit. Is.* Ath. 47; Z. Epit. 60, fr. 160). Ammonianus seems not to have left Alexandria.

[25] Among the students that Syrianus was known to have recruited from Alexandria, Hermeias and Gregory were brothers (*Vit. Is.* Ath. 55; Z. Epit. 75, fr. 123). Ulpian was related to Aegyptus, possibly one of Hierocles' students, and was the older brother of Isidore (*Vit. Is.* Ath. 123A; Z. fr. 324). It is worth noting, however, that much of Damascius' information for the early students of Syrianus and Proclus seems to have been learned from either his mentor Isidore or his previous teacher Ammonius, the son of Hermeias. The stories told by these men would have undoubtedly placed disproportionate emphasis upon the deeds of their family members. Given the interests of his sources, it is not surprising that philosophical families are emphasized in Damascius' work. When the

helped too that both scholarchs were well-connected politically. Syrianus, for example, was able to secure a public professorship in Alexandria for Hermeias, his former student and relation by marriage.[26] Proclus too had well-placed friends and, according to Marinus, enjoyed notable success as a patron for various petitioners.[27]

The distinction and political influence of its teachers made the Athenian Neoplatonic school the intellectual center to which the best Alexandrian students of philosophy were attracted for as long as Proclus was actively teaching. This changed after Proclus' death in spring 485. Under his successors, Alexandrian students no longer made the trip across the Mediterranean. After 485, only one Alexandrian student, Damascius, is known to have journeyed from Alexandria to Athens and he came not for academic reasons but because he was fleeing an anti-pagan persecution. By the 480s Athens no longer stood at the center of the Alexandrian philosophical world. Like the reasons for its development, the decline of the Athenian Neoplatonic school as a destination for traveling Alexandrian students is intimately linked to both the reputation of its teachers and the type of doctrines they presented.

By the 480s the philosophy taught in Athens was no longer unique. All of the Alexandrian students who studied under Syrianus and Proclus followed the lead of Hierocles and returned to Alexandria to begin teaching. The teaching they did there, though it had some specifically Egyptian emphases, was basically the same as that done in Athens. One sees the Athenian influences in the *Anonymous Prolegomena to Platonic Philosophy*, an introduction to and outline of the Neoplatonic school curriculum followed in Alexandria in the late fifth and early sixth centuries.[28] This document bears striking similarities to the curriculum followed in Proclus' school. The same similarity is seen in the surviving commentaries that emerged from Alexandrian schools in this period. As just one

---

narrative seems to have demanded it, however, Damascius does include the names of students who were not members of these philosophical families. Hierocles, Proclus, Asclepiodotus and Zeno all left Alexandria to study in Athens and none had known familial connections to other Alexandrian students at the school. The school was apparently just as appealing to students outside of this familial network.

[26] Hermeias' public position is mentioned in *Vit. Is.* Ath. 56; Z. fr. 124. Though Isidore is not mentioned as the one responsible for securing this position for him, a prominent teacher often had the ability to win a public teaching post for a favored student (e.g. Prohaeresius in Eunapius, *Vit. Soph.*, 493). Since Syrianus had arranged for Hermeias to marry his relative Aedesia, he would have had an additional incentive to find him a prominent professorship.

[27] *Vit. Proc.* 16.

[28] L. G. Westerink (1962), *Anonymous Prolegomena to Platonic Philosophy*, Amsterdam: North Holland. It is generally assumed that the *Prolegomena* came from the Alexandrian school and took its final form under Olympiodorus in the mid-sixth century. The scale of virtues upon which this curriculum was based a central feature of Iamblichan Neoplatonism and played a large role in Marinus' *Life of Proclus*.

example, the commentaries of Olympiodorus, one of Ammonius' students, echo many of the ideas of Proclus.[29] This is not surprising. Proclus was Ammonius' teacher and, when Ammonius returned to Alexandria, he brought knowledge of many of his master's doctrines (and, likely, copies of his books as well) back to Alexandria. A similar thing must have occurred many times over as this collection of Athenian trained Alexandrian teachers assembled in the city. When this happened, all of the doctrines and pedagogic tools of the Athenian school became readily available to students in Alexandria. One no longer needed to travel to acquire them.

The attraction of the Athenian Neoplatonic school was further reduced because Marinus, Proclus' successor, did not enjoy the same high reputation as his predecessors. The possibility of studying under an acknowledged master like Plutarch or Proclus had continued to attract Alexandrian students to Athens even when the brand of Neoplatonism they taught was available locally. Marinus, however, was much inferior to his predecessors both as a scholar and as an influential patron. He is described by a contemporary as 'atonos' and his philosophical production was generally seen as second rate.[30] Marinus was no better as a patron. Indeed, during his short tenure at the head of the school he even managed to alienate the school's most influential political backer.[31] In both of these respects he was quite inferior to the Athenian trained Alexandrian teachers Ammonius and Asclepiodotus.[32]

In a sense, the quality of the education that the Athenian school gave to the Alexandrians who came to it served to eventually stem the flow of students from that city. Young Alexandrians were initially attracted to Athens by the great minds and innovative doctrines that defined the city's Neoplatonic school. It did not hurt that the leaders of the school were politically influential as well. As clusters of Alexandrians studied in Athens, returned home, and began teaching, the features that had made travel to Athens attractive were duplicated beside the Nile. The large number of students who returned to teach in Alexandria

---

[29] For this assessment see R. Jackson et. al. (1998), *Olympiodorus' Commentary on Plato's Gorgias*, Leiden: Brill, pp. 1-3.

[30] The description is found in *Vit. Is.* Ath. 97I; Z. Epit. 275. Though a gifted mathematician, his philosophical production was much inferior to that of Proclus. His first commentary, on Plato's *Philebus*, was so problematic that he cast it into a fire to prevent its publication (*Vit. Is.* Ath. 38A; Z. Epit. 42). His second, on the *Parmenides*, was equally poor but was published nonetheless (*Vit. Is.* Ath. 98J; Z. fr. 245).

[31] *Vit. Is.* Ath. 100A; Z. Epit. 155-6. This was the senator Theagenes. Though apparently a rather difficult man to control, Proclus was able to work with him quite well.

[32] Ammonius' political influence was such that he survived a rather public spat with Erythrius, a man who was three times named Praetorian Prefect of the East (*Vit. Is.* Ath. 78E; Z. fr. 173). Asclepiodotus was the son-in-law of a prominent Aphrodisian aristocrat also named Asclepiodotus and, by virtue of this marriage, shared the advantages of his father-in-law's position.

eliminated the doctrinal originality that the Athenian school had once enjoyed. In addition, the intellectual and political prominence of some of these returning Alexandrians outshone the teachers who remained in Athens. In sum, students stopped traveling from Alexandria to Athens because none of the advantages that had made travel to school necessary remained.

In this context it is fitting to return to the scene from Aeneas' *Theophrastus* with which this study began. After Euxitheos, the former Alexandrian student on his way to Athens, told Aegyptus of the purpose of his journey, his old friend reacted with surprise. 'My dear friend', he responded, 'you have Athens; for if you want to see a wise man instead of the Acropolis, the Propylia, and the shipyard, Theophrastus, the great glory of the Athenians has landed among us and teaches here.'[33] It is perhaps only natural that, like so many other students in the 490s, Euxitheos chose to forego his voyage to Athens and stay in Alexandria.

---

[33] *Theophrastus*, 3.15-8.

References

Primary Sources

Aeneas of Gaza, *Theophrastus*, ed. M. E. Colonna, Napoli: Salvatore Iodice, 1958.
———*Epistulae*, ed. L. M. Positano, Napoli: Libreria Scientifica, 1961.
Damascius, *The Philosophical History*, ed. P. Athanassiadi, Athens: Apamea, 1999.
———*Vitae Isidori Reliquiae*, ed. C. Zintzen, Hildsheim: Georg Olms, 1967.
Eunapius, *Vitae Sophistarum*, ed. G. Giangrande, Rome: Scriptores Gr. et Latini consilio Acad. Lync. editi, 1956.
Hierocles, *De Providentia ap. Photius*, Bibliotheke, Codd. 214, 251, ed. R. Henry, Paris, Belles Lettres, 1959.
Libanius, *Opera*, ed. R. Foerster, Leipzig: Teubner, 1903.
Marinus, *Vita Proculi*, ed. R. Masullo, Naples: M. D'Auria, 1985.
Plutarch, *De Pythiae oraculis*, ed. S. Schroder, Stuttgart: Teubner, 1990.
Procopius of Gaza, *Epistolae et Declamationes*, ed. A. Garzya et R. Loenertz, Ettal: Buch-Kunstverlag, 1963.
Synesius, *Epistulae*, ed. A. Garzya, Rome: Typis Officinae Polygraphicae, 1979.

Secondary Sources

Cameron, Alan and Long, J. (1993), *Barbarians and politics at the court of Arcadius*, Berkeley: University of California Press.
Fitzgerald, A. (1926), *The Letters of Synesius*, Oxford: Oxford University Press.
Jackson, R. et. al. (1998), *Olympiodorus' Commentary on Plato's Gorgias*, Leiden: Brill.
Oliver, J. (1976), 'The Empress Plotina and the Sacred Thymelic Synod', *Historia* 24, pp. 125-8.
Smith, M. F. (1996), *The Philosophical Inscription of Diogenes of Oinoanda*, Wien: Verlag der Osterreichischen Akademie der Wissenschaften.
Westerink, L. G. (1962), *Anonymous Prolegomena to Platonic Philosophy*, Amsterdam: North Holland.

Chapter 3

Letters of Recommendation and the Circulation of Rural Laborers in the Late Roman West[1]

Cam Grey

Skilled wage labor could be extremely valuable at certain crucial times in the agricultural year. This fact did not escape the fifth-century[2] agronomist Palladius, who observed that 'five modii can be gathered from a full field in one day's labor by an experienced reaper, by a mediocre one only three, by a poor one even less'.[3] Palladius' claim that his *Opus Agriculturae* is a treatise aimed at peasant farmers themselves should be treated with caution, but it seems likely that it was designed to be more than merely a theoretical work.[4] On the basis of the organization of the work by month, rather than by theme, it has been plausibly suggested that the aim of the *Opus Agriculturae* was to provide its elite audience with a handbook for the management of their rural estates.[5] It is reasonable, therefore, to expect that there might be some detailed discussion of the ways in which relations with rural laborers such as reapers could be contracted and maintained. Unfortunately, while Palladius provides further evidence of the existence of itinerant and specialist laborers in the rural landscape, he gives no clue as to how they might come into contact with elite landowners.[6] Consequently, the historian is forced to turn to other genres to understand this aspect of rural labor relations in the fourth and fifth century West.

---

[1] I would like to thank Peter Garnsey and John Crook for their comments on drafts of this article, and for ongoing discussion of the arguments expressed here.

[2] For dating, Martin (1976), VII-XX.

[3] *Op. Ag.* VII.2.1: 'Quinque modios recidere potest pleni agri opera una messoris experti, mediocris vero tres, ultimi etiam minus'.

[4] *Op. Ag.* I.1.

[5] Martin (1976), XXV; Frézouls (1980), 195.

[6] *Op. Ag.* I.6.2; VI.4.1; Frézouls (1980), 201-2.

The object of this paper is to examine the evidence of one such genre, namely some letters of recommendation for farmers and rural laborers which survive in the correspondence of aristocratic landowners. These letters are suggestive rather than conclusive, but they offer tantalizing glimpses of a rural landscape in which some agricultural specialists and even farmers moved regularly from estate to estate. Indeed, it can be argued on the basis of these letters that relationships between landowners and peasants—whether tenants, wage-laborers, share-croppers or clients—were fluid, many-faceted and open to negotiation. Letters of recommendation provide a marked contrast to the picture which emerges from the legislation of an immobile peasantry, tied to the land as *coloni*, and large, self-sufficient, self-contained estates owned by aristocratic landowners.

The legislation portrays movement by tenants (*coloni*) as flight from fiscal obligations.[7] Early scholars, adherents of an agricultural crisis hypothesis, interpreted this as evidence for widespread abandonment of land and urban drift,[8] but this conclusion has since been firmly rejected.[9] It is clear that the *coloni* of this legislation are moving. However, their movement is not from country to city, but from estate to estate. The edict of 332 censures 'any person with whom somebody else's tenant is found'[10] and a later law included in the same rubric prescribes punishments for any person who 'through solicitation should receive somebody else's tenant or by concealment should harbor him'.[11] In addition, tenants clearly travel for reasons which have nothing to do with a crushing tax burden. Marriage was one such reason.[12] A young couple from different estates in Gaul, one described as a resident tenant (*inquilinus*), elope together.[13] The *coloni* of the *fundus Thogonoetis* in North Africa threaten to abandon their tenancies and move if an unpopular bishop is imposed upon them.[14] The fact that their grievance against Antoninus is taken seriously by both their landlord and the bishop of Hippo reveals that this was no idle threat.

Mobility of rural labor was embedded in the socio-economic structure of the late Roman period. Peasants could and did move around the rural landscape, as tenants, laborers and even travelers upon their own errands, with their own

---

[7] For example, *Brev.* V.9.1 = *CTh* V.17.1 (332, *Ad Provinciales*).

[8] Clausing (1925) remains invaluable as a summary account.

[9] Whittaker (1976); (1980).

[10] 'Apud quemcumque colonus iuris alieni fuerit inventus'.

[11] *Brev.* V.9.2 = *CTh* V.17.2 (386, East): 'quisquis colonum iuris alieni aut sollicitatione susceperit aut occultatione celaverit'.

[12] *CTh* V.18.1.4 = *CJ* XI.48.16 *mut.* (419, Italy).

[13] Sidonius *Ep.* V.19.

[14] Augustine *Ep.* 20*.10.

motives. A letter of Sidonius Apollinaris reveals a rural laborer undertaking a journey to Vaison.[15] Two estates of Sidonius are known, Avitacum near Clermont-Ferrand in the Auvergne, and his patrimonial estate near Lyon.[16] A journey between either estate and Vaison was no minor undertaking,[17] involving up to two weeks' travel on foot. From Nola, Paulinus sends a letter to Bordeaux asking that the bearer, a former slave, be provided with a plot of land.[18] In his turn, he is sent a kitchen boy from Africa by Sulpicius Severus when his own cooks abandon him.[19] Ruricius of Limoges writes to a Gallic landowner on behalf of a man who has fled his wrath, taking refuge in a church at Userca.[20] Peasants—some, at least, clutching letters from landlord or patron—traveled the roads of the late Roman Empire alongside soldiers, itinerant artisans, Imperial officials and the holy.

Our understanding of the physical environment within which these travelers moved has been transformed by recent historical and archaeological research.[21] It is no longer satisfactory to talk of generalized nucleation of settlement, or to identify a decline in population on the strength of falling numbers of recognizably Roman villa sites. Rather, the rural landscape of the late Roman period was characterized by considerable complexity and diversity. Settlement pattern was a conscious choice, determined by the interplay of a complex collection of environmental, social and economic factors. Within this diversity, however, one common feature can be determined. This is the close association of rich and poor, of large and small sites. Villas might be surrounded by hamlets or farmsteads.[22] Small settlements might be situated close to towns.[23] Farmers might issue daily from fortified towns to farm the surrounding fields belonging to them or their wealthier fellow townsmen.[24] Structures of vertical alliance take as their physical context close relations between town, villa and hamlet or village.

---

[15] Sidonius *Ep.* IV.7; *cf.* VII.4.

[16] Sionius *Ep.* II.2; Stevens (1933), 185-95 for attempts to locate Avitacum.

[17] Lyon to Vaison, upwards of 150km; Clermont-Ferrand to Vaison, some 350km.

[18] Paulinus of Nola *Ep.* 12.12.

[19] Severus *Ep.* 3; Lepelley (1989), 236-8 presents the arguments surrounding the attribution of this letter to Severus and Paulinus; Paulinus of Nola *Ep.* 23.

[20] Ruricius *Ep.* II.20.

[21] A brief survey of the literature for the western Empire includes Lewit (1991); van Ossel (1992); van Dommelen (1993); Garnsey (1996); van Ossel and Ouzoulias (2000); Bender (2001); Bowes (2001); Riggs (2001).

[22] Kehoe (1988), 230-4; Percival (1992), 159.

[23] Augustine *Ep.* 20*.10.

[24] *Vita Severini* 10.1.

These structures are customarily complex, mutually interdependent and fluid. Dealings between laborer and landowner exist within the context of dynamic systems of vertical alliance and economic interaction. It can be assumed that surviving letters of recommendation are paradigmatic or formulaic examples of a practice more widespread than the relative scarceness of the current evidence suggests. The letters which do survive reveal that, in some instances, rural laborers gained employment with a landowner by means of a pre-existing alliance with another landowner or patron. The new alliance became itself part of this fluid system of rural labor, in which one landowner's tenant might work as a casual laborer for another; a farmer might temporarily move from one estate to another; and a skilled laborer might be employed on a casual or periodic basis by a number of landowners simultaneously.

The focus here is upon the relationships between ongoing vertical alliances—such as tenancy or patronage—and periodic or incidental alliances of wage-labor. In broad outline, one might sketch the particular characteristics of each in the following terms. Tenancy is in essence an impersonal relationship, privately contracted and founded upon a mutual interest in the occupation or cultivation of land. For peasant lessees, it is an integral part of a 'multi-stranded dependency relationship'.[25] For elite landowners, it is one option among several in a customarily mixed farm management regime.[26] Tenancy remained a fundamental economic strategy for both in the late Roman period.

Patronage relationships seem to be a feature of most if not all agrarian societies.[27] Briefly, they can be defined as enduring, reciprocal relationships of exchange between individuals of unequal status. They contain more than one point of common interest,[28] and are entered into voluntarily by both parties.[29] At an ideological level, patronage was deeply embedded in Roman society.[30] Recent scholarship has incorporated individual relationships within broader systems of patronage. These systems are characterized by fluidity, ambiguity and flexibility, leading to competitive, adaptable structures of alliance.[31] In the late Roman period, patronage systems expanded and changed in response to a reformulation of

---

[25] Foxhall (1990), 99.

[26] Foxhall (1990), 113; Rathbone (1991), 394-401; Aubert (1994), 129-46.

[27] Bloch (1961), 147; Blok (1969), 366; Gallant (1991), 159.

[28] Saller (1982), 1; 194; Garnsey and Woolf (1989), 153-4; for general theories; Wolf (1966), 86-7; Waterbury (1977).

[29] Wolf (1966), 86; Scott (1977), 22.

[30] Wallace-Hadrill (1989), 10; *cf.* Saller (1982), 38.

[31] Johnson and Dandeker (1989), *passim.*

relations between patronage and fiscal responsibility and the emergence of a multiplicity of patrons in rural contexts.[32]

Wage labor is commonly enmeshed with both tenancy and patronage alliances.[33] For landlords and patrons, wage labor satisfies the periodic, seasonal needs of the estate more effectively than the employment of a permanent, under-utilized labor force. For peasant proprietors and tenants, it supplements the income and resources of the household.[34] Wage labor may also be undertaken by marginal populations, itinerants, the rural poor, individuals with few or no other means of subsistence.[35] Skill levels and terms of employment varied. The highly skilled reapers of Palladius' *Opus Agriculturae* and the famous Mactar inscription of third-century North Africa might be regularly employed in gangs at specified times of the year.[36] At the other end of the spectrum, the unskilled *mercennarii* of Varro were employed irregularly and casually, with little hope of ongoing contact with their employer.[37] Often, however, laborers did have direct or indirect links with the landowner or his estate. Comparative literature suggests that landowners hired seasonal labor on a preferential basis, choosing clients over non-clients.[38] Papyrological evidence from the Appianus estate in third-century Egypt reveals that some casual laborers, at least, were related to permanent employees or tenants of that estate.[39]

The letters which form the source material for this paper, however, reveal landlords or patrons using their influence to facilitate the employment of their clients or tenants on another estate, with another landowner. One can speculate that the individuals carrying these letters had some kind of specialized skill. They may, for example, have been blacksmiths, carpenters, potters or coopers. Palladius—possibly following Varro[40]—recommends that each of these specialists be retained on a rural estate, 'lest a need for wandering into town distract peasants

---

[32] *CJ* XI.52.1 (396S, Thrace); *CTh* XI.24.4 (399, Egypt).

[33] White (1970), 366; Garnsey (1980), *passim*; De Ste Croix (1981), 187; Foxhall (1990), 97-8.

[34] MacMullen (1974), 42 with notes 43-8.

[35] De Ste Croix (1981), 187; Finley (1985), 73.

[36] *CIL* VIII.11824.

[37] Varro *RR* xvii.2-3.

[38] References are collected in Gallant (1991), 164.

[39] Rathbone (1991), 392.

[40] *Geoponika* II.49.

from their important labor',[41] and they are among *rustici* exempted from lustral tax payments.[42] However, not every estate would have merited full-time employment of such specialists.[43] It seems plausible, then, that letters of recommendation were one way in which the movement of these specialists between the estates of wealthy landowners could be effected to the advantage of landowners and laborers alike.

Both unskilled and skilled laborers continued to be employed on a casual or seasonal basis on the estates of wealthy landowners.[44] In some instances, these laborers were not regular participants in sedentary agriculture. Rather, they occupied the margins of that society, taking advantage of its occasional needs. In a letter to Augustine, a certain Publicola observes that nomadic tribesmen might be employed to guard the crops:[45]

> Among the Arzuges, as I heard, the barbarians are accustomed to swear by their demons to the decurion or tribune in charge of the boundary. Those who have been hired to escort baggage, or others to guard the harvest, the various landowners and chief tenants are accustomed to receive, to guard the harvest, as if they were of the faithful, upon the decurion sending a letter.[46]

Publicola's principal concern is that these *barbari*, through their oaths to pagan deities, will pollute the Christian crops which they have undertaken to protect. In passing, he reveals a fascinating and unexpected element to the contract of employment. These crop guardians are hired on the strength of a letter written by a military officer.[47] This type of letter vouched for the trustworthiness of the laborer. In this frontier region of North Africa, then, the rural labor market was partially regulated by members of the military stationed there. Such an arrangement was one way of creating a link between laborer and landowner

---

[41] *Op. Ag.* I.6.2: '*Ferrarii, lignarii, doliorum cuparumque factores necessario habendi sunt, ne a labore sollemni rusticos causa desiderandae urbis avertat*'.

[42] *CTh* XIII.1.10 (374, Italy).

[43] Although cf. Aubert (1994), 176, arguing that specialists could be employed in other tasks throughout the agricultural year.

[44] White (1970), 349-50; Rathbone (1991), 390-3; Banaji (1992), 125.

[45] Augustine *Ep.* 46.1.

[46] '*In Arzugibus, ut audivi, decurioni, qui limiti praeest, vel tribuno solent iurare barbari iurantes per daemones suos. Qui ad deducendas bastagas pacti fuerint vel aliqui ad servandas fruges ipsas, singuli possessores vel conductores solent ad custodiendas fruges suscipere quasi iam fideles epistulam decurione mittente*'.

[47] Goodchild (1950), 31.

through the intercession of another. In an anonymous, seasonal labor market, such a link could be crucial.

Alternatively, rural laborers could obtain a letter from a patron or landlord to introduce them to another landowner. Customarily, such a letter spends more time on the relationship between author and recipient than on that between author and bearer. In his letter to Simplicius, Sidonius observes:[48]

> The bearer of this letter earnestly begs me to let him take a note from me to you, although I should inevitably have asked him to do that very thing, even if he had said nothing about it, as soon as I discovered what way he was going; for it is my love for you rather than deference to the courier that has elicited this message.[49]

This example is hardly typical of the letters written for a fellow aristocrat, or the son of a close friend.[50] There, the bearer's good birth, virtue and talents are highlighted.[51] In this letter, Sidonius appears to be doing just the opposite, stressing the *rusticitas*, the boorishness, the undesirable qualities of the bearer by comparison with the culture he shares with Simplicius. This is best expressed in a series of rhetorically humorous paired opposites:

> I picture to myself how novel everything will be to this fellow, who is scarcely an enviable paragon of gentility, when you bid the stranger welcome to your home, the nervous messenger to a talk with you, the bumpkin to your gaiety, the poor man to your table, and when a man who here behaves as a vulgarian amongst gorgers and men surfeited with an overdose of onions, there finds himself treated with as much courtesy as if he had hitherto made himself sick in the company of gourmandizing Apicii and of posturing carvers from Byzantium.[52]

---

[48] Sidonius *Ep.* IV.7.

[49] *'Baiulus apicum sedulo precatur, ut ad vos a me litteras ferat, cuius a nobis itinere comperto id ipsum erat utique, si tacuisset, orandus; namque hoc officium vester potius amor quam geruli respectus elicuit'.*

[50] For example, Sidonius *Ep.* III.10.

[51] Stowers (1986), 153-5.

[52] *'Videre mihi videor, ut homini, non usque ad invidiam perfaceto nova erunt omnia, cum invitabitur peregrinus ad domicilium, trepidus ad conloquium, rusticus ad laetitiam, pauper ad mensam, et cum apud crudos caeparumque crapulis esculentos hic agat vulgus, illic ea comitate retractabitur ac si inter Apicios epulones et Byzantinos chironomuntas hucusque ructaverit'.*

Here, then, is direct contact between the elite of the late Roman Empire and Peter Brown's elegantly named 'barbarian within'.[53] Sidonius himself is equally elegant in encapsulating the terms of this contact when he concludes:

> But whatever his character or importance, he has enabled me to discharge my incumbent duty to the full. And after all, although persons of that sort are generally insignificant creatures, yet in the matter of paying regard to our friends by letters affection loses much if it is deterred from indulging in more frequent correspondence by the lowliness of the bearers.[54]

Though clearly part of an elaborate joke, Sidonius' less than complimentary remarks about the behavior of this man on his own estate suggests that he is not merely an itinerant traveler. It is also worth observing, through the rhetorical flights of fancy, that this journey is made on the laborer's own initiative. It is reasonable to assume that he intends to return to Sidonius' estate, and certainly Sidonius makes no indication that his interest in the man finishes with this letter. From his concluding remarks, it can even be surmised that Sidonius expects a return letter by the same bearer. Perhaps, then, a laborer with some specialized skills—after all, he has come to Sidonius' attention, even if apparently for the wrong reasons—plans to offer that service to Simplicius on a casual basis. It is plausible to suggest that this man is one of the specialist artisans of Palladius' perfect estate. Perhaps also this represents one instance of periodic travel by such a specialist between the estates of a number of related landowners.

Some letters of recommendation do stress the relationship between author and bearer, using it as the foundation for pious claims of responsibility. In a pair of letters written probably in 397[55] on behalf of a *colonus* appealing a legal decision, Symmachus expresses in fulsome tones the obligations placed upon him in his role as the man's landlord. To Hadrianus, *Magister Officiorum*,[56] he observes that 'my reason for writing to you on behalf of Theodulus is more pressing because he is a *colonus* of my fields and my care for him is more an obligation than it is a favor'.[57] To the *quaestor* Felix, he observes that 'to those whom one knows well and esteems, a prompt recommendation is an obligation, so that through an

---

[53] Brown (1971), 14-6.

[54] '*Attamen qualis ipse quantusque est, percopiose me officii votivi compotem fecit. Sed quamquam huiuscemodi saepe personae despicabiles ferme sunt, in sodalibus tamen per litteras excolendis dispendii multum caritas sustinet si ab usu frequentioris alloquii portitorum vilitate revocetur*'.

[55] *PLRE* I, 406, s. v. Hadrianus 2; *PLRE* II, 459, s. v. Felix 2.

[56] For attribution of this letter to Hadrianus, see Bonney (1975), 369-70. I am grateful to John Matthews for his observations on the language and purpose of this letter.

[57] Symmachus *Ep.* VII.56: '*Pro Theodulo autem scribendi mihi ad te causa propensior est, cum sit colonus agrorum meorum atque illi debita magis quam precaria cura praestetur*'.

honorable recommendation they should come to the acquaintance of good people'.[58] These letters are formulaic, as comparison with similar letters of recommendation written by Symmachus reveals. References to *humanitas*, and hopes that 'having been admitted into your clientele, he might rejoice in having both availed himself of my patronage and entered into yours' are customary.[59] They are evidence for an idealized relationship based on mutual obligation, and a commitment to aiding a client's attempts at initiating multiple, complementary relationships.

These idealized, personal bonds—and their attendant demands—may be found elsewhere, in the correspondence of other aristocrats, and in other types of relationship. Ausonius writes to Paulinus of Nola on behalf of Philo, 'formerly my bailiff who ... is in danger of being driven inconveniently from the shelter which your people afforded him' at Hebromagus.[60] Philo is no longer employed on Ausonius' estate, having set himself up as a grain merchant, but he calls upon Ausonius when he experiences difficulties in this new enterprise. Ausonius' attitude to Philo parallels Sidonius' to his unnamed laborer, but he intervenes nonetheless, asserting:

> Unless you kindly grant this my request—namely that he be permitted to stay on there as suits his purpose, and that a barge or some sort of vessel be furnished him, so that a little of my corn may be transported as far as the town, thereby opportunely delivering Lucaniacus from famine—a literary man's whole household there will be reduced, not to Cicero's *Speech on the Corn Supply*, but to the *Weevil* of Plautus.[61]

In this case, the rhetoric cloaks a complex situation. Although the ideology of patronal obligation plays its part, Ausonius is also moved by self-interest. By intervening on behalf of his former bailiff, Ausonius is also ensuring the relief of his own estate, Lucaniacus, from a grain shortage. This combination of idealized benefaction with material self-interest can also be found in the correspondence of Paulinus himself, who includes in a letter to his former confessor Amandus at Bordeaux a request that Sanemarius, a *libertus* of his, be furnished with a small

---

[58] Symmachus *Ep.* V.48: *'Bene cognitis ac probatis commendatio prompta debetur, ut ad notitiam bonorum sub honesta adstipulatione perveniant'*.

[59] Symmachus *Epp.* II.70; VII.56; IX.57: *'admissus in clientelam tuam et meum sibi patrocinium profuisse et tuum accessisse laetetur'*.

[60] Ausonius *Ep.* 26: *'procuratoris quondam mei ..., quas... concesso ab hominibus tuis usus hospitio, inmature periclitatur expelli'*.

[61] *'Quod nisi indulseris rogante me, ut et mora habitandi ad commodum suum utatur et nauso aliave qua navi usque ad oppidum praebita frugis aliquantum nostrae advehi possit, Lucaniacus ut inopia liberetur mature: tota illa familia hominis litterati non ad Tullii frumentariam se ad Curculionem Plauti pertinebit'*.

plot of land on the estate of the Church—so that the man can care for the *memoria* of Paulinus' parents.[62]

These letters of recommendation reveal peasants accessing the horizontal alliances of the aristocracy, exploiting a series of complementary vertical alliances themselves, and appealing to both the altruism and the self-interest of their patrons and landlords. This is in marked contrast to the picture of rural socio-economic relations which has been constructed on the basis of the legislation. It is true that the 'colonate of the late Roman Empire' has undergone significant revision in the past two decades. *Coloni* are no longer believed to have been bound to their landowners in a relationship of personal dependence which was the precursor of the mediaeval serfdom. The *communis opinio* of current scholarship is that they were still juridically free men.[63] But the legal picture of an inert peasantry needs some explanation.

Coloni were recognized by contemporaries to be of a different status from slaves and freedmen,[64] although that status was surrounded by some confusion.[65] The legislation contains repeated reaffirmations of their free status, while acknowledging that the boundary with slavery was problematic. The earliest preserved law on the subject directs that 'those *coloni* who meditate flight shall be bound in chains in the same manner as if they were slaves, so that they shall be forced to fulfill the duties that befit free men by virtue of the slave's sentence.'[66] Likewise, the late fifth- or early sixth-century *Interpretatio* directs that the *colonus* is to be 'reduced to slavery'.[67] A law concerning *coloni* in Thrace concedes that 'they appear to have the status of free men', although it affirms that 'they must be treated as slaves of the land on which they were born'.[68] This was not merely a

---

[62] Paulinus of Nola *Ep.* 12.12. This letter also reveals that Paulinus maintained a proprietary or patronal interest in the land he had ceded to the church at Alingo; for further discussion, Trout (1999), 148-9.

[63] Lepelley (1983), 335; Whittaker (1987), 109; Sirks (1993), 332; 350-1; Carrié (1997), 94; Scheidel (2000), 727-8.

[64] Lepelley (1983), 335 with note 35; 341 with note 62.

[65] Carrié (1983), 252; Carrié (1997), 87-8; 95.

[66] *Brev.* V.9.1 = *CTh* V.17.1 (332, *Ad Provinciales*): '*Ipsos etiam colonos, qui fugam meditantur, in servilem condicionem ferro ligari conveniet, ut officia, quae liberis congruunt, merito servilis condemnationis conpellantur inplere*'.

[67] '*in servitium redigatur*'.

[68] *CJ* XI.52.1 (396S): '*licet condicione videantur ingenui, servi tamen terrae ipsius cui nati sunt aestimentur*'.

legal problem. Augustine asks Eustochius 'whether it is lawful for the owner to make slaves of his tenant farmers or of their sons'.[69]

Confusion over the status of *coloni* emerged from the foundation upon which the relationship between landowner and tenant rested. The authority granted to a *dominus* over his *colonus* was not conceived of as a private law right, as it would be if it were comparable with the *ius in rem* over a slave. Rather, it pertained in public law and was connected with his ownership of the land which the tenant inhabited or cultivated. The bond of the tenant was to the land, not the landlord.[70] For this reason, the law codes reveal restrictions upon both tenants' freedom of movement and landlords' autonomy in effecting or allowing their movement. A law concerning *coloni* in Palestine directs that 'no *colonus* should rejoice in his own right as if he were unattached and free'.[71] A law of Arcadius and Honorius confirms the edict of 332, declaring that landlords had the legal right to reclaim *coloni* who had moved to another *fundus*.[72] Constraints on the movement of *coloni* amounted to a loss of economic independence. Similarly, they were forbidden to alienate land without the consent of their patron, who was held ultimately responsible for its tax burden.[73]

Landowners also lost some economic independence. They were forbidden to replace or expel *coloni* registered on the tax rolls.[74] In the event that a landowner sold or gave away parcels of his land, the tenants of that land were transmitted with the land to the new landowner.[75] In each case, the aim of the legislation was to ensure that individuals registered in the municipal tax rolls as responsible for the fiscal burden of an area of land continued to fulfill that responsibility. In the ideal world which the legislation presents, an immobile peasantry would fulfill the fiscal needs of the government for easily traced, clearly acknowledged hierarchies of fiscal responsibility.

The reality did not conform to this legal ideal. Peasants retained their freedom of movement. They rented a number of plots of land simultaneously, or rented in addition to owning their own land.[76] They combined with agriculture a diversity of

---

[69] Augustine *Ep.* 24*.1: '*utrum liceat possessori seruos facere colonos uel filios colonorum suorum*'.

[70] Lepelley (1989), 246 at note 37.

[71] *CJ* XI.51.1 (393S, Palestine): '*nullus omnino colonorum suo iure uelut uagus ac liber exsultet*'.

[72] *CTh* IV.23.1 = *CJ* XI.48.14 (400, Gaul).

[73] *Brev.* V.11.1 = *CTh* V.19.1 (365, East).

[74] *CJ* XI.63.3 (383, East); *CJ* XI.48.7 (384, Italy); Vera (1997), 216.

[75] *Nov. Val.* XXXV.1.18 (452, Italy and Africa).

[76] Palladius *Op. Ag.* I.6.6; *CTh* XI.1.14 = *CJ* XI.48.4 (371, East).

activities, including hunting, fishing, small-scale pastoralism, contract plowing, pottery, carpentry and the sale of goods.[77] They were involved in a multiplicity of complementary alliances with a multiplicity of patrons, as the epistolary evidence attests. A patron might intercede with a landlord or another patron on a business matter, or to smooth over a private disagreement.[78] A landlord was expected to intercede with government officials.[79] He was responsible for defending his tenants against the unjust claims of another, as a letter written to a certain Salvius by an anonymous North African landowner reveals.[80] A former landlord might intercede with another landlord.[81] The role of the masses in the late Roman Empire, at least, was not merely to be led, exploited and dominated by elites.[82]

Letters of recommendation exchanged by elite landowners were one means of facilitating the movement of rural laborers in the late Roman West. Beyond this assertion, however, the evidence of those letters does not lend itself to firm statements about the functioning of these systems of regulated movement. Some observations, however, are justified, and are offered by way of conclusion. In spite of the recommendations of Palladius, the estates of large landowners were not autarkic in the period. They continued to rely on periodic and casual labor, and, probably, itinerant specialists as well.[83] These specialists may have been tenants of one landowner while at the same time practicing their trade on the estates of others.[84] They could move of their own volition, upon the initiative of their landowner or patron, or on the prompting of a landowner who offered land or needed extra labor.[85]

Vertical alliances between rich and poor in rural contexts—whether of tenancy, patronage or wage labor—were ideologically constructed as close, personal and mutually binding.[86] In practice, no doubt, relationships between

---

[77] *V.Sim.Styl.(Syr)* 6; 7; Paulinus of Nola *Carm.* 18; *CTh* XIII.1.10 (374, Italy); *cf.* Palladius *Op. Ag.* I.6.2; Drinkwater (2001), 143.

[78] Ausonius *Ep.* 2 = Symmachus *Ep.* I.32; Ruricius *Ep.* II.48; Ruricius *Ep.* II.20.

[79] Symmachus *Epp.* V.48; VII.56.

[80] *Epistula ad Salvium* 2: 'ruricolae mei'. The letter is included in the corpus of Sulpicius Severus, but not written by him; Lepelley (1989), 237-9.

[81] Ausonius *Ep.* 26.

[82] The phrase is taken from MacMullen (1990). He presents a rather bleak picture of relations between rich and poor in the countryside.

[83] Augustine *Ep.* 46.

[84] Sidonius *Ep.* IV.7.

[85] Sidonius *Ep.* IV.7; Paulinus of Nola, *Ep.* 12.12; *Brev.* V.9.2 = *CTh* V.17.2 (386, East).

[86] Symmachus *Epp.* V.48; VII.56; Paulinus *Ep.* 12.12; 15.4; *Epistula ad Salvium* 2.

landowner and peasants were brokered or facilitated by a bailiff or farm manager.[87] Nevertheless, the impression gained from the correspondence of these elite landowners is that the inhabitants of their rural estates occupy a more prominent place in the apparatus of self-representation as men of power and influence than in the world of Cicero or Pliny.[88] Finally, a letter of recommendation was not the end of an alliance between landowner and laborer or tenant. Rather, it was a recognizable event in ongoing relations between the two.[89] Letters of recommendation were one element in the dynamic systems of alignment and alliance of the late Roman West which are visible to the historian only in fragments.

---

[87] Symmachus, for example, learns from his farm manager Amazonius that Marcellus—a man who owned fields adjoining one of his estates—is frustrating the attempts of a certain Ursus for a legal hearing (*Ep.* IX.11); *cf.* the Appianus estate in third-century Egypt; Rathbone (1991), 71.

[88] *cf.* Drinkwater (2001), 140-1 on Gallic aristocrats' alternative life paths.

[89] Ausonius *Ep.* 26; Paulinus of Nola *Ep.* 12.12; Sidonius *Ep.* IV.7.

References

Primary Sources

Augustine, *Opera II.2; Epistulae*, A. Goldbacher, ed., *CSEL* 34 (1898).
————*Opera II.6; Epistolae ex duobus codicibus nuper in lucem prolatae*, J. Divjak, ed., *CSEL* 88 (1981).
Ausonius, *Works*, 2 vols., H. G. E. White, ed. and trans., Loeb, (1961).
Codex Iustinianus, Corpus Iuris Civilis vol. 2, P. Krueger, ed., Berlin, (1954).
Codex Theodosianus, T. Mommsen, ed., Berlin, (1905).
Eugippius, *Vita Severini*, H. Sauppe, ed., *MGH(AA)* 1 *pars posterior*, (1877). *Geoponika*, H. Beckh, ed., Teubner (1895).
Palladius, *Opus Agriculturae*, R. H. Rodgers, ed., Teubner, (1975).
————*Opus Agriculturae*, vol. 1, R. Martin, ed. and trans., Budé, (1976).
Paulinus of Nola, *Epistulae*, G. de Hartel, ed., *CSEL* 29, (1999).
————*Carmina*, G. de Hartel, ed., *CSEL* 30, (1999).
Ruricius, *Epistolae*, in R. Demeulenaere, ed., *CCSL* 64, (1985).
Sidonius Apollinaris, *Poems and Letters*, 2 vols., W. B. Anderson, ed. and trans., Loeb, (1936; 1965).
Symmachus, *Opera*, O. Seeck, ed., *MGH(AA)* 6 part 1, (1883).
The Lives of Simeon Stylites, R. Doran, introd. and trans., *CS* 112, (1992).
The Theodosian Code and Novels and the Sirmondian Constitutions, C. Pharr, trans., Princeton, (1952).

Secondary Sources

Aubert, J. J. (1994), *Business Managers in Ancient Rome: A Social and Economic Study of Institores, 200 B. C.–A. D. 250*, Leiden: E. J. Brill.
Banaji, J. (1992), 'Rural communities in the late Empire A. D. 300-700: Monetary and economic aspects', unpub. D. Phil. Thesis, Oxford University.
Bender, H. (2001), 'Archaeological perspectives on rural settlement in late antiquity in the Rhine and Danube area', in Burns and Eadie, eds. (2001), 185-98.
Bloch, M. (1961), *Feudal Society*, London: Routledge and Kegan Paul.
Blok, A. (1969), 'Variations in Patronage', *Sociologische Gids* 16, 364-78.
Bonney, R. (1975), 'A New Friend for Symmachus?', *Historia* 24, 357-74.
Bowes, K. (2001), ''...Nec sedere in villam': villa churches, rural piety and the Priscillianist controversy', in Burns and Eadie, eds. (2001), 323-48.
Brown, P. (1971, repr. 1991), *The World of Late Antiquity*, London: Thames and Hudson.
Burns, T. S. and Eadie, J. W., eds. (2001), *Urban centers and rural contexts in late antiquity*, East Lansing, Michigan: Michigan State University Press.
Carrié, J. M. (1983), 'Un roman des origines: les généalogies du 'colonat du Bas-Empire'', *Opus* 2, 205-51.
————(1997), ''Colonato del Basso Impero': la resistenza del mito', in Lo Cascio, ed. (1997), 75-150.
Clausing, R. (1925; repub. 1965) *The Roman Colonate: The theories of its origin*, Rome: "L'Erma" di Bretschneider.
De Ste. Croix, G. E. M. (1981), *The class struggle in the ancient Greek world: from the archaic age to the Arab Conquest*, London: Duckworth.
Drinkwater, J. (2001), 'Women and horses and power and war', in Burns and Eadie, eds. (2001), 135-46.

Finley, M. I. (1985), *The Ancient Economy*, 2ⁿᵈ ed., London: Hogarth.

——ed. (1976), *Studies in Roman Property*, Cambridge: Cambridge University Press.

Foxhall, L. (1990), 'The dependent tenant: land leasing and labour in Italy and Greece', *JRS* 80, 97-114.

Frézouls, E. (1980), 'La vie rurale au Bas-Empire d'après l'œuvre de Palladius', *Ktèma* 5, 193-210.

Gallant, T. W. (1991), *Risk and Survival in Ancient Greece: Reconstructing the Rural Domestic Economy*, Stanford: Polity.

Garnsey, P. D. A. (1980), 'Non-slave labour in the Roman world', in Garnsey, ed., (1980), 34-47.

——, ed. (1980), *Non-slave labour in the Greco-Roman world*, Cambridge: Cambridge Philological Society.

Garnsey, P. D. A. (1996), 'Prolegomenon to a study of the land in the later Roman Empire', in J. H. M. Strubbe, R. A. Tybout and H. S. Versnel, eds., *ENERGEIA: Studies on Ancient History and Epigraphy presented to H. W. Pleket*, Amsterdam: J. C. Gieben,135-53 (reprinted in P. D. A. Garnsey (1998), *Cities, peasants and food in classical antiquity: essays in social and economic history*, ed. W. Scheidel, Cambridge: Cambridge University Press, 151-65).

Garnsey, P. D. A. and Woolf, G. (1989), 'Patronage of the rural poor in the Roman world', in Wallace-Hadrill, ed. (1989), 153-70.

Gellner, E. and Waterbury, J., eds. (1977), *Patrons and Clients in Mediterranean Societies*, London: Duckworth.

Goodchild, R. G. (1950), 'The *Limes Tripolitanus* II', *JRS* 40, 30-8.

Johnson, T. and Dandeker, C. (1989), 'Patronage: relation and system', in Wallace-Hadrill, ed. (1989), 219-42.

Kehoe, D. P. (1988), *The economics of agriculture on Roman imperial estates in North Africa*, (*Hypomnemata* 89), Gottingen: Vandenhoeck and Ruprecht.

Lepelley, C. (1983), 'Liberté, colonat et esclavage d'après la Lettre 24*: la juridiction épiscopale <<de liberali causa>>', in *Les lettres de Saint Augustin découvertes par Johannes Divjak: Communications présentées au colloque des 20 et 21 Septembre 1982*, Paris: Etudes Augustiniennes, 329-42.

——(1989), 'Trois documents méconnus sur l'histoire sociale et religieuse de l'Afrique Romaine tardive, retrouvés parmi les *spuria* de Sulpice Sévére', *AntAfr* 25, 235-62.

Lewit, T. (1991), *Agricultural Production in the Roman economy A.D.200-400*, BAR Int. Ser. 568, Oxford: Tempus Reparatum.

Lo Cascio, E., ed. (1997), *Terre, proprietari e contadini dell'Impero romano. Dall'affitto agrario al colonato tardoantico (Incontro studio di Capri, 16–18 ottobre 1995)*, Rome: NIS.

MacMullen, R. (1974), *Roman Social Relations: 50 B. C. to A. D. 284*, New Haven and London: Yale University Press.

——(1990), 'The Historical Role of the Masses in Late Antiquity', in *Changes in the Roman Empire: Essays in the Ordinary*, Princeton: Princeton University Press, 250-76 and 385-93.

Percival, J. (1992), 'The fifth-century villa: new life or death postponed?', in J. Drinkwater and H. Elton, eds., *Fifth-century Gaul: a crisis of identity?*, Cambridge: Cambridge University Press, 156-64.

Perrin, M. Y. (1992), '*Ad Implendum Caritatis Ministerium*: la place des courriers dans la correspondance de Paulin de Nole', *MEFRA* 104, 1025-68.

Rathbone, D. (1991), *Economic Rationalism and Rural Society in Third-Century A. D. Egypt: The Heroninos Archive and the Appianus Estate*, Cambridge: Cambridge University Press.

Riggs, D. (2001), 'The continuity of paganism between the cities and countryside of late Roman Africa', in Burns and Eadie, eds. (2001), 285-300.

Saller, R. P. (1982), *Personal Patronage under the Early Empire*, Cambridge: Cambridge University Press.

Scheidel, W. (2000), 'Slaves of the soil: review article', *JRA* 13, 727-32.

Scott, J. C. (1977) 'Patronage or exploitation?', in Gellner and Waterbury, eds., (1977), 21-39.

Sirks, A. J. B. (1993), 'Reconsidering the Roman Colonate', *ZRG* 123, 331-69.

Stevens, C. E. (1933), *Sidonius Apollinaris and his age*, Oxford: Clarendon.

Stowers, S. K. (1986), *Letter Writing in Greco-Roman Antiquity*, Philadelphia: Westminster Press.

Trout, D. (1999), *Paulinus of Nola: Life, Letters, and Poems*, Berkeley, Los Angeles and London: University of California Press.

van Dommelen, P. (1993), 'Roman peasants and rural organisation in central Italy: an archaeological perspective', in E. Scott, ed., *Theoretical Roman Archaeology: first conference proceedings*, Aldershot: Avebury, 167-86.

van Ossel, P. (1992), *Établissements ruraux de l'Antiquité tardive dans le Nord de la Gaule*, 51e supplément à Gallia, Paris: Editions du Centre national de la recherché scientifique.

van Ossel, P. and Ouzoulias, P. (2000), 'Rural settlement economy in Northern Gaul in the Late Empire: an overview and assessment', *JRA* 13, 133-60.

Vera, D. (1997), 'Padroni, contadini, contratti: *realia* del colonato tardoantico', in Lo Cascio, ed. (1997), 185-224.

Wallace-Hadrill, A. (1989), 'Introduction', in Wallace-Hadrill, ed. (1989), 1-13.

———ed. (1989), *Patronage in Ancient Society*, London and New York: Routledge.

Waterbury, J. (1977), 'An attempt to put patrons and clients in their place', in Gellner and Waterbury, eds. (1977), 329-342.

White, K. D. (1970), *Roman farming*, London: Tharnes and Hudson.

Whittaker, C. R. (1976), '*Agri Deserti*', in Finley, ed. (1976), 137-65.

———(1980), 'Inflation and the economy in the fourth century A. D.', in C. E. King, ed., *Imperial Revenue, Expenditure and Monetary Policy in the Fourth Century A. D.*, BAR Int. Ser. 76, Oxford: Tempus Reparatum, 1-22.

———(1987), 'Circe's Pigs: From Slavery to Serfdom in the Later Roman World', *Slavery and Abolition* 8.1, 88-122.

Wolf, E. (1966), *Peasants*, New Jersey: Prentice-Hall.

Chapter 4

Milestones, Communications, and Political Stability

Ray Laurence

Introduction: An Allusion of Change

Late Antiquity has traditionally been associated with a major change that is now described as a transition. The physical remains of that transition can be found throughout not only Central Italy, but also the rest of the Roman Empire as well. A classic example comes from the Via Flaminia, just north of Carsulae in Umbria. Here, the Romanesque church of San Giovanni de' Butris has been built over the top of a Roman bridge that had originally taken the Via Flaminia across the river.[1] This example of discontinuity between the classical and medieval periods is not unusual, but it remains poorly dated. We do not know: when the bridge collapsed, how an alternative route was facilitated, or what effect did the destruction of the infrastructure of this long distance route have on the social and economic history of the region. However, elsewhere we find continuous use of the road, with Romanesque churches sited by the side, pointing to a continuity of settlement and transportation. A useful example of this phenomenon is the location of the church of San Damiano at Carsulae (Figure 4.2). Literary sources point to a similar contradiction. Procopius observed the survival of the paving of the Via Appia from the turn of the second century AD (he attributes this to the original builder—Appius Claudius):

> After much laborious smoothing, the slabs were cut into polygonal shapes and he then laid them together in such a way without using lime or anything else. And they were fitted together with such care and gaps filled so well that, to the onlooker, they appear not to be the work of man but of nature.[2]

The contrast is often made with Libanius viewing a collapsed marshy road near Chalcis:

---

[1] See Figure 4.1; Pineschi 1997 for details of current plans for an interpretative center on the site.

[2] Procopius *Bell.Goth.*14.6-11.

Figure 4.1 San Giovanni de' Butris (Via Flaminia). Photograph courtesy Ray Laurence

Figure 4.2 San Damiano at Carsulae (Via Flaminia). Photograph courtesy Ray Laurence

> In the territory of Chalcis, I came across a road running through the
> remains of an Antiochan winter camp. The road was, so to speak, half
> marsh, half mountain and hard going. The marshy ground was crossed
> by a layer of stones, seemingly cast there by intent, but in an artless
> fashion, unlike other territories, where, in the case of roads, as for
> masonry, stones are rammed together into the built up soil of a causeway,
> as if it were a mortar wall.[3]

The second passage describes a classic example of a road in collapse. The blocks
of stone become obstacles in their own right. As Hugh Davies, an ex-highway
engineer, has informed me—roads cannot continue in use without maintenance.[4]
There is no such thing as a durable maintenance-free road. There is an important
point that needs to be made with reference to the survival of sections of paving
from Antiquity in the archaeological record. These stretches of paving are for the
most part the final surface of Antiquity, rather than the initial road surface. Its
date should not be seen to occur extensively prior to the second century AD, when
an active campaign to resurface the roads of Italy with stone flags was
undertaken.[5]   However, for the utilization of this surface for wheeled
transportation, there was a need for it to be maintained and repaired. The
discussion of the discovery of the route of the major roads is seldom conducted
with reference to the history of Late Antiquity, instead discussion links these
archaeological survivals to the building of the roads, often recorded in earlier
sources such as Livy's *History of Rome*. The presence of literary sources from the
early empire and an emphasis in the history of technology on beginnings, or in our
case the building of a road for the first time, causes the explanation of roads in the
Roman landscape to concentrate on their initial construction.[6] The absence of
precise dating for the actual sections of road, or their survival and collapse in Late
Antiquity causes us to turn to an alternative form of evidence to gain an overview
of the maintenance of the infrastructure of roads in this period—the milestones.

Milestones: A Particular Type of Evidence

A milestone is a particular form of evidence. By definition, these should appear
every mile along the major roads of the Roman Empire. They are numbered, so
that a traveler will know how far they are from their destination and point of
departure. This form of information, when cross-referenced with an itinerary
causes a person in Antiquity to know physically where they are with reference to

---

[3] Libanius 14.6-11.

[4] See Davies 2002 for full discussion of Roman road engineering.

[5] Laurence 1999: 62-7.

[6] Quilici 1991.

their knowledge of travel.[7]   In a similar way today, in the search for ever increasing amounts of archaeological data, researchers use a global positioning system, or GPS, which is cross referenced to the grid references of a conventional map, or the information is downloaded into a geographic information system, or GIS. In both cases, the end result is that a person can understand their position in the landscape, particularly if unfamiliar, with reference to a system of geography.

Looking at the actual inscriptions on the stone markers, we quickly realize that these are more than simply stones that measure miles. The stones, between two and four meters in height (see Figure 4.3), have ample space on them for additional forms of communication. Most, if not all, milestones mention the name of a Roman emperor and in many cases an action associated with the maintenance of the road. This does not necessarily connect that person with the construction of the road itself, but often refers to specific actions of repair or improvement:

> stravit
> refecit
> restituit
> curavit

In contrast, the milestones of Late Antiquity seldom mention any actual form of work undertaken by a specific emperor. This raises the question of what was the purpose of the renewal of a milestone by a particular emperor. The nature of the inscriptions on the milestones changes after the Severan emperors. Previously, the texts referred to a specific action on the part of the emperor in terms of road improvement: paving, repair of old and collapsed structures or simple restoration. After Caracalla, the text changes to refer to the emperors, such as Aurelian, as the restorer of peace or the world (instead of the road) and are expressed in the dative and have been seen to have been dedications to the emperor.[8] The imagery is reminiscent of Aelius Aristides' oration on Rome[9] written in the second century AD, in a way the roads of the empire held together the unity praised through rhetoric in this text. In a similar way, on the milestones of the third century AD and later, we find expressions of the new emperor as the restorer of that world explained by Aelius Aristides. The relationship of the past to the present can be seen by the association of milestones set up at the same point on the road system. A classic example of this phenomenon is found at Hagenbach on the road leading from Mainz up the left back of the Rhine into Raetia. Five milestones have been found here:

> 1. Decius   Dated 249/50
> 2. Postumus   Dated 267/8

---

[7] On itineraries and their use see discussion of Laurence 1999: 82-90; Adams 2001; Brodersen 2001; Laurence 2001; Salway 2001.

[8] Donati 1976: 162; Basso 1987.

[9] *Orat.*24.

Figure 4.3 Milestone at Alba Fucens (Via Valeria).
Photograph courtesy Ray Laurence

3. Carus	Dated 282/3
4. Licinius	Dated 308
5. Licinius Junior	Dated 317

The mode of communication would appear to have changed from a message about the nature of the road and the creator of the ease of that journey[10] to a dedication to the current emperor or the restorer of the world in the case of Aurelian.[11] Milestones of an earlier time, such as those of the disruptors of the world, for example Caracalla, could be turned around and inscribed with a new inscription referring to Constantius 80 years later;[12] whilst in the intervening period a new stone with Probus' name was erected next to the original stone. Hence, we may read the milestones of the empire as a means of propaganda or a means of asserting loyalty to an individual emperor or usurper.[13] The removal and replacement of milestones would seem to be one way to explain the absence of certain emperors from the record, but much depended on local circumstances.

However, although their appearance may have depended on local circumstances, the inscriptions on them are formulaic and have their origins with a centralized authority at a distance. The milestones of Magnentius in the mid-fourth century are a case in point. They are formulaic and find a corollary between their vocabulary and that of coins minted in his brief reign. They read as follows:[14]

> To the Liberator of the Roman world, the restorer of Liberty and of the res publica, the saviour of soldiers and provincials, our lord Magnentius, invicible princeps, victor and triumphator, always Augustus.

The formula is found in Italy, France, Spain, and North Africa.[15] It is repetitive and standardized pointing to an origin with a centralized authority that controlled and stipulated the exact phrasing to be used. However, there is an interesting variation in Central Italy that brings the presence of milestones back to their association with public road building. At Alba Fucens, we find the normal Magnentius inscription with the addition that:[16]

---

[10] Compare Statius *Silvae* 4; Laurence 1999: 42-52.

[11] *CIL* 17.31.

[12] *CIL* 17.13a and 13b; compare examples in Donati 1974: 160.

[13] Isaac 1990: 304-9.

[14] Basso 1986 no.64.

[15] Basso 1987.

[16] Donati 1974 nos 68 and 90.

Flavius Romanus vir clarissimus consularis Flaminiae et Piceni curavit

The verb *curavit* is a classic milestone statement from an earlier era. It certainly refers to some form of work that was overseen by Flavius Romanus. The emperor is honored in the usual way, as found on other milestones, but the extra lines create a reference point to the consul of the region of the Flaminia and Picenum. It makes a specific reference to some undefined work that was conducted in the reign of Magnentius. In other cases, where we do not find the last lines referring to the regional authority, we may assume that the lines were simply not added, but some unspecified form of work was undertaken.

Regional Patterns

The problems of interpretation of the evidence of milestones were raised by Isaac and Roll. They observed in Palestine that the pattern of the surviving milestones did not reflect a survival rate of a uniform distribution across the province. Instead, they suggested that the milestones were concentrated in areas of habitation and were seldom found in desert regions. This questions the utility of the milestone as a marker of distance and position.[17] Moreover, they also question their usage by a local population because they were inscribed in Latin rather than the local language of the area. Hence, they assume that the milestones were set up for usage by the military.[18] However, maybe this underestimates the nature of bilingualism in the region. The local population may not have chosen to speak or write Latin, however they may have been able to identify the meaning of a milestone with its inscription in Latin referring to the number of miles from a place and the imperial, titulature. Signs in languages other than those of the native population need not have been simply ignored. Instead, they would have been incorporated into their understanding of the language of geographical knowledge.[19] Also, the example of Palestine studied by Isaac raises a further question: was the pattern they observed localized to that area of the Roman Empire? Should this pattern of a region that included deserts also be found generally for example in the Western Empire also?

The sample size and the proportion of milestones surviving from Late Antiquity, as opposed to the high empire, are quite striking. Taking the milestones published in *CIL* for Italy as a whole we find 223 coming from the period post AD 284 ending with two milestones set up by King Theoderic in the fifth century. This is a higher number of surviving stones than those found from the first two centuries AD—a period of road construction and maintenance much studied by

---

[17] See Isaac and Roll 1982: 91-8 and more recently Isaac 1990: 304-9.

[18] Isaac 1990: 305; see also Alcock 1993: 120-4 on the absence of milestones from Achaia; in contrast to North Africa, see Salama 1987.

[19] Compare Creighton 2000: 146-73 on responses to coin legends in pre-Roman Britain.

scholars both in Italy and beyond. This highlights the importance of milestones as markers of distance and as a form of communication to travelers in Late Antiquity. There is considerable variation in the data sets for the empire as a whole. For example, from Britain a total of 101 inscribed milestones survive,[20] a much smaller sample to the survival of 450 inscribed stones studied by Isaac and Roll. In contrast, elsewhere, large bodies of material survive and have been published. However, a relatively large sample, of say a thousand milestones from Asia Minor, still represents a poor survival rate, if every major Roman road was marked every mile by at least one large inscribed stone. To examine the broad patterning of the data three regions with a large number of milestones recorded were selected: Italy, Gaul and Asia Minor. Also, the three regions have quite different histories. Italy, at the very center of the empire, provides us with a control on the more militarized provinces such as the Rhine frontier in Gaul or Palestine studied by Isaac and Roll. Gaul, including Germany, had a strong military presence on its borders and hence should identify the role of the army in milestone creation when compared to Italy. Asia Minor offers a further comparison that of the east.

Many milestones simply do not survive. Hence, along a stretch of road, we will be missing evidence that remains unaccounted for. This factor prevents a localized approach to the data that does survive. For example, in the Veneto, a total of 100 milestones have been recorded of which 88 are from the fourth century AD.[21] This pattern may seem exceptional and depends on the low survival rate from the earlier periods alongside a massive loss of stones—if they were set up at intervals of one mile originally. Instead, we need a different approach to the data and to look at the overall data that survives from individual provinces in order to make broad comparisons across the empire. This is done with a view to understanding the data itself and to make a comparison between different parts of the empire. The data is presented as a series of bar graphs in order to compare the variation within the pattern of the data itself.

The pattern of milestone construction in Italy can be cross-referenced to the dated inscriptions set up by the *curatores viarum*.[22] The pattern of evidence through time points to an initial period of the establishment of the road system across the Italian peninsula by the end of the first century AD. There followed a massive interest in the care for roads in the early to mid-second century with just over 30 per cent of all milestones from Italy dated to this period (Figure 4.4). After this period there is a sharp decrease in the number of milestones surviving from the second half of the second century through to the time of Diocletian. It is in the period of the first half of the fourth century that we find the largest number of milestones surviving from Italy as a whole. Even after the mid-fourth century

---

[20] Isaac and Roll 1982; Sedgley 1975.

[21] Basso 1986.

[22] See Ertmann 1976 on the epigraphy of the *curatores viarum*.

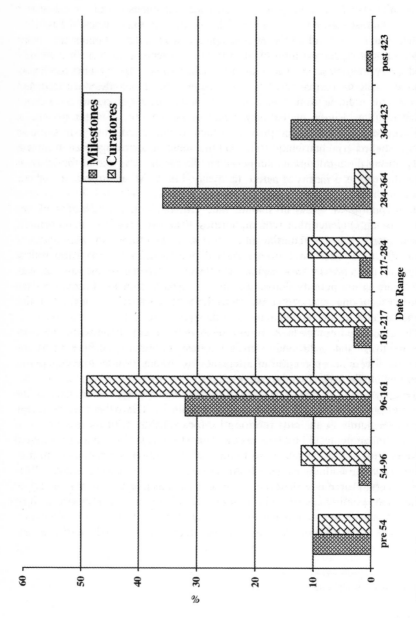

Figure 4.4 Comparison of Milestones and Inscriptions of *Curatores Viarum* in Italy (from Laurence 1999)

down to the time of Theoderic we find a higher number of milestones survive than from the equivalent periods in the third century or even the first century.

The pattern found from the milestones, now published as *CIL* XVII.2, from Gaul, Helvetia and Germania provides our second sample with the last milestone set up in 435. We find in this pattern a period of establishment of the road system in the first half of the first century AD, followed by a period of renewal later than in Italy in the second half of the second century (Figure 4.5). In contrast, to the Italian evidence the largest number of milestones survives from the third century with some continuation into the first half of the fourth century. This patterning follows the observation made by Isaac in 1990 that milestones represent actions of allegiance by military commanders or provincial governors during periods of political conflict. Hence, our example from Hagenbach of five milestones set up in the same place points to that place as a focus of the assertion or expression of loyalty to the imperial household. The fact that these actions are not so prominent in Italy during the third century suggests that during the third century milestones take on this role as a means of asserting loyalty, but it was only relevant to those regions in which there was a military presence. In contrast, in Italy milestones appear in periods of political stability and can be seen as indicators of the assertion of stability by the central authorities. The evidence from Asia Minor[23] shows a pattern that is different again (Figure 4.5). Milestones were set up fairly consistently through second, third and early to mid-fourth centuries. They peak at the time of the tetrarchy in a period of stability and some would say renewal. Where there is a similarity across all sample regions is in the decrease in the number of surviving inscribed stones from the later fourth century and an almost disappearance of the phenomenon in the fifth century.

The evidence from the western provinces only in part supports the thesis of Isaac and Roll[24] that milestones were set up for the military to be read by the military and were an expression of allegiance by the military to a new emperor. The overall chronological pattern supports their case for the third century, but the reappearance of milestones in the less than militarized provinces of Italy in the fourth century suggests a pattern of greater complexity. Here, we may be seeing forms of emulation of the past referring to, for example, Trajan's restoration of Italia.[25] Ultimately, road building in this context emulated the past and asserted the value of road building and the restoration of a treasured tradition that could be traced back to the building of the Via Appia by Appius Claudius in 312 BC. This would suggest that milestones like coins created the imagery of a new era of stability and reconstruction. The absence of milestone construction in Italy reflects a concentration of propaganda or requirement for statements of allegiance to have been made by the military. In the late third and early fourth centuries, the ideals of reconstruction and stability were focussed on Italy as opposed to the

---

[23] Collected by French 1981.

[24] Isaac and Roll 1982; Isaac 1990.

[25] See Laurence 1999: 47-52.

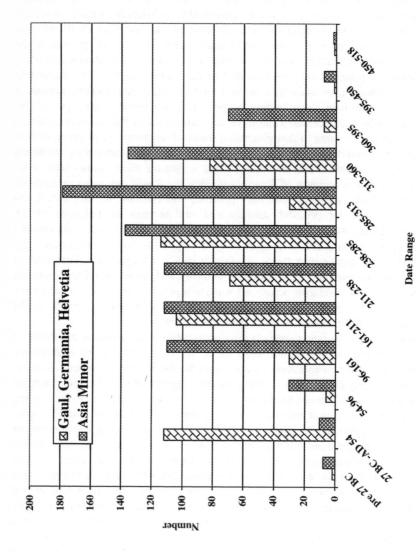

Date Range

Figure 4.5 Existing Milestones: A Comparison across Provinces

provinces of the legions. Hence, we can find a total absence of milestones through the period 161 to 284 from regions of Italy, for example the Sabina and Samnium or the Veneto (Figure 4.6). The presence of milestones in Italy represented an ideology of renewal, which associated the new emperors with earlier examples including: Trajan, Nerva, Claudius and Augustus.

The survival of milestones from the first century AD into the periods of renewal in Late Antiquity reveals something of the experience of the traveler on the roads of the empire. Looking at the milestones to be informed of their position, the traveler encountered inscriptions referring to new or current emperors alongside, quite literally in some cases, earlier ones. A good example is the Via Domitia from Arles to the Pyrenees.[26] Ninety-three milestones survive, two from the time of construction in the Republic, 20 are Augustan (no action is stated), 18 refer to *refecit* or *restituit* under Tiberius, followed by another 26 from Claudius' reign (note the blank for Gaius' principate). Then there are 26 referring to restoration under Antoninus Pius. There remain nine stones from Late Antiquity with a maximum of four being associated with any one emperor—in this case Constantine. The trend here is for an initial period of construction and reconstruction in the first two centuries AD and then in the third and fourth centuries to see a sporadic siting of milestones without the concentrations in any one reign.

Milestones may be interpreted in a similar way to coinage within the period in question. Coins circulated as a means of exchange and carried messages about the centralized power of the emperor. As a corollary, travelers circulated and were presented via the milestones with information in a similar fashion with the emperor's name prominent at each milestone. We could see this as a form of product awareness in Late Antiquity that is contrasted with the direct relationship between the messages on the milestones and the state of the road in the first two centuries AD. This would cause the milestones to be read as signifiers of the history of the present, in which certain individual emperors had ceased to appear on the surviving stones. The primary purpose of the milestone was to measure distance, but the renewal and preservation of them caused the viewpoint to focus on the centralized power. Hence, we should see the milestones as a means of communication to the traveler by those with authority to set up the stones. Certain points on the road system where today we find more than one milestone, for example Hagenbach, became places or points, which were associated with displays of loyalty. This, in part, accounts for the survival of more than one milestone at certain points in the road system, but also identifies these places as locales of politics and the expression of loyalties. The question remains who this might have been—milestones do not give away the secret of their creator, they are often anonymous statements about a distant authority, which may be the key to their strength as a means of propaganda or ideological legitimization.

---

[26] Rivet 1988: 103; Clavel 1970: 414-20.

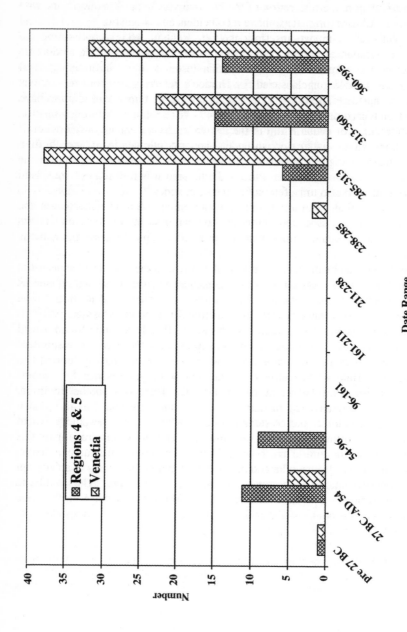

Figure 4.6 Regional Variations: Venetia and Regions 4 and 5 in Italy

Theodoric and the Via Appia

Nowhere is this pattern of propaganda and use of the tradition of road building made clearer than in the restoration of the Decennovius under Theodoric, the first Gothic king. We are fortunate to have a coincidence between our epigraphic and literary evidence. The two inscriptions (*CIL* 10.6850, 6851) proclaiming the action of restoration are confirmed and explained by the text of Cassiodorus.[27] The inscriptions were found near Terracina close to the Decennovius canal system, made famous for classicists by Horace's *Satire,* and record the actions taken under the King Theodoric. The road and canal system would seem to have collapsed and become marshy and action was taken under the direction of a *praeco*—Caecina Mavortius Basilius Decius (ex-prefect of the city, ex-prefect of the praetorian guard, and ex-consul). Cassiodorus is categorical that through neglect arable farming had given way to woodland and marshes. Moreover, he notes that by re-opening the drainage canals the land was restored but we would also expect the road also to be restored at the same time.[28]

The language of the inscriptions are interesting, because it combines the signifiers of power associated with late antique milestones and the actions described in second century milestones from the Via Appia. The King's name is in the nominative, but he is described as: 'Our Glorious and celebrated King Theodoric, victor and triumphator, always Augustus' in the manner of milestones from the third century onwards. The description of the work undertaken is detailed and reminiscent of the actions of *silice sua pecunia stravit* under Nerva and Trajan found on milestones on the Via Appia (*CIL* 10.6839, 6840, 6841). It confirms a reason for the comparison between Theodoric and Trajan found elsewhere.[29] Trajan as rebuilder of the Via Appia and Theodoric as restorer of Trajan's works recreates an image of a golden age from the past, in contrast to Procopius' assertion of the stones of the Via Appia established by Appius Claudius (quoted at the beginning of this article). There was another tradition, often forgotten or ignored by modern authors, reported by Dio Cassius[30] that it was Trajan who built the road of stone through the Pontine Marshes and provided the road with magnificent bridges and mansiones. Theodoric was drawing on this tradition in the restoration of the region, whereas Procopius' text, quoted above, makes no mention of later works and refers only to Appius Claudius in an attempt to break the association between the road and the Gothic King. The politics of road reconstruction as a means to asserting the power of the Gothic King has here

---

[27] *Var.*2.32.

[28] Cassiodorus *Variae* 2.32 reference to the damage to the area and the recreation of marshland, might have been caused by bradyseism or the rise in sea level observed in fifth century. See Arthur 2002: 9-11 on the submergence of Puteoli resulting in its abandonment.

[29] *Anonymous Valesianus* 60.

[30] 68.15.31.

caused Procopius to ignore the role of Trajan. In looking at the Via Appia in the light of this passage, modern authors are drawn to the origins of the road as reported and miss the ideological message of contemporary road reconstruction or the legitimizing tradition of the past and its re-invention. The physical remains of the milestones asserted a different tradition that accounted for a view of history that had been extended into the present by the actions of restoration of drainage on then part of Theoderic. Thus the traveler on the Via Appia could find the link that placed the Gothic King into the traditions of the principate, from the second century of the *Optimus Princeps* and even back to the republic and its builder Appius Claudius more than eight hundred years earlier.

Travel and Communication across Geographical Space

Inscribed milestones were placed on the roads across the empire, initially in the first two centuries AD, to create a sense of measured space and reference to position. Additional milestones were set up, next to those that had originally marked out or measured the road, when repairs or major projects of renewal were undertaken. The latter is particularly apparent in the second century in both Italy and Gaul. In Late Antiquity, the pattern of milestone placement and the message that the inscription contains became quite different. In Italy, in the third century, milestones virtually cease to appear; whereas closer to and on the frontier, we find concentrations of milestones during the third century across provinces associated with concentrations of military units. After AD 284, we see a re-appearance of milestones in Italy, which continues into the later fourth century. Finally, we see a disappearance of these inscribed markers of distance in the fifth century.

  As an epigraphic pattern, the milestones present us with an apparatus for imperial communication between the centralized state and its subjects. The third and fourth century milestones place a stress in their format on the renewal of a world that had been lost. The messages were constructed with an exactitude that points to a centralization of communication that is only found in a similar format in the coinage, or on commemorative arches—such as that of Constantine in Rome.[31] However, even the shortest-lived emperor's titulature appears repeated in the same format on milestones, whether in the east or in the west. The audience for these inscribed stones was the traveler, often an influential civilian, administrator, or soldier. Such minor, and yet more frequent, forms of communication were supplements to the major monuments—not only those famous ones from Rome, for example the arch of Constantine;[32] but also those actually on the roads themselves outside the imperial city, for example the arch of Constantine at Malborghetto on the Via Flaminia.[33] The insertion of milestones of

---

[31] Elsner 2000.

[32] Elsner 2000.

[33] Messineo and Calci 1989.

the new emperor alongside those of Augustus, Claudius, Trajan, and Antoninus Pius were attempts to create an image of a new age.[34] All emperors from Late Antiquity attempted these associations with the past, which we are familiar with on the major monuments.[35] The milestones surviving from Late Antiquity point to how common this phenomenon was, not just in the major towns and along the roads not only of Italy, but in the provinces as well. The new milestones created a juxtaposition, between the name of the emperor in the present and those of the past. If work was done on the road itself, the impression of renewal and restoration was not simply metaphorical—it had a physical manifestation that could for the traveler become a simple proof of the new age, return to the golden eras of the past or restoration of the world. The road as an arena of communication and propaganda points to the continuing importance of travel and the utilization of the road network in Late Antiquity. The pattern of change, as seen in the re-use of a bridge on the Via Flaminia as the foundation for the Church of San Giovanni de' Butris, occurs after Theodoric. More importantly, we should associate the undated bridge not with the documented period of reconstruction of the Via Flaminia under Augustus[36] but instead with the continued use of the bridge in Late Antiquity. The positioning of the surviving literary evidence creates an image of decay and decline in Late Antiquity through a modern perception of its absence. The need for attention to the road system in the first and second centuries is well attested[37] and continued into Late Antiquity. The milestones surviving with a greater frequency in the later period point to repair, renewal and the continuing use of the road system into the early fifth century AD.

---

[34] For the tradition of these emperors see Eutropius' *Breviarum* especially 8.5 on Trajan.

[35] Elsner 2000: 152-3.

[36] *Res Gestae* 20.5; see Ballance 1951.

[37] Laurence 1999: 27-38.

References

Adams, C. 2001. '"There and back again": getting around in Roman Egypt', in C. Adams
    and R. Laurence (eds.) *Travel and Geography in the Roman Empire,* Routledge:
    London, pp. 43-72.
Alcock, S. 1993. *Graecia Capta. The Landscapes of Roman Greece,* CUP, Cambridge.
Arthur, P. 2002. *Naples from Roman Town to City-State: An Archaeological Perspective,*
    Archaeological Monographs of the British School at Rome 12, London.
Balance, M.H. 1951. 'The Bridges of the Via Flaminia', *Journal of Roman Studies* 49: 78-
    119.
Basso, P. 1986. I miliari della Venetia Romana (*Archeologia Veneta* 9).
———1987. La propaganda imperiale lungo le strade romane: il caso miliare di
    Magnenzio al museo civico di Oderzo, *Quaderni di Archeologia del Veneto* 3:
    167-71.
Brodersen, K. 2001. 'The Presentation of Geographical Knowledge for Travel and
    Transport in the Roman World: *Itineraria non tantum adnotata sed etiam picta*',
    in C.Adams and R. Laurence (eds.) *Travel and Geography in the Roman Empire,*
    Routledge: London, pp. 10-26.
Clavel, M. 1970 *Beziers et son territoire dans l'antiquite,* Les Belles Lettres, Paris.
Creighton, J. 2000. *Coins and Power in Late Iron Age Britain,* CUP, Cambridge.
Davies, H. 2002. *Roads in Roman Britain,* Tempus, Stroud.
Donati, A. 1976. I miliari delle regioni IV e V dell'Italia, *Epigraphica* 36: 155-65.
Elsner, J. 2000. 'From the Culture of *Spolia* to the Cult of Relics: the Arch of Constantine
    and the Genesis of Late Antique Forms, *Papers of the British School at Rome* 68:
    149-84.
Ertmann, P.C. 1976. *Curatores Viarum,* Ph.D dissertation, University of Michigan, Ann
    Arbor.
French, D. 1981. *Roman Roads and Milestones of Asia Minor,* BAR Int. Ser. 105, Oxford.
Isaac, B. 1990. *The Limits of Empire. The Roman Army in the East,* Clarendon, Oxford.
Isaac, B. and Roll, I. 1982. *The Roman Roads in Judaea I: The Legio-Scytlopolis Road,*
    BAR Int. Ser. 141, Oxford.
Laurence, R. 1999. *The Roads of Roman Italy: Mobility and Cultural Change,* Routledge,
    London.
———2001. 'The creation of geography: an interpretation of Roman Britain' in C. Adams
    and R. Laurence (eds.) *Travel and Geography in the Roman Empire,* Routledge:
    London, pp. 72-99.
Messineo, G. and Calci, C. 1989. *Malborghetto* (Lavori e Studi di Archeologia 15), De
    Luca, Rome.
Pineschi, I. 1997. 'Dalla ricerche alla valorizzazione alcune proposte concrete', in I.
    Pineschi (ed.) *L'Antica Via Flaminia in Umbria,* Editalia: Rome.
Quilici, L. 1991. 'Le strade romane nell'Italia antica', in R. Cappelli (ed.) *Viae Publicae
    Romanae,* De Luca, Rome, pp. 17-24.
Rivet, A.L.F. 1988. *Gallia Narbonensis,* Batsford: London.
Salama, P. 1987. *Milliare d'Afrique Proconsulare. Un Panorama historique du Bas
    Empire Romaine,* (Coll. Ec. Fr. Rome 101), Rome.
Salway, B. 2001. 'Travel, *Itineraria* and *Tabellaria*', in C. Adams and R. Laurence (eds.)
    Travel and Geography in the Roman Empire, Routledge: London, pp. 27-71.
Sedgley, J.P. 1975. *The Milestones of Roman Britain: their petrography and probable
    origin,* BAR 18, Oxford.

PART TWO
ELITE COMMUNICATION
NETWORKS

Part Two

Elite Communication Networks

Introduction

The four papers in this section address an issue of current scholarly discussion, the growth of large-scale, long-distance communication networks in Late Antiquity. Claire Sotinel explores the geography of information dissemination across the Adriatic Sea based on 'a prosopographical study of information agents'. She concludes in her paper that 'exchanges of [ecclesiastical] news followed a pattern different and independent from other forms of communication, such as trade or pilgrimages'. The next three papers discuss a distinctive phenomenon of the Late Antique world, the multiplication of large-scale letter collections. They show why these collections came into being and discuss the many purposes they served for their creators. Scott Bradbury examines the letters of Libanius to show how new kinds of long-distance networks of travel and epistolary communication were necessary to further the ambitions of the East Roman aristocracy in the centralized political system of the Late Roman state. Michele Salzman also shows how Symmachus' letters built long-distance social networks in the West. She then goes on to show how Symmachus used letters on travel to express the point of view and values of a traditional pagan aristocrat and thereby contributed to a dissemination of his social identity and that of his class. Finally, Wolf Liebeschuetz turns to another large-scale letter collection, that of Symmachus' adversary, Ambrose of Milan, to show how Ambrose used this burgeoning genre to sum up his position on the relations between the Church and the Empire in a 'political testament' intended to present himself not only to his contemporaries but to posterity as well.

Chapter 5

How Were Bishops Informed?
Information Transmission across
the Adriatic Sea in Late Antiquity[1]

Claire Sotinel

Introduction

This paper concerns the reception and dissemination of information in
ecclesiastical matters, with specific focus on the Adriatic Sea. As an indispensable
tool for exercising power and control, information dissemination can be studied as
a way to characterize institutions. This case study of information dissemination
during a specific period of Late Antiquity in the regions bordering on the Adriatic
Sea, re-examines the commonplace understanding that the church in the West took
the place of the Roman imperial state. The study focuses upon the following
questions: how did the churches concretely exercise control over their
communication networks, what did they borrow from the imperial power, and in
what ways did they depend upon the imperial power in doing so? Approaching
these questions in terms of the regions which surround the Adriatic Sea is
worthwhile because the area, in effect, forms both a border separating and a
channel uniting the Greek-speaking East and the Latin-speaking West. The
Adriatic offers abundant documentation insofar as its shore belongs to distinct
ecclesiastical provinces over which a number of different influences were
simultaneously felt: Rome, Milan, Aquileia and Constantinople. A
prosopographical study of information agents active in the area will provide data
contributing to an evaluation of the quality of the dissemination (speed, routes,
efficacy) and of the volume of exchanges, allowing us to measure the evolution of
the geography of influence in the region between the fourth and sixth centuries.

Information is intended here as in the definition proposed by Marco Mostert
in the recent volume, *New Approaches to Medieval Communication*: 'Information
comprises both statements (knowledge, ideas, beliefs) and instructions (purposes,

---

[1] This paper is part of a larger project of the University of Bordeaux involving historians of
Classical Antiquity, Late Antiquity, medieval and pre-modern eras, regarding the history of
information prior to the Enlightenment.

values and norms)'.[2] I employ the term more restrictively than he does, because I am interested primarily in what he refers to as statements, those statements, to be precise, which are expressed in verbal communication. This definition intersects partially with that of 'news' as described by Sian Lewis in her seminal book, *News and Society in the Greek Polis*, where she intends it to mean 'new information about the subject of some public interest that is shared with some portion of the pubic'.[3] Unfortunately, Lewis' book has not yet inspired similar studies in the Roman world. Usually, when historians of Roman antiquity take up questions regarding communication, they concentrate on issues concerning either the technical aspect of road-constructions and speed of journeys[4] or, more recently, the relationship between written and oral communication or the 'diffusion' of culture. Studies of the *cursus publicus* remain concerned with its primarily institutional basis.[5] One finds as a result that these subjects are mentioned in the most classical, the most narrative histories, without being conceptualized. In terms of Late Antiquity, one exception is Lee's *Information and Frontiers in Late Antiquity*, which focuses mostly on foreign policy.[6] Studies concerning letter-bearing couriers would be closer to the subject of this paper, if their attention were more focused on their specific functions than on the sociology of couriers.[7]

Method

This study will examine information and the concrete way in which it is disseminated as one index among others of the nature of power and of the definition of institutions. I have therefore decided to work exclusively on authenticated exchanges in which the vectors of information are explicitly, if only partially, known. I began the research by examining the trove of data amassed in the recently published *Prosopographie chrétienne du Bas Empire – Italie,*[8] which excludes many persons living in other parts of the Empire outside Italy, as well as anonymous messengers. Thus, the results are exhaustive only as far as the data it

---

[2] Mostert, 1999, p. 9.

[3] Lewis, 1996.

[4] Forbes 1955; Achard, 1991.

[5] Di Paola, 1999.

[6] Lee, 1993.

[7] McGuire, 1960; Perrin, 1992.

[8] PCBE It.

provides concerning Italians; in all 148 pieces of information involving 109 messengers and 99 different missions.[9]

I took into consideration reports concerning all the churches located on the sea coast, for the most part Ravenna, Salona and Aquileia (for total of 19 pieces of information). But a study of the transmission of news across the Adriatic obviously represents, in some respects, a contribution to a wider study of relations between Rome and Constantinople, or between Italy and the East. Allowing for the fact that itineraries are rarely precise, I included in the study all documented exchanges of information between Rome and Constantinople, as long as I had no evidence of another routing than the Adriatic. That 126 of these exchanges involved the church of Rome is itself significant in terms of documentation. The assembled documentation may be too small and too anomalous to be used as a sample to characterize communication, but it offers a rich matrix for reflection.[10]

Itineraries

The study showed the point at which indications of itineraries are rare. In only two cases is the route followed by Adriatic travelers precisely described. In 406 a legation which was dispatched to Constantinople in order to carry letters about John Chrysostom from Rome, Milan and Aquileia followed the route of the imperial courier.[11] We know from reports of Palladius that they benefitted from the privilege of *euectio*, but instead of using the Via Egnatia, they went by sea, perhaps from Brindisi to Athens,[12] from where they tried to reach Thessalonica. On the return journey, the legates took a ship which carried them first to Lampsascus (Hellespont), then to Italy, reaching Hydruntum (Otranto) after 20 days of sailing. We also know why Palladius detailed the route: it developed into a major problem. The legates found themselves denied entry first at Thessalonica, then at Constantinople. Meanwhile, the return trip, entirely by sea, was viewed as an imperial sanction, their long crossing of 20 days was a trial, and their arrival all but involved shipwreck. The second case involves a legation sent by Pope Hormisda in 519 to seek reconciliation between the eastern and the western

---

[9] Some people perform several missions (see below the case of Gerontius or Paulinus), but some legations may have as many as eight members.

[10] About the use of prosopographical material: Sotinel 1997, pp. 194-196.

[11] The legation is composed of five bishops (we know the names of Aemilius of Benevento, Gaudentius of Brescia, Marianus and Cythegius), two Roman priests (Bonifacius and Valentinianus) and an anonymous deacon: Palladius, *Dialogues* 3, 118-132, *SC* 341, p. 82; 4, 1-3, 4, 38, *ibid.*, p. 83, p. 90.

[12] The political situation could explain this choice: Illyricum was then at stake between Stilicho and Anthemius.

churches.[13] The pontifical letter which reports the voyage recalled specifically the legates' arrival at Apollonia (Aulon, Albania), their progress through Scampia,[14] Lychnidos (Ohrid, Serbia), Thessalonica, and their arrival at Easter in Constantinople, two and half months after their departure. The slowness of their journey is noteworthy, even though they used the Via Egnatia and clearly had the support of imperial officials. But the aim of their voyage was not only to bring information in Constantinople; it was a mission in search of reconciliation, a mission which successfully began as soon as they landed in Aulon. That explains Pope Hormisdas' interest in recording it.

In 69 other cases, we have to content ourselves with indirect evidence. An Adriatic itinerary can be deduced with assurance when either the sender or the receiver of the message lives on the seacoast. This study includes all the contacts exchanged between Aquileia, Salona, Ravenna or, more generally, Istria or the Dalmatian region. We may suppose that messengers carrying letters which originated in northern Italy and were directed to the East were more likely to use the Adriatic route; however, this conclusion more often represents a mere supposition. For example, we may be sure that Sabinus, a deacon at Milan, traveled from Palestine to Aquileia when he carried a letter from Basil of Caesarea to the bishop Valerianus. But we cannot be sure that, in this voyage, he did not travel from Palestine to Rome first.[15] One unique case concerns a Christian from Parentium (Porec), in Istria, who went to Ravenna to tell King Theodoric how badly he had been treated by local churchmen.[16] Aquileia was involved in the exchange of information across the Adriatic only when information was directed south, because the overland route via Sirmium (Sremska Mitrovica, Serbia) to Constantinople served as the regular line of communication with eastern cities since the second century AD. Aquileia appears in our documentation mostly through the messages sent by or to Jerome, during his stay at Bethlehem,[17] which explains the disappearance of that line of communication in the fifth century, though archaeological data confirm the importation of oriental and African

---

[13] The legation comprises the bishops Germanus of Capua and Iohannes, the Roman deacons Felix and Dioscoros, the priest Blandus and the *notarius* Petrus: Hormisda, *Ep.* 50, *Coll. Avell.* 149, *CSEL* 35, 2, pp. 594-598; PCBE It., pp. 304-309.

[14] Unidentified city in *Epirus Noua*.

[15] Basilius, *Ep.* 91. For Sabinus, a Nicean deacon of Milan when Auxentius was bishop, who made several voyages in the Orient between 368 and 372, see PLRE It, Sabinus 2, pp. 1969-1973.

[16] Cassiodorus, *Variae* 4, 4; PLRE It., Stephanus 16, p. 2117.

[17] In PCBE It, we can find the deacon Heraclius 3, p 977, the *hypodiaconus* Niceas p. 1538 and the nauclerus Zeno (unfortunately forgotten). For the relationships between Aquileia and Palestine, see Duval 1977, pp. 267-289. We have to remember, too, the presbyter Moyses who brings in 347 to Alexandria the letter sent by Valens and Ursacius seeking reconciliation with Athanasius: Hilarius Pict., *Fragm. Hist.* B II, 8, *CSEL* 65, p. 145.

ceramics at least to the end of the sixth century.[18] Thus, our information is concentrated on Ravenna, whose role increases until the end of the period. One notes the absence of mention of any other cities along the Italian coast, such as Rimini, Ancona or Otranto, which at the time were still flourishing urban centers.[19] The specific routing which characterizes the flow of information is different from the more diversified trade routes.

An indirect clue may be provided by the speed of travel. Clearly, the professionals follow the shortest route, the Via Appia until Brindisium, the Adriatic crossing, the Via Egnatia. It was usual for imperial couriers using the *cursus publicus* to make the journey in winter as well as in summer in about twenty days.[20] It can be safely assumed that all imperial couriers followed this route, as well as some of the official church messengers. It is the only route which can explain the rapidity of the journey undertaken by the *subadiua* Gerontius,[21] who departed from Constantinople for Rome in September 450 and returned with a letter on the 6th of December, and only to return again to Rome before Spring. The *agens in rebus* Eulogius who completed three round-trip journeys between Constantinople and Rome between June 519 and October 520 certainly used the same road.[22] The extraordinary travels undertaken by the *defensor* Paulinus, who completed three round-trip journeys between Rome and Constantinople between April 519 and January 520 (one of which saw him leaving the capital in December), leads us to suppose that he, too, availed himself of this most expedient of routes.[23] As Paulinus is a *defensor ecclesiae romanae*, one should suppose that the emperor placed the resources of the imperial post at his service, and that the Gothic king permitted him to use it as well. This example provides a precious indication of the political relations between the church of Rome and the eastern imperial power during the last years of the reign of Theodoric. In fact, it is one of the very few testimonies of an actual collusion between the Catholic church and the imperial power; six years later, Theodoric was to send Pope John to Constantinople in a very different embassy.[24]

---

[18] Panciera 1957; Carre-Cipriano 1987; Arthur 1990.

[19] Panella 1986; recent excavations in Ancona have proved that the harbor was still in use in the sixth century: Salvini 2001; Otranto: Arthur 1994.

[20] According to the rate of nearly 50 miles per day for 1,110 miles, mostly on land, as the crossing from Brindisium to Dyrrachium may take only one day: Ramsay 1925; Riepl 1913.

[21] *PCBE* It., Gerontius 3, pp. 926-927 and PLRE 2, Gerontius 7, p. 509.

[22] *PCBE* It., Eulogius 3, p. 684-685; PLRE 2, Eulogius 8, p. 420. Eulogius is quoted as *agens in rebus* until January 520, *tribunus* and *notarius* later.

[23] *PCBE* It, Paulinus 18, pp. 1664-1665.

[24] *Excerpta Valesiana*, 90.

Finally, we can also reconstruct the routes taken by messengers carrying the letters of Pope Gregory. As Robert Markus has shown in a recent study, because the letters were published in an almost perfect chronological order, 'groupings of letters often provide a clue as to the circumstances of their dispatch and the route taken'.[25] These groupings permit us to affirm that at the end of the sixth century, the main route for contacts with the East follows the Via Flaminia to Ravenna, from where the Adriatic Sea is crossed to Salona.[26] When for several years, the Via Flaminia was also caught up in the military operations of the Lombards, relations between Rome and Constantinople were effectively interrupted.[27] These indirect clues allow us to hypothesize itineraries in 69 cases. Still, there are 68 cases in which it is not possible to ascertain the routes followed.

The conclusions which can be drawn from this study are both modest and interesting. An important point is the significance of the use of the Ravenna–Salona route as the obligatory route to Constantinople at the end of the period covered by this study. We do not know precisely at what point between the beginning of the sixth century and the reign of Pope Gregory the change occurred. The Byzantines concentrated their efforts in defending the Via Flaminia, abandoning the southern road at least after 570 when Benevento became the headquarters of the Lombards in southern Italy. Such a political choice suggests that the Rome-Brindisi road had already lost its importance. After 570, the traditional route of the *cursus honorum* cannot be followed any longer, but neither is the maritime route by Sicily and Malta utilized. This situation may indicate some deterioration in the condition of the Tyrrenian Sea,[28] but for the most part it suggests the arrival on the scene of a new polarization of communications which required couriers to pass through the headquarters of political authorities, or even the complete dependence of the church of Rome upon the Empire where communication was concerned. It would be interesting to know whether church messengers were controlled by imperial authorities in Ravenna. On the other hand, both senders and receivers of information seemed completely indifferent to the route which was taken, and did not engage in any discussion of this subject. The sole exception consists in the commonplace reference to the dangers involved in traveling on the high seas which is, however, normally expressed only in regard to journeys involving friends or acquaintances who are charged with carrying information. The issue of the speed involved in the transmission of information, which is raised less than one would normally imagine, is never mentioned in relation to any specific itinerary. In this, the spreading of news is considered as a strictly technical matter, which does not affect the nature of information.

---

[25] Markus, 1997, pp. 206-209.

[26] Markus, 1997, p. 207. The letters sent in the Orient systematically are associated with letters destined either for Ravenna or Salona: Markus, 1997, p. 209.

[27] Gregorius, *Ep.* II, 28; Feliciangeli, 1908.

[28] Carandini, 1986, pp. 9-10; Panella, 1986, pp. 451-459.

Some Observations on Chronology

The assembled documentation can be exploited in order to convey something about the variations in the flow of information. The documentation is obviously too sporadic to permit any systematic analysis; furthermore, it may be useful to remember that the use of prosopographical data allows us to study only the part of information transmission which concerns the messengers. Still two significant observations are possible. First, no decrease in the number of exchanges is noticeable during the period. On the contrary, a tendency toward an increase in exchanges of information can be observed throughout the period: ten missions are attested between 325 and the end of the reign of Theodosius, 32 between the death of Theodosius and 476, 35 during the period when Italy is politically independent of the Byzantine emperor and seven during the Gothic war (535–52) then, following a period of decline, with only two identified journeys between 552 and 590, the registry of Gregory informs us of eight missions specifically concerned with the transmission of information between Italy and the East.

Reports of these exchanges are unequally distributed over the given time period. Clearly, certain cases are marked by an intensification of exchanges; such is the case in regard to the Council of Chalcedon (451), which might not in itself be surprising. However, it is important to draw attention to the fact that Chalcedon provides much more material concerning transfers of information than does the Arian crisis of the fourth century.[29] Chalcedon is even surpassed by the schism of Acacius and the various attempts at its resolution. The schism, in fact, is responsible for generating a massive assembly of documentation between 484 and 536.[30] In contrast, the Three Chapters controversy, which is known both in the East and the West, provides only a small number of exchanges. On the other hand, there are long periods during which the subject of this enquiry cannot be studied at all, owing to a lack of evidence. One such lacuna extends for 14 years between the Council of Nicea and 339; we observe another one of 23 years' duration between 375 and 398, a further one lasting 11 years between 439 and 449, inclusive, and, finally, a lacuna between 565 and 584. These are the longest periods of unrecorded exchanges and they lead to some reflections. Only the last lacuna mentioned can be partially attributed to a military situation. The brutality of the Lombard invasion and the difficulties attested by a number of contemporary witnesses were clearly the cause of the rupture in contacts between Italy and the East, as the letter of Pope Pelagius II, which restored exchanges after a long interruption, explicitly claims. Pelagius was the first Roman bishop since the end of the Gothic war who was consecrated without the assent of imperial

---

[29] The council of Chalcedon may have been a turning point in the history of information in more than one way. Not by chance can we observe only after 450 a clerical staff devoted to diplomatic missions: Sotinel, 1998, pp. 113-114.

[30] No less than 34 people are involved in the negotiations about Acacius between 484 and 536.

authorities.[31] But not even in this unique case is the war a sufficient explanation because the lacuna in our documentation begins two years before an invasion which at first affected only northern Italy. None of the other lacunae can be related to any specific trouble arising from political life. Instead, for the most part, they coincide with those moments in which political power was physically present in the West. It is an apparent paradox that relations between western and eastern churches (or between the western churches and the eastern political milieux) seem more intense during periods of political separation. Moreover, the schism of Acacius, a period of both political and ecclesiastical independence, is the period in which the greatest number of messengers is attested.

The two explanations which can be suggested for this apparent paradox clarify two completely distinct aspects of the history of information and its links with the history of institutions. On the one hand, it demonstrates the importance of the contacts between the Italian churches and imperial power. The contact is so strong that when the political power vanishes or grows more distant, it does not create the conditions for a *de facto* autonomy, but, rather, a need for contacts across a longer distance. Remote information is nothing but a substitute for more immediate relations, such as those attested between the emperor and the northern Italian churches of the fourth century. One could make an argument concerning the clearly involuntary manner in which the western churches, Rome included, learned *malgré elles* to live in this relative independence from political power which was to be, in later centuries, such a strong point of Roman pontifical ideology. On the other hand, let us recall that we are only considering those exchanges of information the vehicles of which merited particular attention. It appears, not surprisingly, that attention to vectors of information is not explicitly paid unless they exercise an influence on the content of information. Thus, the more delicate the matter, the more likely that the vector of information determines the quality of the transmission. Indeed, the density of our documentation in periods of political or religious turmoil attests simultaneously a marked determination to maintain contacts and the increasing difficulty in attaining this objective. Only a major military catastrophe, as during the worst moments of the Lombard invasion, can impede the travels of information couriers.

Conclusion

From a methodological point of view, this paper has demonstrated the usefulness of the *PCBE* corpus, which allows us to collect more consistent series of data revealing new forms of historical evidence. On the other hand, despite its systematic character, this prosopographical corpus is, by nature, very selective and should never be considered as representative of any aspect of reality in the late

---

[31] Pelagius II ep., in Gregorius, *Epistulae*, Appendix, in MGHep. II, pp. 440-441.

ancient world.[32] This feature does not signal a failure on the part of the prosopography; on the contrary, it makes it more useful. In the present study, the selective nature of the *PCBE* permitted us to define a specific type of information, the high political and strategical value of which justifies the interest in information vehicles. In this way, the prosopographical approach establishes a typology of information.

From the point of view of the history of information, the present study demonstrated ways in which the exchanges of news followed a pattern different and independent from other forms of communication, such as trade or pilgrimages. We have observed that the geography of information transmission does not conform entirely to that of Adriatic traffic as a whole,[33] and that its chronology does not simply comprise periods of political or religious history. As a result, this study might provide a first step toward a history of western churches and information in Late Antiquity.

---

[32] In this, it differs from the PLRE, which can be used in a very different way for administrative history.

[33] Sotinel, 2001.

References

Achard, G. (1991), *La communication à Rome*, Paris: Les Belles Lettres.
Arthur, P. (1994), 'Ceramics and early Medieval central and Southern Italy: a potted History', in Francovitch T., and Noyé G. (eds), *La Storia dell'Alto Medioevo italiano (VI-X secolo) alla luce dell'archeologia Convegno Internazionale (Sienna, 2-6 dicembre 1992)*, Firenze: All'insegna del Gillio, pp. 412-421.
———— (1990)'Anfore dall'alto adriatico: il problema del''Samos Cistern type', *Aquileia Nostra* 61, pp. 281-295.
Carandini, A., 'Il mondo della tarda antichità visto attraverso le merci', in Giardina, Andrea ed, *Società romana e impero tardoantico* vol. 3: *Le merci, gli insediamenti*, Roma-Bari: Laterza, pp. 3-19.
Carre, M.-B., Cipriano, M. T. (1987), 'Note sulle anfore conservate nel museo di Aquileia', in *Vita sociale, artistica e commerciale di Aquileia romana, Antichità Altoadriatiche* 29, pp. 479-494.
Di Paola, L. (1999), *Viaggi, trasporti e istituzioni: studi sul cursus publicus* (Pelorias 5), Messina: DiScAM.
Duval, Y.-M. (1977), 'Aquilée et la Palestine entre 370 et 420', in *Aquileia e l'Oriente mediterraneo, Antichità Altoadriatiche* 12, pp. 263-322.
Feliciangeli, B. (1908), *Longobardi e Bizantini lungo la via Flaminia nel secolo VI*, Camerino.
Forbes, J.R. (1955), 'Land transport and road building', in *Studies in ancient technology* II, Leiden: Brill, pp. 126-186.
Lee, A.D. (1993), *Information and Frontiers: Roman foreign relations in Late Antiquity*, Cambridge-New York: Cambridge University Press.
Lewis, S. (1996), *New and society in the Greek Polisi*, London: Duckworth.
Markus, R. A. (1997), *Gregory the Great and his time*, Cambridge: Cambridge University Press.
Mostert, M. (ed.) (1999), *New approaches to medieval communication*, Turnhout: Brepols.
Panciera, S. (1957), *Vita economica di Aquileia in età romana*, Venezia: Associazione nazionale per Aquileia.
Panella, C. (1986), 'Le merci : produzioni, itinerari e destini', in Giardina, A. (ed.), *Società romana e impero tardoantico* vol. 3: *Le merci, gli insediamenti*, Roma-Bari: Laterza, pp. 431-459.
PCBE It: Pietri (C. + et L.) dir., J. Desmulliez, Chr. Fraisse-Coué, E. Paoli-Lafaye, Ch. Pietri, L. Pietri et Cl. Sotinel, *Prosopographie Chrétienne du Bas-Empire*, 2, *Prosopographie de l'Italie chrétienne (313-604)*, vol. 2, Rome, 1999-2000.
Perrin, M.Y. (1992), '*Ad implendum caritatis ministerium*. La place des courriers dans la correspondance de Paulin de Nole', *MEFRA* 104, 2, pp. 1025-1068.
Ramsay, A.M. (1925), 'The speed of the roman imperial post', *Journal of Roman Studies* 15, pp. 62-74.
Salvini, M. (2001), *Lo scavo del lungomare Vanvitelli: il porto romano di Ancona*, Ancona.
Sotinel, C. (1997), 'Le recrutement des évêques en Italie aux IVe et Ve siècles: pour une enquête prosopographique', in *Vescovi e pastori in epoca teodosiana. XXV Incontro di studiosi dell'antichità cristiana Roma, 8-11 maggio 1996*, 1, Rome, pp. 193-204.
———— (1998), 'Le personnel épiscopal, enquête sur la puissance de l'évêque dans la cité', in Rebillard, É. and Sotinel, C. (eds.), *L'évêque dans la cité: image et autorité*, table ronde organisée à l'École française de Rome, 1-3 décembre 1995, Rome: Collection de l'École française de Rome 248, pp. 105-128.
———— (2001), 'L'utilisation des ports dans l'arc adriatique à l'époque tardive (IVe - VIe siècles)', *Antichità Altoadriatiche*, 46, pp. 55-71.

Chapter 6

Libanius' Letters as Evidence for Travel and Epistolary Networks among Greek Elites in the Fourth Century

Scott Bradbury

The great letter-collections of the fourth and fifth centuries bear indirect witness to a prodigious amount of travel in Late Antiquity, travel on a scale unparalleled in earlier periods of the ancient world. The correspondence of Libanius of Antioch constitutes the largest of these collections, some 1544 letters falling into two distinct groups: a larger corpus of roughly 1250 letters composed in the single decade 355–65 and a smaller corpus of 300 letters written between 388 and 393.[1] We do not know whether Libanius decided, for reasons of political security, *not* to keep copies of letters between 365 and 388 or whether they were simply lost. If he did maintain anything like his rate of composition between 355 and 365 (an average of one letter every three days), then we could assume that some 2000 letters have—mercifully!—not survived.

How are we to account for the phenomenon that Libanius wrote so many letters and, more generally, that Late Antiquity, as opposed to earlier periods, witnessed the production of so many great letter-collections?[2] My interest here is

---

[1] I cite the letters of Libanius in the standard Teubner edition of Richard Foerster. O. Seeck, *Die Briefe des Libanius zeitlich geordnet* (Leipzig 1906), is the fundamental work on the letters, but must be supplemented with A. H. M. Jones, J. R. Martindale, et al., *The Prosopography of the Later Roman Empire*, vol. 1 (A.D. 260-395) (Cambridge 1971) and P. Petit, *Les Fonctionnaires dans l'oeuvre de Libanius* (Paris 1994). Individuals included in *PLRE* are referred to by their *PLRE* number; persons of curial status are referred to by their number in Seeck's *BLZG*.

[2] There exists no general study of letter writing or letter-collections in Late Antiquity. An observation of Giles Constable about medieval letter-collections could apply equally well to their Late Antique counterparts, 'The serious study of letters and letter-collections as a type of historical source is one of the least developed branches of medieval historiography' (*Letters and Letter-Collections*. Typologie des sources du moyen-âge occidental 17 [Turnhout 1976] 7). On ancient letters and letter-collections, see H. Koskenniemi, *Studien zur Idee und Phraseologie des griechischen Briefes bis 400 n. Chr.* (Helsinki 1956), K. Thraede, *Grundzüge griechisch-römisch Brieftopik* (Munich 1970), S. K. Stowers, *Letter Writing in Greco-Roman Antiquity* (Philadelphia 1986), A. J. Malherbe, *Ancient Epistolary Theorists. Sources for Biblical Study*, no. 19 (Atlanta, Ga. 1988), J. T. Reed, 'The Epistle',

not in the literary motives for which men of letters compiled the great collections and wished them preserved. Libanius, for example, undoubtedly wished his letter-collection to be preserved as a 'style book' for other correspondents. The actual content of the letters only becomes meaningful after painstaking historical reconstruction and the rich prosopography of the corpus would have been virtually impenetrable within a generation after Libanius' death. My concern is rather with the social conditions that promoted the high volume of travel and epistolary communication implicit in a vast letter collection like that of Libanius. By virtue of its sheer size and geographical range, Libanius' corpus can moreover serve as a window on the travels and epistolary communication of a wide sampling of the provincial elites of the Greek East in the fourth century. I will argue that the provincial aristocracies of the Greek East of the fourth century engaged in more travel and expended more effort in the creation and maintenance of extended networks of influence via personal visiting and the exchange of letters than their predecessors of earlier periods of antiquity.

Due to the period's social, political and religious developments, the Later Roman Empire saw the creation and expansion of large inter-provincial networks of influence that could only be forged and maintained through extensive travel and carefully cultivated lines of communication. The growth of Christian networks paralleling and promoting the growth of the Church is the most obvious example. It is hardly surprising that most of our great Late Antique letter-collections were written by bishops.[3] Libanius' corpus was also produced to service a vast network of connections, though it is directed to a quite different social and religious milieu, namely, the traditional, still predominantly pagan, provincial aristocracies of the Greek East. His letters suggest quite clearly that travel and the maintenance of social networks between cities and across whole provinces were both increasingly obligatory in the fourth century for prominent families who wished to maintain their wealth, status and power.

In the early empire, prominent Eastern families might dominate their home cities through purely local resources and local networks of influence. Few Greek provincials had political opportunities beyond their native cities.[4] By comparison,

---

in *Handbook of Classical Rhetoric in the Hellenistic Period (330 B. C. - A. D. 400)*. Ed. S. E. Porter (New York 1997), M. L. Stirewalt, *Studies in Ancient Greek Epistolography* (Atlanta, Ga. 1993), J. L. White, *Light from Ancient Letters* (Philadelphia 1986).

[3] For an up-to-date study employing social network theory to analyse one bishop's personal network, see M. Mullett, *Theophylact of Ochrid: Reading the Letters of a Byzantine Archbishop* (Aldershot, England; Brookfield, Vt., USA 1997). There are also useful studies employing social network theory in M. White (ed.), *Social Networks in the Early Christian Environment: Issues and Methods for Social History* (Atlanta, Ga. 1992).

[4] By 249 AD there were still only 182 officials of equestrian rank in office in the empire, according to H. G. Pflaum, *Les procurateurs équestres sous le haut-empire romain* (Paris 1950) 102. On the slow arrival of Easterners to senatorial status, see A. Chastagnol, 'Remarques sur les sénateurs orientaux au IVe siècle', *ActaAntHung* 24 (Budapest, 1975) 341-56.

the expansion of the provincial system and the growth of the imperial government in the fourth century created an age of opportunity, at least for those with influence in the imperial consistory, the body which actually dispensed the high offices of the empire.[5] Those sorts of connections needed to be developed through the cultivation of a personal network, whether through physical travel or through letters. In addition to creating opportunities for ambitious notables, the expanded provincial system of the fourth century also created complications for prominent families accustomed to dominating the local politics of their cities. The imperial government interfered more in their affairs than it had ever done in the early empire, and former imperial officials (*honorati*) would return home after a term of office, having built up personal networks in other provinces and often at court. These wider connections naturally gave them advantages in social and political dealings at the local level. The heavy hand of the *honorati* is best attested in Antioch, but the problem was faced by local aristocrats of smaller cities as well.[6] Consequently, there was pressure on all families who wanted to stay competitive to cultivate extra-local networks of influence.

Libanius is not of course a representative correspondent. His status as a sophist and a personal predilection led him to forge and maintain an epistolary network of unusual proportions. Some 700 letters involve sophistic activity and fully 500 involve present or former students.[7] Although Libanius does not openly recruit students via letters, recruitment and promotion of his students' careers are a fundamental motive behind the extraordinary breadth of his connections. He seems normally to have had between 50 and 80 pupils and we know the social origins and/or career paths of 204 of them.[8] Although half the school was perhaps recruited from Antioch itself, the other half came from surrounding provinces, virtually all the provinces of the Greek East. The largest contingents of students came from Phoenicia and Palestine, Cilicia, Galatia, Cappadocia and Armenia, and finally, Constantinople itself.[9] As we would expect, his epistolary network and the home regions of his known students overlap to a considerable degree. The central artery of this epistolary network is the imperial post road running from Antioch through Tarsus, Ancyra, Nicomedia and on to Constantinople. Hundreds of letters travel that route and not just because of Constantinople's political

---

[5] P. Heather, 'New men for new Constantines? Creating an imperial elite in the eastern Mediterranean', in P. Magdalino (ed.), *New Constantines: the Rhythms of Imperial Renewal in Byzantium, 4th–13th Centuries* (Aldershot, England 1994) 11-33.

[6] Heather, 'New men' pp. 25-32; W. Liebeschuetz, *Antioch: City and Imperial Administration in the Later Roman Empire* (Oxford 1972) 186-92.

[7] P. Petit, *Les Etudiants de Libanius* (Paris 1957) 137.

[8] Petit, *Les Etudiants*, pp. 68-70.

[9] Petit, *Les Etudiants*, p. 114.

prominence. Libanius had spent his early teaching years in Constantinople and Nicomedia, and he remained very well connected in both cities, which explains how he was able to recruit so successfully from them, despite their distance from Antioch. The prominence of students in the letters is important for the theme of travel and epistolary networks because we are offered the opportunity to observe a good sampling of Greek provincial aristocrats at different periods of their lives, from their initial sojourn away from home for study in Antioch and later when their political careers would carry them away from their home provinces.

Were the young men who set out for Antioch to study with Libanius likely to engage in more travel during their lives and to maintain more extensive epistolary networks than their counterparts in earlier periods? I would argue that they did because the social and political conditions of the day required them to do so. Travel for the purpose of rhetorical studies was hardly new, but the career paths pursued by these young men after leaving school were different because so many sought social and political advancement away from their native cities. The boys' families were of course prominent, often the *protoi* or *principales* of their cities or imperial office-holders, and they were on the whole still pagan. In the best-documented regions, nearly all the boys who study with Libanius can be linked together. They usually belong to a series of extended, intermarrying families, many of whom send their sons to Libanius. In Armenia, for example, 18 of the 20 known students can be linked in such a network of local, prominent families.[10] Often we discover an old schoolmate of Libanius who was probably the catalyst for local recruitment.[11] For a solid majority of these students, the study of rhetoric at Antioch was the first step in a career path involving travel and the opportunity to develop personal connections well beyond their native cities.

Just over one-third of Libanius' students were recruited among the sons of imperial officials.[12] Those boys almost invariably pursued high office, initiating their careers in a palatine bureau or as advocates at the bar of a prominent official. Some maintained their native city as a place of residence, but many seem to have taken up residence in another city. Further, nearly 50 per cent of Libanius' students were of curial origin, whereas only 21 per cent returned to their home cities and fulfilled their duties as decurions.[13] Those who did not return home were thus active participants in one of the most conspicuous social phenomena of the day, the 'flight' of the decurions.[14] Wealthy students of curial origin were lured by imperial service, occasionally by advocacy, provided that it offered curial immunity. Poor decurions, by contrast, seem to have lacked the support to secure

---

[10] Petit, *Les Etudiants*, p. 132.

[11] Petit, *Les Etudiants*, pp. 132-34.

[12] Petit, *Les Etudiants*, p. 172.

[13] Petit, *Les Etudiants*, pp. 165-78.

[14] On curial flight, see Liebeschuetz, *Antioch*, pp. 174-86.

an imperial post. They tended to gravitate toward advocacy as a way to make money, but again they do not appear to have had enough backing to secure the positions conferring curial immunity. Unlike their wealthy counterparts, who often belong to extended clans and benefit from a succession of letters of recommendation, the 'poor boys' appear in isolated letters, often addressed to a governor of a neighboring province where the boy has traveled in the hope of escaping his city council.[15]

Tarsus offers a good example of a successful extended clan that illustrates the themes I have been discussing. Of the 14 students known from Tarsus, ten can be related to a network of inter-connected families.[16] The central family is represented by three older brothers, Hierocles 3, Demetrius 2 and Julianus 14, along with two unnamed sisters.[17] Hierocles had been a rhetor (in fact, he had been a teacher of Themistius), and an advocate. Demetrius was himself a sophist, that is, he composed orations, which he exchanged with Libanius, and he played a key role in Julian's pagan revival in Tarsus. Amongst them, those three brothers held five governorships in neighboring provinces during the 340s and 350s, and Themistius summoned Julianus to be a senator in 359. Of the three sons known in the next generation, one had been a fellow student with Libanius—he died in 355. Another son, Alypius 4, is unusual in that he sought an imperial post in the west. We find him as *vicarius* of Britain in 358 and a loyal supporter of Julian in Gaul. He was later the *comes* charged by Julian with the rebuilding of the Temple in Jerusalem. Alypius' brother, Caesarius 1, was *vicarius* of Asia in 362–63, *comes rei privatae* in 364 and Prefect of Constantinople in 365. In all, this large family sent four sons to study with Libanius. Due to the break in the letters after 365, those boys' careers are unknown, but they too undoubtedly entered imperial service. What is striking about this single family in a single decade is that one of them is always in office and two sons are very well connected at court. They offer a particularly successful example of a pattern that is reduplicated in other regions where Libanius is well connected.

Libanius personally loathed travel and never left Antioch again after his return in 354. Moreover, he deplored his contemporaries' tendency to set off for Constantinople or the court in the pursuit of power. Although his most vehement outbursts about the 'flight' of the best men from their cities belong to his later years, when he had become increasingly alienated by the pace of social change, his personal inclinations emerge occasionally in the early correspondence as well. For example, in 358 he wrote to a young kinsman, Thalassius 2, who had just taken up a post at court in Sirmium, where he was reported to be working very hard:

---

[15] On the distinction to be drawn between 'rich' and 'poor' decurions with lists drawn from Libanius' letters, see P. Petit, *Libanius et la vie municipale à Antioche au IVe siècle après J.-C.* (Paris 1955) 338-42 and Petit, *Les Etudiants*, p. 121.

[16] Petit, *Les Etudiants*, pp. 122-24.

[17] *PLRE* 1, *Stemma* 15, p. 1139.

> I expected you to do that [that is, work hard], once you had gone there, but
> I expected you to consider staying at home better than going there.
> Whoever has a wife, young and good, but no children yet, and moreover
> has great wealth, enough so as to bring him happiness, why does he need
> to give up shepherding what he has and preparing for heirs from his own
> line and, instead, to be all agog at something else? To me, at any rate, *that*
> seemed to be the advantageous course, both back then and now, but you
> chose departure on the pretext that you would be coming back again in
> summer.   Instead, you've fastened on the Pannonians [the court at
> Sirmium] and disregarded your promises! (*ep.* 377)

Libanius' most intimate friends shared his prejudice against imperial service; most declined to hold office. But the fate of Libanius' own family illustrates the problem with 'staying local'. There were two branches to the family, a staunchly municipal branch, represented by Libanius and his favorite uncle Phasganius, and an office-holding branch, represented by an uncle Panolbius.[18] The municipal branch disappeared with the death of Libanius himself. Panolbius' branch, by contrast, married children of the Praetorian Prefects, Thalassius 1 and Helpidius 4, both conspicuous examples of the Christian aristocracy of service that had prospered under Constantius. That branch of the family became Christian and office-holding; they owned properties across several provinces, and despite setbacks under Julian and Valens, they prospered and produced a Consul in 404. Moreover, a cousin from that branch, Spectatus, was a *notarius* at court and entrusted with important imperial business involving constant travel: two embassies to Persia in 356 and 358 as well as frequent trips between the court in the west and Constantinople and Antioch.   Spectatus served as Libanius' most trusted letter-carrier and his principal contact at court for Libanius and his friends in the 350s. He played a vital role in establishing and servicing Libanius' network of contacts at court in Italy and Pannonia.

Most of Libanius' friends and students served as governors and rose no higher. Many held only one governorship, but many others held several. By law they were not normally allowed to govern their native province, so they island-hopped in the surrounding regions.   Indeed, it would not be much of an exaggeration to say that they served as governors in each other's provinces. For example, Libanius' old friend Priscianus 1 practiced as an advocate both in his native Beirut and at Antioch before being appointed governor of Euphratensis for 360–61. He was succeeded there by Julianus 14, one of those older three brothers from Tarsus. After a year out of office, Priscianus was appointed governor of Cilicia.   During that year he had the opportunity to extend and deepen his connections with the Tarsus families we have already met. In 364, he became governor of Palestina Prima, adjacent to his native Phoenicia, and thereafter passes out of the historical record as the letters break off. Priscianus' multiple

---

[18] *PLRE* 1, *Stemma* 18, p. 1141.

governorships allowed him the opportunity to extend his connections in several provinces near his native Beirut and his adopted home in Antioch.

Libanius treats his friends' service as governors as an extension of the normal activities of a prominent *principalis*. For example, his formula for how to be a model governor is remarkably uncomplicated. All one had to do was to 'make the cities flourish', that is, one respected the rule of law, promoted the interests of admirers of Hellenic culture, and left office poorer than when one entered it.[19] In his letters, as in honorific inscriptions, we find the same attention to the governor's culture, justice, and liberality. The emphasis on lavish spending is particularly interesting, since it is, in effect, the old ideal of civic *philotimia* projected into a larger political arena. Provincial elites of the second century competed by decorating their home towns. Provincial elites of the fourth century competed by holding governorships in which, ideally at least, they decorated the capital of a neighboring province.[20]

A substantial majority of Libanius' contemporaries thus pursued careers involving some form of imperial service and all of these posts could only be secured through the patronage of powerful functionaries with influence in the emperor's consistory. Prominent families needed to mobilize their resources to create the network that would incorporate the necessary high officials. To do so, they travelled and corresponded with an eye to forging and extending their connections of friends and allies, both through office-holding and through cultivation of friendships. The result, as we observe it in Libanius, is a world which seems constantly in motion and constantly working at networking.

As governors Libanius' friends had real authority, but there were also serious checks on their power. Their office was temporary, the permanent imperial staff might frustrate their plans, and the province's resident *honorati* might well have connections and influence more powerful than the governor. Prudence was advisable. Libanius occasionally wrote letters of introduction for new governors who wanted to meet the people that counted in their new provinces. When the Antiochene sophist Marius 1 was appointed governor of Phoenicia in 363–64, Libanius wrote to two former governors there, Andronicus 3 and Gaianus 6. *Ep.* 1460 is an excellent example of this practice, 'I said to the governor [Marius] that Andronicus was a friend of mine, and he said "Well, why don't you write to Andronicus?" So I'm obeying him and I'm writing to tell you and all the Phoenicians that you have what is best from Antioch!'[21] Libanius' friend Sabinus

---

[19] Cf. *Epp.* 150, 332, 391, 438, 459, 747, 1217, 1261.

[20] On Greek evergetism in the early empire, see P. Veyne, *Bread and Circuses* (London 1990) 71-200; for the transfer of 'la manie du bâtiment' from *curiales* to provincial governors and *honorati*, see Petit, *Libanius et la vie municipale*, pp. 291-293 and 318-319; Liebeschuetz, *Antioch*, pp. 132-36.

[21] *Ep.* 1460 to Andronicus 3, a native of Constantinople who had settled in Tyre after serving as governor of Phoenicia in 360–61. *Ep.* 1461 is addressed to the outgoing governor, Gaianus 6, also a resident of Tyre. Gaianus is an example of a man governing

5 as governor of Syria in 358 had run afoul of powerful interests. He was hounded with prosecution in his year after office and refused to serve again. Whoever governed Cilicia had to contend with the network of connections of the Tarsus clan I described earlier. So governors exercised caution, conciliated powerful local families and used their term of office to extend their own network of connections.[22] Extended prominent families holding multiple governorships developed a web of connections stretching across several provinces. The successful placement of a family member at court greatly enhanced their access to the key patrons who handed out imperial offices. These conditions taken as a whole made it difficult for prominent provincial families to 'stay local' and they help to explain why the fourth century seems so much more international and cosmopolitan in character than earlier periods.

---

his native province. *Ep.* 799 alludes to the unusual nature of his post. *Ep.* 107 also alludes to a recommendation to a departing governor.

[22] Brown, *Power and Persuasion*, pp. 20-21, 24, 29.

Chapter 7

Travel and Communication in
The Letters of Symmachus

Michele R. Salzman

A reader might expect to find reflections on Roman society or exciting descriptions of new experiences in the accounts of travel narrated by Symmachus in his *Letters*. That reader would be disappointed. Nor would that reader find a notion of travel as a means to personal or religious progress. Yet travel, with its inconveniences, its earthly pleasures and its opportunities for social interaction, figures prominently in many of the letters of this key figure in late Roman society. Symmachus was, despite his protests about disliking travel, a man in motion. His accounts of his travels advertised his ties to the world of the elite—friends, villas, patronage, pleasure. They also reveal the importance of his ties to the past of his family and of Rome. Thus, for Symmachus, travel and his accounts of it served to communicate his values and perspectives to other Roman aristocrats of the fourth century, many of whom shared his views.

This paper will explore, first, where Symmachus and the Roman elite in his circle in the late fourth century Western empire went and what they say about why they went there. Then, I will look at Symmachus' expressed attitudes toward travel and his accounts of particular places, for they reveal much about the persona that Symmachus wished to manifest in his relations with family and friends. I will focus on travel in *Book 1* of the *Letters of Symmachus* since these can be set within a specific time period, ca. 370–84, a period that established the foundations for Symmachus' reputation as a writer, orator, and statesman.

Before I begin traveling through the *Letters* of Symmachus, however, I think it important to emphasize certain aspects concerning the circulation of these letters that show how public these *Letters* were. Although written as private correspondence to specific individuals, each of Symmachus' letters, when received, was read aloud to the members of the household and to friends; typically, the confidential bits of information or controversial views on public affairs would be conveyed by the letter carrier in private, oral conversation.[1]

---

[1] References to Symmachus' *Letters*, *Books 1-8* are to the text published by J.P. Callu, *Symmaque, Les Lettres* Vols. 1-3 (Paris, 1972-1995). References to *Letters*, *Books 9-10* and to his *Orations* are from the text published by O. Seeck, *Symmachi Opera, MGH AA 6.1* (Berlin, 1883). Symmachus mentions information being delivered orally by letter carriers often; see for example, *Ep.* 1.11, .46, .87.2, .90.1; 2.11, 2.21; 3.30, 4.44; 6.13, 8.31,

Symmachus kept copies of the letters he wrote and at some time in the 380s or 390s, it was probably Symmachus himself who, in my view, collected the correspondence of *Book 1* and circulated it; the remaining books of letters—*Books 2-7* certainly, and *Books 8-10* possibly—were collected for publication between 402 and 407/8, either by Symmachus himself, who died before he could finish the project, or by Symmachus' son, Quintus Fabius Memmius Symmachus, whose name appears in subscriptions to books.[2] Thus, Symmachus' letters in *Books 1-7* were collected for publication by Symmachus and/or his son; *Books 8-10* of the letters were likely a later addition, possibly compiled from family archives in the fifth century, as S. Roda suggested, perhaps in response to Symmachus' growing reputation as an epistolographer.[3] Indeed, Symmachus' letters were read, in part because they were viewed as exemplars of stylish, elegant correspondence, and in part because they were of general social and historical interest, for the people with whom Symmachus corresponded were among the leading figures of his day.[4]

I stress the public nature of these letters for this explains much about them. It explains why, for example, there is no mention of Symmachus' embarrassing support for the usurping emperor Maximus in 388.[5] But, more immediately, their

---

9.37. *Ep.* 6.18, notes that Symmachus gave oral information about a grain shortage to his letter carrier, so that the recipient of the letter will learn more by listening than by reading.

[2] The explicits to the letters of Symmachus that name Memmius as the compiler of the correspondence after Symmachus died are only extant for *Books 2 and 4*. This led S. Roda, *Commento storico al Libro IX dell'epistolario di Q. Aurelio Simmaco* (Pisa, 1981), pp. 69-79 to argue, rightly I think, that Memmius only published *Books 2-7*. *Books 8-10* appear to follow a different organizational pattern than *Books 2-7*, and contain some anonymous letters as well as some letters to correspondents already included in earlier books. And the subscription to *Book 10* indicates the inclusion of speeches as well as senatorial *sententias*. Hence, I follow Roda in seeing *Books 8-10* as a later compilation, perhaps drawn from the family archives. Because *Book 1* of Symmachus' letters is thematically unified and fits within such a narrow chronological time frame, I see much reason to agree with Roda's suggestion that *Book 1* was published by Symmachus himself. For discussion of the thematic unity of *Book 1*, see P. Bruggisser, *Symmaque ou le rituel épistolaire de l'amitié littéraire. Recherches sur le premier livre de la correspondance, Paradosis 35* (Fribourg, Switzerland 1993).

[3] A. Cameron, 'The Real Circle of Symmachus', Unpublished paper, makes this argument, developing the ideas of S. Roda (1981), pp. 69-79.

[4] For the interest in reading and preserving Symmachus' letters, see H. Peter, *Der Brief in der römischen Literatur* (Hildesheim, 1965 rept.), pp. 142-143 and Symm. *Ep.* 2.48.1; 2.12. For the reception of letters, see M. Mullett, *Theophylact of Ochrid. Reading the Letters of a Byzantine Archbishop. Birmingham Byzantine and Ottoman Monographs* Vol. 2 (Aldershot, Hampshire U.K. 1997), pp. 31-37 with remarks pertaining to fourth and fifth century practice; and P. Cugisi, *Evoluzione e forme dell'epistolografia Latina* (Rome, 1983).

[5] Symmachus composed and delivered a panegyric to Maximus, but he notes only the fact that he delivered a speech of apology to Theodosius and obtained pardon; *Ep.* 2.13; 2.28,

public function explains why Symmachus, and later his son, were conscious of the degree to which these letters could serve as 'advertisements' for their reputations and for that of their family. Because representation of self and family was a key motivation behind the selection and publication of these letters, Symmachus' travels and his description of these travels, I will argue, must be read not as a simple account of his movements, but as one component, consciously shaped, of Symmachus' and his family's reputation. Thus, Symmachus' descriptions of his travels serves to communicate his literary persona, as do the letters that include these descriptions.

Symmachus' Travels

In ten books of correspondence extending over a period of some 28 years, Symmachus mentions only a handful of places as travel destinations. Almost all of these are in Italy, in the areas near Rome, to Latium, and Campania, and especially to the Bay of Naples. These are the traditional resort destinations of the Roman elite mentioned in literary accounts from the second century BC on, and noted as desirable destinations in no small part because they were also close to the City. There are a few brief references to travel further afield, but these are limited. Symmachus notes trips to the court at Milan and there is reference in passing to time in Trier in Symmachus' youth. Symmachus also mentions time spent in Africa as proconsul. However, there are no descriptions of these places further afield.[6]

It is hard to believe that Symmachus' travels had such a limited scope. In the first place, it was typical for late Roman landowners to visit their estates to assure a steady source of income and to keep an eye on their physical upkeep.[7] Indeed, from his letters we know that Symmachus had at least 15 country villas in Latium and in the southern part of Italy as well as income producing estates in Samnium, Apulia, Sicily and Mauretania; he may have had more estates in other provinces, not explicitly mentioned in his correspondence.[8] In fact, Symmachus does, in

---

.30, .31 (*Ain panegyrici defensione*), .32, 8.69; Soc. *H.E.* 5.14.6; Lib. *Ep.* 1004.8 (ed. R. Foerster).

[6] For Symmachus' travel to Milan, see Symm. *Ep* 7.13; to Trier, *Ep.* 9.88; for reference to his proconsulship of Africa, see *Ep.* 8.5, 8.21, and 9.115. Symmachus does not note travel to Sicily, but he did have reason to go there; see *Ep.* 9.52.

[7] D. Vera, '*Simmaco e le sue proprietà: Struttura e funzionamento di un patrimonio aristocratico del quarto secolo d.c.*', in F. Paschould (ed.), *Colloque genevois sur Symmaque* (Paris, 1986), pp. 231-275. So, for example, Ambrose's brother, Uranius Satyrus, visited Africa in 374 to check on his properties there: Ambr. *De exc. Sat.* 58.

[8] O. Seeck (1883), pp. XLV-XLVI.

Book 1, tell us of his visits to estates in Campania and Latium to assure the upkeep of his property.[9]

The limited range of named destinations in Symmachus' letters is all the more striking if we take into account that Symmachus and his circle also traveled on public business. As members of senatorial legations or imperial delegations, they went with some frequency to the imperial centers at Milan and Trier. Symmachus, for example, was chosen by the senate in 368/9 to go to Trier to deliver an oration and a gold offering for Valentinian's *quinquennalia*, and to recite a panegyric to Gratian.[10] Although Roman aristocrats probably used the public post for such a trip, travel for this purpose is represented, if at all, as uncomfortable and unpleasant, especially if it involved travel to a distant, foreign city. According to Symmachus, Nicomachus Flavianus the Elder alleged as a reason for considering resignation of his office the fact that he had to travel to Constantinople.[11]

One frequent reason for travel noted in the letters of Symmachus is the consular games. This is not surprising, given that these were annual events of great public and private import. Indeed, consular inaugurations seem much like presidential ones. An invitation was an important sign of distinction, where one's presence and demeanor were judged. A decision not to attend might have important political as well as social ramifications, requiring considerable tact. When Symmachus sent his regrets for not attending a certain set of consular games, he sent apologies not only to the consul designate but to the friends of the consul designate as well as to the emperor. So for example, when he could not attend the consular games of Syagrius in 380 or 381, he sent apologies not only to Syagrius, but to Syagrius' friend, Proculus Gregorius, and to another anonymous friend as well.[12]

There are six occasions of refusals to attend consular ceremonies in 28 years of Symmachus' correspondence. From these we can extract a set of acceptable excuses. One could cite the difficulties of travel, and one could emphasize these by noting the impact on one's health. In *Epistle 6.7*, addressed to Symmachus' daughter and her husband, Nichomachus Flavianus the Younger, Symmachus explains why he will not leave Rome for Milan for the consular ceremonies of Honorius in 398:

---

[9] Symm. *Ep.* 1.5; and in another letter, *Ep.* 1.10, again to his father, Symmachus boasts of improvements made to a villa at Capua, although he would rather be on vacation: "*Ita desiderato et expetito otio ad negotium concessimus sumptuosum.*" In the final letter to his father, *Ep.* 1.12, Symmachus notes his habit of 'doing what he has been ordered to do' (*Mos gestus est imperatis*) as reason for traveling to an estate of unknown location so he can make repairs.

[10] Symm. *Or.* 1; *Or.* 3.

[11] Symm. *Ep.* 2.8, .17, .23; 5.36.

[12] Symm. *Ep.* 5.34, .38.

> For you (both) know of my weakened health, and you understand that my son would be left alone; and you have learned that the rivers have swollen to the point that I fear a flood. The news has also reached you, I think, that the bridges are down and there are landslides.[13]

As is clear from this letter, travel in winter was most problematic, especially if going as far from Rome as Milan. Travel arrangements took time; a late arriving invitation could be cited as reason enough for not attending Neoterius' consular ceremonies in 390 in Milan or Petronius Probus' in 371 in Trier.[14] In another letter, Symmachus claims that two days' notice is not enough time to get from Naples to Rome to attend some praetorian games.[15]

Symmachus' Attitudes to Travel

Unwillingness to appear far from Rome may perhaps explain why most of the consular inaugurations that Symmachus declines were held either in Milan or Trier.[16] Distance from Rome was a consideration, even when Symmachus could use the services of the public post or a government servant (*apparitor*), which he did when traveling to the consular inauguration of Valentinian in Milan in 387 and that of Stilicho, probably also in Milan in 400.[17] We know that Symmachus was willing to go to some consular ceremonies held in Rome; he mentions doing so for Atticus in 397.[18] Hence, in considering Symmachus' refusals to attend consular inaugurations it is not so much merely the desire to advance his career, as William

---

[13] Symm. *Ep.* 6.7.1: *Nam et fractam valetudinem meam nostis, et unici mei solitudinem contemplamini, et eruptiones fluminum usque ad metum diluvii conperistis, pontium quoque ruinas et montium labes apud vos, ut arbitor, fama non tacuit.*

[14] Symm. *Ep.* 5.38 for Neoterius' inauguration; *Ep.* 9.112 should be identified with Probus' inauguration, as demonstrated by S. Roda (1981), pp. 247-249.

[15] Symm. *Ep.* 9.125.

[16] The consular inaugurations that Symmachus declines were held either in Milan, as were those of Syagrius (*Ep.* 1.101) in 380 or 381, Valentinian 2 and Flavius Neoterius (*Ep.* 5.38) in 390, Honorius (*Ep.* 6.7) in 398 and Manlius Theodorus (*Ep.* 5.4, 5.5) in 399, or Trier, as were those of Sextus Petronius Probus (*Ep.* 9.112) in 371, and Ausonius (*Ep.* 1.19, .20) in 379.

[17] Symm. *Ep.* 3.52; 3.62; 4.69 for Valentinian's games; *Ep.* 4.31, .49; 7.4, .7 .8; 8.21; 9.8 for Stilicho's inauguration, on which, see also Claudian, *De consulatu Stilichonis.*

[18] Symm. *Ep.* 7.30.

McGeachy argued, as a host of personal and public considerations in which the distance to be traveled, location, and personal comfort were significant factors.[19]

Travel did present certain challenges, made more pressing when long distances had to be considered and when the times of the year were taken into account. Rising waters, poor road conditions, landslides and cold weather made travel in winter, as already noted, least desirable. Indeed, Symmachus may exaggerate, but it would appear that travel was postponed and communications were disrupted in winter.[20] But even in the best of circumstances and seasons, travel could be dangerous. Unexpected rains could wash out roads even in spring.[21] Robbers could make one hesitate to travel to a distant estate, or civil unrest with unruly soldiers, even in Campania, might frighten a wealthy traveling aristocrat.[22] The more distant the travel, the more likely that a band of barbarian invaders might make travel difficult, as was the case for Symmachus on an embassy to Milan in 402.[23]

Regardless of distance or mode of travel, and regardless of the fact that he had use of state servants or the public post, Symmachus almost invariably expresses a strong distaste for travel on public business. Typical is *Epistle* 7.54: 'Since you are well informed in all matters, you know how much worry an embassy involves, how much difficulty a distant journey'.[24] This distaste for travel might lead an aristocrat to avoid office. So, for example, Symmachus explicitly urges Nicomachus Flavianus the Elder to 'forget the delights of Baiae which are so threatening to virtue' and to turn, instead, to the rewards of public office.[25] This attitude toward travel—which Symmachus himself articulates—could easily lead to insularity and deter an aristocrat from seeking offices that entailed frequent movement or foreign embassies. Such an attitude would be counterproductive to a career in public office. Yet, in the empire of the fourth century, travel was a necessary requirement if one were to serve the emperor or be part of the ever-expanding imperial bureaucracy or imperial entourage. Paradoxically, the very goals of aristocratic life—namely office and public honors—could be threatened by giving in to this quite understandable

---

[19] J.A. McGeachy, *W. Aurelius Symmachus and the Senatorial Aristocracy of the West*, Ph.D. Diss. (Univ. of Chicago, 1942), pp. 99-100.

[20] Symm. *Ep.* 1.65: *Quid hiems faciet quae terra et mari morabitur commeatus?*

[21] Symm. *Ep.* 7.7.

[22] Symm. *Ep.* 2.22 for the robbery; 7.38 for soldiers.

[23] Symm. *Ep.* 7.13, .14.

[24] Symm. *Ep.* 7.54: *Ut es rerum omnium sollers, scis quantum legatio habeat sollicitudinis, quantum peregrinatio difficultatis.* Cf. *Ep.*1.14.

[25] Symm. *Ep.* 2.8, .17.

foreign travel. Hence, it is with a sense of the noblesse oblige that Symmachus, the dutiful aristocrat that he presents himself as being, will urge others and will, himself, put up with foreign travel on public service.

But there is more than just dislike of the inconveniences of travel at work here, for Symmachus' distaste for travel on public business is coupled, in his *Letters*, with a marked unwillingness to celebrate or even describe at length untraditional locales. Although Symmachus did travel to new centers of power—notably Milan and Trier—he does not describe these cities in positive terms as attractive places to visit or reside.[26]

This negative view of travel when on business—*negotium*—is in sharp contrast to Symmachus' generally positive attitude and warm descriptions of places in Latium or along the Campanian coast. Only when he visits these traditional elite venues does Symmachus express pleasure. His *Letters* make frequent mention of his trips to seaside estates and mountain retreats, either his own or those of friends, at Baiae, Bauli, Capua, Cora, Cumae, Formia, Fundi, Laurentium, Naples, Ostia, Praeneste, and Puteoli. Symmachus dwells happily on his travels to these areas, debating the relative merits of residing by the ocean at Formia or Naples, or retreating to the mountains of Laurentium or Praeneste. Indeed, one of Symmachus' epistolary commonplaces is to contrast the pleasures of a seaside to a mountain retreat.[27]

When describing travel to these venues, travel itself becomes a pleasurable social event—an extension of the *otium* traditionally associated with Roman aristocratic life. The elite on such trips traveled more comfortably than when traveling on business. Often, Symmachus and his friends would take small ships from Rome to Campania, a cause for some concern but not so extreme as to prevent their continued use.[28] If going by land, Symmachus would travel via carriages drawn by horses or mules (*iumenta*) rather than on horseback.[29] This mode of travel was slower, but it was preferred. It allowed for the ostentatious display of an elegant carriage. And time was not an issue for Symmachus who, like his peers, traveled at a leisurely pace, stopping at villas, his own or one of his friends. One of Symmachus' trips shows the pattern; Symmachus left Rome in spring or early summer of 396 (*Ep.* 5.93). After summering in Puteoli and Bauli,

---

[26] The one foreign place described in a positive light is the River Moselle, but this description occurs in a letter to Ausonius in which Symmachus, in gently mocking tones, calls into question the veracity of the poem describing the river; Symmachus' description in *Ep.* 1.14 is not of a real journey.

[27] Symmachus writes in favor of the mountains: *Ep.* 7.35; cf. *Ep.* 7.15, .18, .20, but he can also write in favor of visiting a seaside resort, as in *Ep.* 2.55, 7.31, .37.

[28] Symm. *Ep.* 2.4, .5, .6, appear gently mocking Nicomachus Flavianus' fears about such short sea voyages on the Bay of Naples.

[29] Senators usually traveled in carriages drawn by horses or mules. See Symm. *Ep.* 6.12.4, .15, and .26.2.

he left for Naples at the end of October. After two days there, he left for Capua. He evidently planned to spend the month of November returning to Rome, but it was nearly January before he got to the city.[30] It is the pleasures of this sort of travel as a social occasion that led Symmachus to see a trip to Campania as 'solace from movement'.[31] This view of travel surprises, given Symmachus' frequent references to the inconveniences of travel on public business; it makes sense only in reference to the leisurely socializing that travel offered the elite, the sort of travel that Symmachus wants to be seen as engaged in. So, playing on his notion of the solace offered by travel, Symmachus indicates in a later letter in *Book 5*, that only the presence of his friend, Helpidius, will offer some consolation for his undertaking a trip, even if it is just a short one to Campania. The key to Symmachus' professed reluctance to travel is that this trip was necessitated by some sort of official business.[32]

Symmachus' limited list of travel destinations and descriptions casts him in the image of the traditional Roman senator and landowner, enjoying the pleasures of a private life surrounded by powerful friends and family. This image emerges most prominently in the programmatic opening letter to the correspondence, *Epistle* 1.1. Here, Symmachus makes much of his travel from his wife's estate at Bauli (a bit beyond Baiae, in the direction of Cape Misenum) on the Bay of Naples to his place on the Lucrine Lake (north of Baiae and southeast of Cumae). It was not because he was tired of Bauli that he moved; quite the contrary, he claimed. He feared that he would not be able to tear himself away to visit other of his properties.[33] Yet, Symmachus dwells on the villa he has left at Bauli. He boasts of a portrait gallery there that included the villa's famous former owners, the consul Septimius Acindynus and Symmachus' father-in-law, Memmius Vitrasius Orfitus signo Honorius. Symmachus composed some verses that celebrated the public offices of these two men and included these in this first letter.

> My father-in-law wears the palla, an Attic cloak, my father, the toga picta; the former was in charge of sacred rites, the latter set law for Roman citizens. I, whose broach fastened military attire, governed as a

---

[30] Symmachus left Rome in early summer of 396: *Ep.* 5.93. His itinerary is outlined by O. Seeck (1883), pp. LXI-LXII.

[31] Symm. *Ep.* 5.12.

[32] Symm. *Ep.* 5.93. Although the text is not entirely clear, public business of some sort furnished the reason for this visit to Campania where the presence of Helpidius is said to be the solace for Symmachus' trip. I follow the text offered by J. P. Callu, Tome 2 (1982), pp. 222-223: '*Ipse memento promissi quo te ob causas publicas peregrinationis meae fore solacium spopondisti*', and translate as 'You remember your promise that you would be a consolation for my trip which was undertaken for official reasons'.

[33] Symm. *Ep.* 1.1.2.

praetorian prefect of the emperors among the peoples of the East. But my image makes no note of my consular fasces; look back at the list of offices [to find it].[34]

Symmachus emphasized the glory of this villa further when he turned to versifying the history of Bauli. Symmachus notes, in verses that were also included in this letter, that Bauli had a legendary heroic founder, Hercules. It attracted famous inhabitants, like the republican orator Hortensius, and the above-mentioned consul Acindynus, Symmachus' father-in-law Orfitus, and himself!

> Here the god Alcides brought together his flocks to be stabled,
>> flocks torn away from the home of the three-bodied Geryon.
> As a result, a more recent age has altered 'Boalia'
>> and calls it Bauli, with a suggestive hint of its [original] name.
> Fortune has descended from this god to distinguished masters,
>> so that this famed place not endure obscure owners.
> Hortensius, fortunate in his wealth, lived in this hall,
>> the man who competed in eloquence against the man from Arpinum.
> Here, the consul Acindynus has led an outstanding life,
>> and here Orfitus [lived], who ruled over the descendents of Aeneas.[35]

Symmachus thus chose to use this letter to open his first book, and to dwell on Bauli as a means of establishing Symmachus' persona as a cultured Roman noble, distinguished by his classical learning, his family, and his civic prominence. By dwelling on his villa and his family's accomplishments, Symmachus asserted his link to a glorious past, one tied to venerable pagan deities, like Hercules, and to illustrious holders of public office, as were members

---

[34] Symm. *Ep.* 1.1.3:

> *Attica palla tegit socerum, toga picta parentem:*
> *Praefuit iste sacris, hic dixit iura Quiritis;*
> *At mihi castrensem quod mordet fibula vestem,*
> *Aurorae in populis regum praetoria rexi,*
> *Sed fasces pictura tacet; tu respice fastus.*

For Septimius Acindynus, see *PLRE* 1 p. 11; for Memmius Vitrasius Orfitus signo Honorius, see *PLRE* 1, pp. 651-653.

[35] Symm. *Ep.* 1.1.5:

> *Huc deus Alcides stabulanda armenta coegit*
> *Eruta Geryonae de lare tergemini.*
> *Inde recens aetas corrupta boaulia Baulos*
> *Nuncupat occulto nominis indicio.*
> *Ab divo ad proceres dominos fortuna cucurrit,*
> *Fama loci obscuros ne pateretur heros.*
> *Hanc celebravit opum felix Hortensius aulam,*
> *Contra Arpinatem qui stetit eloquio.*
> *Hic consul clarum produxit Acindynus aevum*
> *Quique dedit leges Orfitus Aeneadis.*

of his wife's family; by such associations, Symmachus attains greater distinction, and his own achievements, present, past and future, are amplified.[36] Symmachus also evokes his position as upholder of Roman traditional religiosity and civic virtues, emphasizing too his own expertise in rhetoric and literature.

This positive image of Bauli and the environs of Baiae is evoked in another of Symmachus' letters, *Epistle* 1.8, again addressed to his father and placed at the beginning of the collection. When trying to convince his father to visit, he dangles as incentives the 'quiet of his estate on the Lucrine Lake, the pleasures of the waters of Baiae, Puteoli with its stylish crowds and the vast silences of Bauli'. Again, Symmachus resorts to poetry to express the venerable associations of the area with Greek gods and mythology. So he describes it as:

> Where horned Lyaeus
> Covers the summits of Gaurus,
> [Where] Vulcan heats the
> Middle regions from his steamy caverns,
> [And where] Thetis and her sisters, among the many fish of Baiae,
> hold the lower regions.
> The water is warm, the air is cool,
> [And] in the midst of a chorus [of water nymphs],
> [she] swims, beaming down on Amathus, the,
> ruler of Sea and Sky,
> Flower of the stars, Dione.[37]

In this place, 'where horned Lyaeus [Bacchus] covers the summits of Gaurus', Symmachus can evoke for Baiae, the presence of Thetis and her sisters as he describes 'the warm water and cool breezes' that bring even Amathusian Venus here. Such a place, depicted with classicizing allusions and Greek mythology, underscores Symmachus' literary skills, the mark of the true aristocrat. Though he denies his own abilities as a poet, claiming that 'he has exercised more the duties of the place rather than of his talent',[38] Symmachus intentionally depicted

---

[36] See P. Bruggisser (1993), pp. 68-87.

[37] Symm. *Ep.* 1.8:
> Ubi corniger Lyaeus
> Operit superna Gauri ...
> Volcanus aestuosis
> Medium coquit cavernis
> Tenet ima pisce multo
> Thetis et Baiae sorores.
> Calet unda, friget aethra,
> Simul innatat choreis,
> Amathusium renidens,
> Salis arbitra et vaporis,
> Flos siderum, Dione

[38] .Symm. *Ep.* 1.8: *loci potius quam ingenii mei munus exercui*

Baiae and its environs, Puteoli and Bauli, as a locus of respectable senatorial life, where the elite occupy themselves in literary and cultural pursuits amidst friends and family. Not insignificantly, the pagan deities reside here too.

Yet this image of Bauli and the area around Baiae emphasized in *Book 1* with positive poetic and personal allusions, contrasts with Symmachus' evocation of these places in other letters. In *Epistle* 8.23, Symmachus describes a trip to the area but emphasizes its well-known entertainments—singing on cruises, dinners with friends, and 'youths swimming shamelessly [that is, nude] in the waters'. The shift in emphasis underscores the rhetorical end of this letter, expressed through different symbolic meanings attributed to trips to two very different images of Bauli and the seaside resorts around Baiae. In *Book 1*, the image of this area was consistent with the traditional, conservative Roman values with which Symmachus wanted to be identified in the eyes of his father and other readers of these letters which date from the 370s, a period when Symmachus was establishing his reputation. In this later letter (8.23), written around 396, well after Symmachus' position in society has been secured and a series of high offices held, Symmachus' concern for establishing his credentials had diminished. Moreover, since this letter is in *Book 8*, it was likely chosen for publication by neither Symmachus nor his son, and that too may contribute to the differences in associations noted for this place. Now Bauli and Baiae are depicted as pleasurable retreats for the Roman elite, but potentially dangerous too for the reputations of established men. So, Symmachus emphasizes the fact that he himself still acts with appropriate consular dignity, despite the considerable pleasures of the area:

> I am not afraid that you may think I am being wanton in places so
> pleasant and so abounding in good things. Everywhere I lead a life
> befitting a consul and I am serious at my Lucrine Lake estate. There is
> no singing on my yachts, no gluttony at my banquets, no frequenting of
> the baths or any shameless swimming on the part of the youths. Be
> assured that in dissipation the blame is not to be laid on the places.[39]

Another letter, written in the following year, ca. 397/8, returns to the dangers of the area. But now, the dangers are to women and, more specifically, to his daughter. So, in a letter to his daughter and her husband, Symmachus emphasizes how important it is that she resist the temptations of Baiae and not spend her time 'sweeping the shores' in countless, potentially dangerous social calls.[40] Rather, his daughter should remain at home, working amidst spinning wheels and wool.

---

[39] Symm. Ep. 8.23.3:
Non vereor ne me lascivire in tanta locorum amoenitate et rerum copia putes. Vbique vitam agimus consularem et in Lucrino serii sumus. Nullus in navibus canor, nulla in conviviis helluatio, nec frequentatio balnearum nec ulli iuvenum procaces natatus. Scias nullum esse in luxuria crimen locorum.

[40] Symm. *Ep.* 6.67.

Since wealthy elite women in the fourth century did not generally spin their own clothes, this advice should be read as a literary allusion that harkens back to Penelope, replete with the traditional value placed on the chaste, hardworking *matrona*. Of course, Symmachus claims, he is confident that his daughter will maintain a modest lifestyle, thereby showing that she is worthy of her husband and her origins. In this way, she will strengthen the bond between the families.[41] Clearly, Baiae and its reputation can be shaped to advance the image of Symmachus and his family, be it as a source of family pride and honor, as in *Book 1*, or as a dangerous playground of the rich and powerful, against which background he and his daughter can emerge as representatives of the old Roman virtues.

Travel and Epistolary Collections: Building Social Networks

If Symmachus' travel letters lacked a reflective component, they nonetheless were central to his presentation of himself and his world. Travel, as discussion of the *Letters* of Symmachus has shown, served to delimit the boundaries of elite Roman society and to retain an image of a world unchanged in time or space. The traditional venues of the Roman elite are celebrated and provide opportunities for frequent trips. Indeed, it is not surprising to find Symmachus lauding the Campanian coast, the traditional retreat of the Roman elite for centuries and the area where Symmachus and many of his friends owned villas.[42] Moreover, in his accounts of travel, Symmachus notes not only the age-old pastimes of the Roman elite—hunting, villa maintenance, seaside socializing, literary pursuits—but also the presence of pagan deities. These descriptions are especially concentrated in *Book 1*, which, I have argued, was likely the result of Symmachus' own editing. The references to travel, thus, present Symmachus in the light of a traditional, Roman senator, tied to a classical, still largely pagan world.

In contrast, references to the new imperial capitals, Milan and Trier, evoke little in the way of positive comment. No mention is made of new imperial constructions there nor, for that matter, of Christian sites or institutions. Moreover, travel to imperial courts or to foreign lands is viewed as uncomfortable, and dangerous—like a disease ('morbi instar')—especially if the traveling is to be done on public business and not for private ends.[43]

Unlike modern travelers who put up with discomfort or danger in search of liberation and new experiences, Symmachus traveled primarily to reinforce the known physical and social fabric of the upper class, as he wished to present that group. Only then did he travel, happily enough, to visit with friends and would-

---

[41] Symm. *Ep.* 6.67.2.

[42] John D'Arms, *Roman on the Bay of Naples* (Cambridge, Mass., 1970), pp. 203-232.

[43] Symm. *Ep.* 8.31.

be friends and family, along well-worn routes. Paradoxically, travel and travel accounts serve in Symmachus' *Letters* as a means of resisting the changes taking place in his own times. New religious sites are not acknowledged. New centers of imperial power are noted, but they are not heralded as centers for aristocratic society. Hence, travel and its description served to communicate Symmachus' notion of how the elite—especially the pagan aristocracy of Rome—should live in the midst of the wide-ranging religious and social transformation of his age.

But if Symmachus' professed attitude to travel is at all typical, it may explain why, too, the fourth and fifth centuries was the age of great letter writing, at least judged on the basis of the number of the many extant epistolary collections from this period.[44] For, although Symmachus appears unwilling to travel to imperial cities or distant lands, it is clear that his letters did. Symmachus' many references to letter carriers, servants or friends, who are passing through Rome or Campania on their way to foreign places shows the reality of frequent travel in the period, and the exploitation of such travel to maintain communications within a far-flung social network. As Symmachus' letters indicate, it was customary for the slaves or retainers of important people to visit the friends of their masters before leaving the city in order to ask for letters to bring back to their masters, who were either in office or at play in other cities or areas. To refuse such a request was considered an insult to the master.[45] Moreover, slaves or friends who brought letters were expected to bring letters back; many of Symmachus' letters are no more than brief salutations, acknowledging the existence of a bond of friendship and written in haste as some impatient letter carrier awaited Symmachus' speedy reply to his own delivered letter.[46]

This movement of men throughout the late antique world, coupled with a distaste for travel, makes it is understandable why Symmachus relied on his letters to, literally, make the journey for him; he used letters instead of visits to maintain even close personal ties. Of course, it was always better if friends could visit, and so Symmachus sent invitations to friends to entice them to travel to join him. Typical is *Epistle* 3.23, which tries to convince Marinianus to join Symmachus on his country estate by describing his rustic life there. But for his own part, Symmachus turned down invitations made to him, and most often, these were occasioned by the consular inaugurations, as discussed above. Unwillingness to attend or visit friends had to be politely justified. But if a visit was not possible, a letter could serve to at least keep up the social connection. Indeed, ever since

---

[44] M. Mullett (1997), p. 11, estimates some 150 major collections of Byzantine letters; of these, a very large number, she notes, date from the fourth and fifth centuries. On the great increase in epistolary collections of the fourth and fifth centuries as compared to the classical period, see too H. Leclercq, '*Lettres chrétiennes*', in F. Cabrol and H. Leclercq (eds.), *Dictionnaire d'archéologie chrétienne et de liturgie*, 15 vols., in 30 pts. (Paris, 1907-1953), VIII, cols. 2683-85.

[45] Symm. *Ep.* 5.61.

[46] See the references to Symmachus' *Epistles* in note 1, above.

Cicero, it was standard epistolary theory to see letters as a kind of mirror of the soul, a means of continuing a conversation with a person and hence a means of bridging the distance between two people who, for whatever reasons, could not travel to one another.[47] Thus, a letter could replace a visit, and travel where and when a busy man like Symmachus would not. And while invitations to visit could be refused, if done politely, what Symmachus could not refuse to do was to send a letter in his place. And he, in turn, demanded a letter in response. Admittedly, even the best, most stylish letter was inferior when compared to a personal visit; indeed, this sentiment was so widespread that it, too, became a *topos* among letter writers.[48] Nonetheless, Symmachus' unwillingness to travel makes the emphasis on an exchange of letters as the second best option quite understandable.

The necessity of penning letters pertaining to travel—accepting or declining it—was part of the aristocrat's duties in building social networks. Indeed, it is striking that Symmachus presents himself most often as proffering invitations to his friends, even though he so often expresses his own irritation at the discomforts of travel outside of his own limited horizons. We do not know how often Symmachus' friends accepted his invitation, but one suspects that if they lived far from Rome and the Campanian coast, they did not visit all that often. Ausonius, for example, featured so prominently as a friend and mentor in *Book 1*, never visited Rome at all. And, so, the necessity of learning how to write to politely decline an invitation to travel and the reliance on the letter to maintain the personal tie emerge as key themes in Symmachus' letters.

To conclude, the movement of Symmachus' letters across the late antique world shows how central travel was to the building of social networks for men like Symmachus who saw letter writing as a substitution for their own travel. Moreover, Symmachus' attitudes toward travel elucidate the habits of letter writing among the elite of the fourth and fifth centuries, and these, in turn, help us to better understand the popularity and ultimate survival of the many epistolary collections from Late Antiquity.

---

[47] Cicero, *Ad Fam.* 16.16.2: *Te totum in litteris vidi.* See also Pseudo Libanius, *Epist. Char.* 2: 'A letter then, is a kind of written conversation with someone from whom one is separated', in *Libanii Opera*, ed. R. Foerster (Leipzig, 1927), 9. See too K. Thraede, *Grundzüge griechisch-römischer Brieftopik, Zetemata* 48 (Munich, 1970), pp. 157-87 on letter writing replacing conversation in person.

[48] Lib. *Ep.* 83, ed. F. Foerster (Leipzig, 1921), 10, p. 84; Synesius *Ep.* 138, ed. A. Garzya, *Synesii Cyrenensis epistolae* (Rome, 1979), pp. 240-241.

Chapter 8

The Collected Letters of Ambrose of Milan: Correspondence with Contemporaries and with the Future[1]

J. H. W. G. Liebeschuetz

Ambrose (AD 337/8–97) was bishop of Milan from 374–97, and, among bishops, he is reckoned as one of the most renowned.[2] As father of the Church he ranks with Augustine, Jerome and Chrysostom. Ambrose is legendary above all for standing up to Roman emperors, for speaking out for what he thought right to the most powerful men in the world. His most celebrated action was to make the emperor Theodosius, who had just been victorious in a civil war, do penance for a massacre of civilians that he had ordered at Thessalonica in Greece. But this was only one of a number of such episodes. So Ambrose exemplified the role of the Church as the moral conscience of society, with a duty to proclaim Christian values, and to condemn wickedness not only of individuals, but also of rulers and governments, no matter how powerful and dangerous.

Ambrose is well-known for other attributes. He was extremely hard working and wrote prodigiously on theological and moral topics. He was ordained after a secular career and so came to theology comparatively late in life. So he taught as he learnt[3] and many of his letters are about his reading. Ambrose made a deep impression on Augustine, and, in fact he played a decisive part in Augustine's

---

[1] I want to thank Dr Carole Hill, my colleague in the task of translating letters of Ambrose for the Liverpool Translated Texts, for helpful comments.

[2] Recent work: Neil B. McLynn, *Ambrose of Milan, Church and Court in a Christian Capital*, Berkeley, Los Angeles, London 1994, which is innovative in the application of historical analysis and criticism to the activities and writings of Ambrose. D.H. Williams, *Ambrose of Milan and the End of the Nicene-Arian Conflicts*, Oxford 1995. But there is still much to learn about many aspects of Ambrose from the older works, of men like S. Mazzarino, *Storia sociale del vescovo Ambrogio*, Rome 1989; J.-R. Palanque, *Saint Ambroise et l'empire romain*, Paris 1933; H. von Campenhausen, *Ambrosius von Milan als Kirchenpolitiker*, Berlin 1929; and F.H. Dudden, *The Life and Times of St. Ambrose*, 2 vols., Oxford 1935.

[3] Ambrose *De officiis* I.4.

conversion to Christianity. Augustine expressed his gratitude by arranging for Paulinus' biography of Ambrose to be written.[4] Augustine had already written Ambrose a very good 'report' in the *Confessions*, his autobiography. This is how he describes Ambrose:

> The multitude of people full of business whose infirmities he gave himself unto, prevented me from hearing and speaking with him. When he was not taken up with them, which was not very often, he either refreshed his body with necessary sustenance, or his mind with reading. But when he was reading, he drew his eyes along over the leaves, and his heart searched into the sense, but his voice and tongue were silent. Often when we were with him, for no man was debarred from coming to see him, nor was it his fashion to have anybody who was coming to speak to him announced, we watched him reading silently, and never otherwise: and after we had long sat without speaking, for we dared not be so bold as to interrupt him when he was so intent on his study, we went out again.[5]

As a writer and theologian, Ambrose was a 'high-popularizer' rather than an original thinker. But there were not many original theologians writing in Latin, and even fewer who read Greek easily, as Ambrose did. So his works, which fill four volumes in the *Patrologia Latina*, became one of the principal authorities on Christian doctrine, and on the duties of the priesthood in the Middle Ages. One innovation of his has remained a conspicuous part of church services to the present day: as a poet and composer of hymns, Ambrose started hymn singing in the West.[6] Characteristically he had made this invention during a situation of confrontation: having been ordered to hand over a church for a service of the Arian sect, Ambrose refused, and organized a sit-in. Then, as the church was surrounded by troops, he kept up the morale of his congregation by getting them to sing hymns, until his opponents gave in. Churches everywhere quickly took up the innovation.[7]

Ambrose's letters have come down to us in a collection of ten books, with two further series of altogether 16 letters transmitted outside the collection.[8] It

---

[4] Paulinus, *V.Ambrosii* 1; for a translation see Boniface Ramsey, *Ambrose*, London/New York 1997, 195-118. The book also includes translations of hymns 1-4 and of the documents concerning the Altar of Victory, and some other works.

[5] *Confessions* 6.2.

[6] Jacques Fontaine, *Ambrose de Milan: hymnes*, Paris 1992 (text, French translation and full commentary). On the circumstances see also McLynn 1994, 200-201.

[7] *Confessions* 9.7.

[8] Latin Text: Otto Faller, Michaela Zelzer *CSEL* 82.10. i-iv. *Book X* and the *Epistulae extra collectionem* are in vol. iii, edited by Michaela Zelzer, whose introductions to vols. ii and iii are fundamental to this paper. Translations: Sister Mary Bayenka, *Saint Ambrose Letters*, Fathers of the Church 26, Washington 1954 (her text is pre-Zelzer); and (if it can be obtained) a very good Victorian version translated in the words of a blurb '*partly by the*

appears that Ambrose published the *Collection* in ten books himself, towards the end of his life, and after the death of the emperor Thedosius I in 395. While we cannot prove that he published them himself, he seems to tells us, in a letter to a friend called Sabinus, that he intended to publish at least some of them: 'these preliminary remarks I am sending you, and I will insert them, if you please in the book of our letters, and place them among their number, so that they may be promoted by the inclusion of your name...'.[9] The letters in the *Collection* had certainly already been published when Paulinus wrote his *Life of Ambrose*, sometime after 410. [10]

If Ambrose did publish the collection of letters between 395 and 397, they constitute his last work. At that stage in life he preferred writing letters to writing another book. To quote the letter to Sabinus once more 'For the present we have chosen that which old men find more easy, the writing of letters in ordinary and familiar language including such passages from the Scriptures as happen to come to mind'.[11] Ambrose thought of the writing of letters an activity suitable for an old man, which he felt himself to be.[12] As a letter-writer Ambrose was consciously following the example of Paul the Apostle, and approvingly quotes Paul's words: 'that what we say by letter when absent, we do when present';[13] and when he says that Paul 'imprinted the image of his presence on his letters',[14] this is clearly what he tried to do himself. Ambrose not only wished the recipients of his letters to sense his personal presence, but also that, through his letters, his presence, like that of Paul, would be experienced, long after he himself was dead and gone.

Numerous letter collections have survived from antiquity. The letters of the highly educated had correspondingly high literary ambitions, but they followed more or less the same conventions, as Scott Bradbury has shown for the letters of Libanius, and Michele Salzmann for those of Symmachus.[15] For men like Libanius or Symmachus, the letter was more than just a form of communication—

---

late *S.F.Wood, M.A. Oriel'*, and revised by the Rev. H. Walford: *The Letters of Ambrose*, in A Library of the Fathers of the Catholic Church 45, Oxford 1881. References are to Zelzer's edition, with the number of the old Benedictine edition printed in *PL* cited in brackets.

[9] *Ep.* 32(48).

[10] Paulinus could assume that the full text of a letter cited by him was available to readers (*Life of Ambrose* 19 on *Ep.* 30 of *Book VI*).

[11] *Ep.* 32(48), 7, see also *Ep.* 37(47), 2.

[12] *Ep.* 28(50), 16; 34(45), 1.

[13] *2Cor.*10.11.

[14] *Ep.* 37(47), 6-7.

[15] See their contributions to this volume.

it was an art form, a creative activity open to all educated people.[16] It was a way people could utilize and display their often painfully acquired literary culture and taste. From this point of view what was important about a letter was not its message, but its formal artistic quality; not the light it throws on its writer's character, or on some exciting episode of his life, but what it tells the reader about its author's education and use of language. So letters were collected not for the information they would provide about their authors and the events they were involved in, but as works of art, to provide models for imitation in the many and various situations that called for the writing of a letter.

Today when we read letters from the past we are of course much more interested in the events and personalities, than in language and style. That is why we are often disappointed by the ancient letter collections, on first reading at least. It is also an obstacle to appreciation, and even to understanding, that the typical letter collection is not structured, either chronologically—except by chance[17]—or artistically. The single letter is the work of art, not the collection as a whole.

But we have at least one collection that is obviously structured in a very sophisticated way so as to convey a picture of the author, his friends and the society in which they lived—the collection in ten books of the letters of Pliny. The *Collection* of Ambrose is not a random assembly of letters, but it resembles the collection of Pliny in that its letters have clearly been selected and probably also arranged in a deliberate[18] order. The order is, however, neither chronological nor by topic, but rather one of variety, with letters concerned with practical problems, or with personal relations, interspersed among what are in fact mini-treatises or sermons in the form of letters.[19] Like those of Pliny, Ambrose's letters have been published in ten books; and their Austrian editor Professor Michaela Zelzer has pointed out that this cannot be a coincidence.[20] Ambrose has evidently modelled

---

[16] See K. Thaede, *Grudzüge griechisch-römischer Brieftopik*, Zetemata 48, Munich 1970.

[17] When the edition follows the order of the author's book of copies, as in the case of the letters of Libanius, see O.Seeck, *Die Briefe des Libanius zeitlich geordnet*, Leipzig 1906, repr. Hildesheim 1967; and the last part of the collection of the letters of Symmachus; see O. Seeck's Introduction to his edition, *Q.Aurelii Symmachi quae supersunt*, Berlin: M.G.H. 1983, repr. 1961.

[18] Consider the intriguing juxtaposition of the two letters in *Book VIII*: 56(5) and 57(6) to Syagrius, bishop of Verona. In 56 Ambrose aggressively rebukes his colleague for the savage treatment of a dedicated virgin allegedly guilty of sexual trespass. In 57 he retells the sensational and lubricious story of *Judges* 18-21, as expanded by Josephus *J.Ant.* 5.8.136-74. He claims that it teaches a moral relevant to the previous letter. Perhaps it does, but it also calls on Syagrius to enjoy a well-told tale, composed according to the rules which both have learnt at school.

[19] For example, *Ep. extra collectionem* 14.

[20] M. Zelzer, 'Plinius Christianus', *Studia Patristica* 23 (1989), 187-204; 'Zu Aufbau und Absicht des zehnten Briefbuches des Ambrosius', in *Latinität und Alte Kirche: Festschrift R. Hanslik*, Wiener Studien Beiheft 8, Vienna 1977, 351-362. See also F. Trisoglio, 'Sant

his collection on that of Pliny. One conspicuous parallel is that in each case, the tenth book deals with public business: Ambrose's relations with emperors occupying the center of the picture.

The first nine books of Ambrose's letters, like the first nine books of the letters of Pliny, contain letters addressed to friends and colleagues. But Ambrose has not selected letters with a view to displaying the social distinction of his correspondents, or to illustrate their way of life. He has not in fact included many letters whose evident purpose had been either to initiate or to maintain influential friendships. Nor has he included very many examples of what one might call the staple of the typical letter collection, that is letters of recommendation of various kinds: for travelers in need of hospitality, for litigants hoping for a favorable hearing, for men seeking employment or promotion. Over the years Ambrose must have written hundreds of letters to senators, high officials and to individuals of every kind in a position to exercise patronage. But if he had duplicates of such letters made, they eventually went into the wastepaper-basket, or at any rate not into his *Collection*, which only contains enough of them to show that he could also write polished letters in that genre also.[21] Nor do the letters in the *Collection* include many samples of the ordinary everyday business correspondence of a bishop. In this respect they are much less representative than, say, the letters of Basil or of Augustine. The majority of his letters are concerned with questions of theology, the proper behavior of clergy and above all biblical exegesis. The addressees, whether clerics or lay-men, are above all persons interested in the understanding the Bible;[22] people who had asked Ambrose to explain a passage that was puzzling, or who would at any rate be grateful rather than bored if Ambrose sent them a lengthy piece of exegesis, often one which he had come across in his reading of a Greek author, notably Philo and Origen.[23] Zelzer has pointed out that many of the 'letters' are probably not real letters at all, but mini-treatises, or sermons in letter form.[24] At any rate, when writing such pieces Ambrose probably did not have in mind any particular correspondent, and it is likely that some of the exegetical letters were in fact sent to more than one

---

Ambrogio connobe Plinio il giovane?' *Rivista di Studi Classici* 20 (1972), 363-410. Though Ambrose imitated the form of Pliny's collection, allusions to individual letters of Pliny appear to be found only in *Ep.* 32.

[21] *Ep* 5(4) to Felix, bishop of Como, on the occasion of the anniversary of his consecration and 43(43) to the same, thanking for a gift of truffles, are just two examples of Ambrose's skill as the writer of occasional letters.

[22] Ambrose's allegorical interpretation of the Bible in Sunday sermons helped Augustine's conversion *Confessions*, 6.3-4.

[23] See the M. Zelzer's annotations to numerous letters in *Ed.* vol. ii.xx-xxxv, H. Savon, *Saint Ambroise devant l'exégèse de Philon le Juif*, Paris 1977.

[24] *Ed.* vol. iii.xxxvii.

addressee.[25] One might perhaps say that Ambrose and his circle were interested in figurative meanings of the Bible in the same way as friends of the pagan senator Praetextatus were interested in arcane meanings of Virgil, the subject-matter—if we are to believe Macrobius—of their table talk during the Saturnalia. McLynn has suggested that among the functions of the letters was that of accrediting the men who received them as followers of Ambrose.[26] But surely the allegorical arguments Ambrose employed in the interpretation of the Bible were not simply the stylized and idiosyncratic discourse of a would-be exclusive circle. They also provided welcome instruction of how to overcome the difficulties of a literal reading of the Bible, a problem of deep concern to both addressee and writer of the letter.[27]

But *Book X* is different. There Ambrose has assembled letters and other documents related to his dealings with the emperors Gratian, Valentinian II and Theodosius I, just as the tenth book of Pliny's letters contains his correspondence with the emperor Trajan.[28] That the *Collection* is made up of nine books of 'religious' letters and only one of 'political' letters is surely significant. It suggests that for Ambrose theology and pastoral work were much more important than one might gather from McLynn's brilliant biography, with its focus on Ambrose the politician.

Book X not strictly speaking a collection of letters at all, but a series of dossiers of letters and other documents related to a small number of incidents, all of which illustrate sensational, not say heroic, episodes in Ambrose's life, and at the same time exemplify principles that he thought should govern the relations of Church and State. The book is therefore in a sense autobiographical, like Augustine's *Confessions*.

Book X is constructed as follows: it starts with two self-contained documents, *Ep.* 70(56) written in 392 and addressed to Theophilus bishop of Alexandria on the subject of the schism at Antioch and *Ep.* 71(56a) of 393 to the bishops of

---

[25] *Ep.* 65 addressed to Clementianus refers to *Ep.* 64 as 'my previous letter', even though in the *Collection* it is addressed to Irenaeus. The answer must be that 64 had been sent Clementianus as well as Irenaeus, and probably to yet others as well. Similarly *Ep.* 68 (to Irenaeus) seems to be a continuation of 50 (to Studius). So it would seem that Irenaeus had received a copy of 50 as well.

[26] McLynn 1994, 282.

[27] *Cf.* the experience of Augustine, *Conf.* V.14.

[28] According to Sherwin White, *The Letters of Pliny, a Historical Commentary*, Oxford 1966, 52-56, Pliny published the first nine books in separate batches himself. The tenth book was published after his death, but a collection including all ten books can be traced back to a manuscript of the sixth century (Sherwin White, *op.cit.* 83). It is likely that the edition in ten books is older than that, and therefore old enough to have been known by Ambrose. Unlike Pliny, Ambrose did not include the letters he received from emperors in his *Collection*. The letter of Gratian (*CSEL. lxxxii.* 10. iii, p. cxvi) has not been transmitted with Ambrose's letters, but with the tract *De spiritu sancto*.

Macedonia, concerning bishop Bonosus, alleged to have taught that the virgin Mary had given birth to sons after Jesus. These surely are real letters.

Next we have a group of three documents: *Ep.* 72(17) of 384 addressed to the emperor Valentinian II, *Ep.* 72a(17a), which is not by Ambrose at all, but by Symmachus, the famous *Third Relatio* pleading for the retention of the Altar of Victory, and *Ep.* 73(18), Ambrose's formal reply to Symmachus. The three documents constitute a single dossier recording Ambrose's success in preventing the emperor from restoring the Altar of Victory to the senate chamber. Incidentally, of the three documents only *Ep.* 72 is a real letter.

The next letter, *Ep.* 74(40) written in 388, is addressed to the emperor Theodosius on the subject of the destroyed synagogue at Callinicum. The letter urges the emperor not to punish monks and others who had destroyed a synagogue in distant Mesopotamia. This is presumably a real letter. A second, only slightly different, version of *Ep.* 74 has been transmitted as 1a (40) *Extra Collectionem*, where it is followed by a letter to Ambrose's sister giving a much amplified version of the same argument, but this time in the shape of a sermon delivered in the presence of Theodosius, ending with a dramatic description of how Ambrose confronted the emperor at the climax of mass (1(41)). I suspect that Ambrose originally wrote the letter to his sister with the intention of publishing it together with that written to the emperor in the *Collection*,[29] but that for some reason he changed his mind.

There follows another dossier: *Ep.* 75(21) was addressed to the emperor Valentinian II in January or early February 386. *Ep.* 75a(21a), also known as *Contra Auxentius,* was—if its heading is to be believed—presented to the emperor Valentinian II, but its aggressive tone makes this most unlikely. Its most likely date is January 386.[30] *Ep.* 76(20) was sent to Ambrose's sister around Easter 386. Of these documents *Ep.* 75 is a real letter, and 76, though addressed to his sister, includes the text of a sermon. It was surely composed from the first with a view to reaching a much wider public, intended as a pamphlet rather than a personal communication. *Ep.* 75a is simply a sermon and in no sense a letter. Together the three documents record the story of Ambrose's resistance to repeated demands that he should hand over a church for a service, or services, of the Arian sect, which would be attended by the emperor.

The next document in the *Collection* is the oration '*On the death of Theodosius I*' *(CSEL* 73, 369-401) of February 395.[31] Ambrose delivered this speech at Milan when the body of the dead emperor was about to be sent for burial to Constantinople. Ambrose praises Theodosius as the ideal emperor, and as an example to all of how a Christian emperor should behave, especially in his dealings with the Church.

---

[29] Like *Ep.* 76.

[30] Otherwise McLynn 1994, 196-208.

[31] This is not printed in Zelzer's edition, but see Sister Mary D. Mannix, *Sancti Ambrosii oratio de obitu Thodosii,* Text, Translation and Commentary, Washington 1925.

The book ends with *Ep.* 77(22), of spring or early summer 386, a letter to his sister, incorporating the text of a sermon, and describing the finding of the remains of the martyrs Gervasius and Protasius. This discovery is represented as a divine sign. In the context of the *Collection* it must be read as an indication of divine approval of Ambrose and especially of the stands Ambrose had taken in the incidents documented in *Book X.* The letter makes a powerful conclusion to the *Collection.*

Not all surviving letters of Ambrose have been transmitted within the *Collection.* Two series, of respectively 12 and five letters, have been transmitted separately, *extra collectionem.* The documents of the first group are documents of the same kind as the letters of *Book X* of the *Collection.* All but one are addressed to emperors. The exception, *Ep.* ex. 1, which has been mentioned earlier, is addressed to Ambrose's sister, but it describes Ambrose's dispute with the emperor Theodosius over the burning of the synagogue of Callinicum. It therefore supplements *Ep.* 74 in the *Collection. Ep. ex.*10 addressed to the usurper Eugenius deals with a later episode in the Altar of Victory affair, which is documented by *Ep.* 72, 72a, and 73 in the *Collection. Ep. ex.* 4, 5, 8, 9 is a dossier of letters to Valentinian II and Theodosius reporting on the Council of Aquileia of 381, a key episode in Ambrose's episcopacy. Though Ambrose had excluded these letters from the *Collection,* he evidently kept them in a very accessible place, so that after Ambrose's death Paulinus, looking for material for his biography of Ambrose sometime after 410, could easily find, and use them. The *Life* has allusions to 1, 2, 3, and 10. It may well be that Ambrose had intended that they should be used in this way. Why Ambrose omitted these letters from his own *Collection* is an interesting question.

The second group of letters *extra collectionem* is more miscellaneous, though they are not ordinary letters either. *Ep.* 11 is the famous letter to Theodosius protesting over the massacre at Thessalonica. It could well have been part of the *Collection.* Ambrose presumably had a reason why he excluded it, and preferred the version of that incident which he gave in the *De obitu Theodosii. Ep.* 12, addressed to the emperor Gratian, is a document which must be discussed by anyone trying to reconstruct the obscure early part of Ambrose's episcopacy, even though it does not raise or illustrate any issue of lasting significance. *Ep.* 13 is a sermon-like treatise on the date of Easter, which informs north Italian bishops of the Alexandrian views on the proper date of Easter, when, as was about to happen in 387, the 14th moon in spring falls on a Sunday. This letter is therefore comparable to the many letters which bring Greek allegorical interpretation of the Bible to the notice of the Latin-speaking West. *Ep.* 14 is a very long sermon addressed to the church of Vercelli, where internecine disputes had held up the election of a successor to the deceased bishop. *Ep. Sir.* and *Ep. ex.* 15 are, respectively, a letter of Pope Siricius and a reply to it written by Ambrose in the name of a synod of north Italian bishops, strongly supporting the pope's excommunication of Jovinianus, a monk who had been preaching and writing against the superiority of the ascetic life and especially of virginity over the married state. *Ep. ex* 14 also has a long section upholding the ascetic life, evidently directed against Jovinianus. One would like to know when this small group of letters was assembled and for what purpose. Paulinus, Ambrose's biographer, does not seem to have known them, at least he does not allude to any of them in the *Life*.[32]

It is evident that the episodes highlighted in the *Collection,* that is the issues on which Ambrose was proud to have made a stand, were more often than not far from what would today be considered politically correct. The message of *Book X* is—with a little simplification—that, in the field of religion, a Christian emperor must not make concessions of any kind to the religious requirements of his pagan, sectarian Christian, or his Jewish subjects. In the letters about the synagogue at Callinicum, Ambrose goes as far as to insist that acts of criminal damage the perpetrators of which would normally be punished, or at least compelled to pay compensation, are to be ignored, if the damage was inflicted in the name of orthodox Christianity on Jews or heretics. The letter describing what to modern minds is the most admirable of Ambrose's acts of confrontation of secular power, his compelling the emperor Theodosius to do penance for the massacre of 7000 civilians in the hippodrome of Thessalonica, has been transmitted only *extra collectionem*, and was not included in *Book X*.[33] Theodosius' penance for the massacre at Thessalonica is however emphasized in the sermon 'on the death of Theodosius', which is in the *Collection.* But whatever we think of the causes Ambrose took up, nobody can question that he always displayed exemplary courage, both moral and physical.

Book X is certainly not simply a miscellaneous collection of business letters that Ambrose happened to find in his files. A number of the documents read as if they had, from the first, been composed for publication. They appear to be addressed not so much to their addressees as to the general public of the present, and also to the future. This is obviously true of the oration, in praise of the late emperor Theodosius, which Ambrose held at Milan 40 days after the emperor's death. It is also true of the second and longer letter to the emperor Valentinian II on the Altar of Victory. This, so-called letter, was not in fact the document which performed the decisive act of persuasion.[34] It is a very carefully written oration, making a point-by-point refutation of the submission of Symmachus—but only after it had already been rejected. In writing it Ambrose can be seen to have had two aims: first, to expound once and for all the Christian case for the abandonment of the ancient and time-honored public religion of the Roman people; and secondly to display his own skill as an orator and to demonstrate that he was at least the equal of Symmachus, the most distinguished orator of his time.[35] Then there are the three letters Ambrose wrote to his sister. Now it has

---

[32] If he had known it, one would have expected him to allude to *Ep. ex.* 11 when relating the Thessalonica episode.

[33] Perhaps because it was confidential (cf. *extra collectionem* 11.50). That its terms are extremely diplomatic suggests that it is a real letter, which was actually sent to the emperor.

[34] *Ep.* 72.1.

[35] Hence an unusually large number of allusions to Virgil.

been known for brothers and sisters to be good friends, and for a brother to keep his sister fully informed of all interesting things that happen to him. But the letters of Ambrose to his sister go beyond the reporting of news—each of them is a careful composition comprising both a narrative of exciting events, and a sermon which Ambrose had held while they were happening. The letters give his sister a dramatic account of how Ambrose stood up for what he thought was right, and a theological justification, backed up by numerous citations from the Bible, of the stand he had taken. They were surely intended for the widest possible public, from the very beginning. In fact the letters give Ambrose's view of the affair, the way that he wanted the issues at stake, and also his own behavior, to be seen and judged not only by contemporaries, but also by posterity.

There is no reason to doubt that some, and perhaps the majority, of the letters are genuine communications between Ambrose and the person, be it the emperor or to whomever they are addressed, though it is difficult to be certain in individual cases. But in view of the fact that the *Collection* has surely an overall purpose, the question arises whether any documents have been altered for publication, and if so, which documents, and how much. The evidence of letter 74, which has been transmitted both within, and as letter 1a outside the *Collection*, suggests that there was some but not very much editing.[36] Though one letter does not provide a sufficient basis for a generalization.

But as Zelzer has shown, the 'real letters' are undoubtedly supplemented by letters written for the sake of publicity, whose status is in fact not very different from the political orations of Libanius. That some of the 'letters' have in fact been written for publicity, rather than for negotiation or diplomacy, is something the historian must bear in mind, if one wants to reconstruct what really happened in the course of Ambrose's conflicts with the court, or indeed the functioning of late Roman government. Perhaps the clearest example is *Ep.* XXX (24) in *Book VI*. This letter purports to be Ambrose's report to the emperor Valentinian II on his embassy to Gaul to the usurper Maximus in 386/7. It would seem to provide invaluable information about the politics of the empire at this critical time. In fact most of the letter is a report of a discussion between Ambrose and the usurper Maximus in the course of which Ambrose defends his own behavior in a previous embassy, and shows himself being remarkably outspoken and even impudent towards the usurper. This was certainly not what Ambrose had been sent to Trier to discuss. In any case Ambrose was far too skilful a politician to let a delicate mission turn into a slanging-match. What Valentinian must have required from his ambassador was a summary of how far his mission had been successful, not an account of his ambassador's fearless outspokenness. In short, if Ambrose wrote a report of his second embassy, this letter was not it. Of course we must ask why Ambrose thought it worthwhile to write and publish this so-called 'letter'. But we

---

[36] Cf. Sherwin White's thought on the editing of Pliny's letters had undergone in the introduction to his *Commentary* on the letters.

can be sure that it was not to inform Valentinian of what had been gained—or not gained—by the embassy.[37]

If Ambrose's *Collection* is not simply a collection of letters, what is it? Taking up the classical genre of the collection of literary letters, particularly in the sophisticated form given it by Pliny, he has turned it into something like a political and theological testament. Ambrose was a gifted orator and a very original poet. It is not altogether surprising that he should create a new genre for his own use. His letters are something new—an aspect of the recasting of the Roman literary tradition in the service of Christianity.[38]

Ambrose's *Collection* of letters is a literary innovation, like *The Confessions* of Augustine, which was in many ways the first autobiography in the modern sense of the word. But Ambrose's letters are not an autobiography. For one thing they are not in chronological order, and furthermore Ambrose was not concerned to document the whole of his life, or even his episcopacy. For us this is unfortunate, since Ambrose has not given us information we would very much like to have either about his early life, or about his early years as bishop.[39] But Ambrose was not concerned to explore his own intellectual and spiritual development, or with showing how he had found God, or with demonstrating how God had guided him over the course of his life. He was concerned with documenting a limited number of remarkable episodes in which he has been actively involved, and in explaining the principles that had governed his conduct in them. But in doing this, he produced the first statement of the Church's claims on the State.

What was the impact of Ambrose's self-presentation? In perhaps 403 the Christian poet Prudentius wrote the second book of his *Contra Symmachum*, in which he refuted the third *Relatio* of Symmachus, as Ambrose had done 20 years earlier in Ep. 73. He therefore discussed material already covered by Ambrose. Prudentius seems to have taken two important ideas from Ambrose. He has adopted the argument that the issue at stake in the conflict between the old and the new religion is a conflict between *mos maiorum* and human progress (II.277-302), and like Ambrose he insists that it was Roman *virtus*, not pagan piety, that enabled the Romans to win their empire (II.551-550). But seen as a whole, Prudentius' poem, far from being a versification of Ambrose's letter, is an independent and

---

[37] But M. Dörner, 'Ambrose in Trier', *Historia* 50 (2001) 217-244 argues that the terms of the letter do make sense in the circumstances of Ambrose's embassy. I am not convinced.

[38] In the same spirit Ambrose recast Cicero's *de officiis,* into a treatise on Christian duties. See K. Zelzer, 'Zur Beurteilung der Cicero-Imitatio bei Ambrosius *de officiis*', *Wiener Studien* 90 (1977) 168-191.

[39] For lack of evidence see D.H. Williams, *Ambrose and the End of the Arian-Nicene Conflicts*, Oxford 1995, esp. 128-140.

original creation, which does not include as much as an allusion to the bishop of Milan. One would like to know why.[40]

Perhaps ten years after Ambrose's death, the format of his *Collection* was adopted by the son of Ambrose's pagan antagonist Symmachus, when he came to make a collection of his father's letters. For he assembled them in ten books, the last of which contains letters to emperors and other public business; and like the letters of Ambrose they are not in chronological order.[41]

Sometime after 410, St Augustine[42] persuaded Paulinus, deacon and procurator of the Church of Milan,[43] to write a life of Ambrose. Paulinus made use of the *Collection* of Ambrose's letters as well as some of the letters preserved by Ambrose but not included in the *Collection*. He described the great episodes of Ambrose's career, but above all he presented him as a saint capable of working miracles.[44] It can be surmised that at this time Ambrose's reputation did not depend on literature. Nobody who had met him would have forgotten the experience, though the memory will not in every case have been a pleasant one.

But subsequently Ambrose's reputation depended on his writings, of course on his theological writings as much, and even more, than on his letters. It is certainly the case that if we did not have the letters, and Paulinus' *Life*, which is partly based on them, our picture of Ambrose would be significantly different. Ambrose does figure in the ecclesiastical historians Rufinus (c. 400), Socrates (c. 440), Sozomen (c. 446) and Theodoret (c. 450). But he is much less prominent than one would expect after reading the letters. None of the ecclesiastical historians mentions Ambrose's part in the affair of the Altar of Victory, or indeed the affair itself. Nor do they mention Ambrose's intervention on behalf of the monks who had destroyed the synagogue at Callinicum. Moreover, they represent the conflict of 386 not as an issue of principle over the surrender of a church for use by Arians, but as an attempt by the Arian empress Justina to have Ambrose banished. Only Theodoret draws attention to that aspect of Ambrose which Ambrose himself had emphasized so strongly in *Book X*. Heightening further the already dramatic episode between Ambrose and Theodosius after the massacre of

---

[40] W. Evepoel, 'Prudence et la conversion des aristocrats romains', *Augustianum* XXX.i (1990) 31-43.

[41] Ms. note: *Q. Aurelii Symmachi epistularum liber X continens epistolas familiares ad imperatores, sententias senatorias et opusculas editus post eius obitum a Q.Flavio Memmio Symmacho v.c.* Most of the book has been lost but the *Relationes*, which may have been part of *Book X*, have survived as a separate collection.

[42] One motive could have been that Pelagius, whom Augustine was fighting, had cited Ambrose in support of his doctrine that man can live without sin. See D.H. Williams 1995 cited in n. 39 above, pp. 106-107.

[43] Anonymous, 'Praedestinatu', *PL* 53.617D.

[44] Lellia Craco-Ruggini, 'Prêtre et functionaire, le modèle ambrosien', *Antiquité Tardive* 7 (1999) 175-186.

Thessalonica, Theodoret hammers home Ambrose's point that it is the duty of a bishop to discipline an emperor who has sinned, and that a pious emperor must submit to the bishop's discipline.[45]

The history of the influence of Ambrose has not yet been written. We know that when Pope Hildebrand, Gregory VII excommunicated the German emperor in 1076, he justified this daring act by citing as a precedent what Ambrose had done to Theodosius after the massacre at Thessalonica.[46] Ambrose was regularly cited in debates about the relations of Church and State in Elizabethan England.[47] But I suspect that it was only in modern times, when people have become less interested in theology and miracles, that the letters have really come into their own.

For modern historians, from Gibbon to McLynn, Ambrose is the man who could speak his mind to the most powerful men in the world, and not only get away with it, but even to get his way. So, to quote Gibbon, 'posterity has applauded the virtuous firmness of the archbishop, and the example of Theodosius may prove the beneficial influence of those principles which could force a monarch, exalted above the apprehension of human punishment, to respect the law and ministers of an invisible judge'. More recently the Catholic Encyclopedia sums up what Ambrose strove and fought for: 'He annunciated the principle that the Church is supreme in its own domain, and is the guardian of morality. Even emperors despite their lofty dignity and absolutism are subject to the moral laws as defined by the Church' (I.375). This is the Ambrose that interests and fascinates historians. They do not necessarily approve of him. Gibbon had very strong reservations: 'The cause of humanity and that of persecution have been asserted by the same Ambrose with equal energy and equal success'. Ambrose would not have understood the implied criticism, because it is based on Ambrose's own letters. For Gibbon's Ambrose is precisely the Ambrose of *Book X* of the letters. He is the man who wrote to an emperor: 'It is my way to show respect to emperors but not to yield to them',[48] and: 'in matters of Faith it is usual for bishops to pass judgment on emperors, not emperors on bishops'.[49] In other words, the modern view of Ambrose, whether of theologian or historian, is based precisely on Ambrose's own publicity. I can think of several contemporary politicians who would be happy if they could control posterity's view of themselves as successfully as Ambrose did.

---

[45] *HE*.V.17. But Theodoret's drama is his own composition—it is not derived from Ambrose's letter. Theodoret had his own reasons for distrusting emperors: see H. Leppin, *Von Constantin dem grossen zu Theodosius II*, das christliche Kaisertum bei den Kirchenhistorikern Socrates, Sozomenus und Theodoret, Göttingen 1996.

[46] Greg. VII, *Ep*. 4.2; 8.21.

[47] P.Collinson, '"If Constantine, then also Theodosius": St Ambrose and the integrity of the Elizabethan *Ecclesia Anglicana*', *Journal of Ecclesiastical History* XXX (1979) 205-29.

[48] *Ep*. 76 (21a), 2.

[49] *Ep*. LXXV (21), 4.

PART THREE
RECONSIDERING LATE
ANTIQUE PILGRIMAGE

Part Three

Reconsidering Late Antique Pilgrimage

Introduction

The complex functions of pilgrimage and the different ways in which it was understood in the Late Antique world are the focus of this final section of papers. Noel Lenski examines the political and religious dimensions of pilgrimage to the Holy Land as they were created by a series of out-of-favor Empresses who constructed new spaces in Palestine in which to exercise their power and built the shrines that were to make pilgrimage to this part of the Mediterranean world a central feature of Christian piety from that day to this. Maribel Dietz analyzes the close connection between monastic asceticism and early Christian pilgrimage, arguing that it often took the form of an open-ended 'itinerant spirituality' that considered the journey itself, and not the arrival at a holy site or person, as the heart of the matter. She thereby warns us against an anachronistic conceptualization of pilgrimage based on its later medieval form. Like Lenski, she emphasizes the central role that women played in the early development of this type of Christian piety. Daniel Caner takes us in another direction as he shows how the distinctive cultural and physical geography of pilgrimage to Mount Sinai, when shaped by the conventions of the classic Greek romance, could be constructed imaginatively and used as a basis for re-examining a timeless theological conundrum—why do the innocent suffer and the evil prosper? Finally, Gillian Clark, like Maribel Dietz, warns us against overly simple and anachronistic assumptions about the conceptualization of pilgrimage in the Late Antique world. She shows us that Augustine of Hippo, that seminal figure in the formation of Latin Christianity, understood pilgrimage and the pilgrim in the classical philosophical sense of a 'foreigner ... who want[s] to go home'.

Chapter 9

Empresses in the Holy Land:
The Creation of a Christian Utopia in
Late Antique Palestine

Noel Lenski

In 382 John Chrysostom, still a junior priest in Antioch, wrote a letter to a young widow whom he hoped to dissuade from remarriage. Among other things he argued that married life was far too risky for a sound-thinking woman to undertake a second time. To drive home the point, Chrysostom catalogued several empresses of recent memory who had been driven to grief by the downfall of their once exalted husbands:

> As to the emperors' wives, says Chrysostom, some perished by poison, others died of mere sorrow; while of those who still survive, one, who has an orphan son, is trembling with alarm lest those who are in power should destroy him (probably Jovian's wife Charito); yet another only after many entreaties has returned from the exile into which she had been driven by him who formerly held the chief power (probably Severa, Valentinian's estranged first wife).[1]

Chrysostom's examples were easy enough to come by, for Late Antiquity, as indeed any period of history, had its fair share of cast-off queens. For all its glamour, this royal job was, after all, hardly without risks. Though it entailed power and prestige, it also brought ominous dangers, especially if an emperor preceded his wife in death or his marital affections soured.[2]

To be sure, this problem, the problem of the rejected or deposed empress, had existed since Octavian divorced his second wife Scribonia in order to marry the first Roman empress Livia. Yet its complications were exacerbated in the third through fifth centuries as frequent usurpations and dynastic squabbles left behind a coterie of ex-empresses, and as Christian prohibitions against divorce began to

---

[1] Joh. Chrys. *Ad vid. iun.* 4 (*SCh* 138.139).

[2] See for example *PLRE* I Charito; Constantia 1; Constantina 2; Faustina; Marina Severa; Prisca 1; Galeria Valeria; *PLRE* II Licinia Eudoxia 2; Iusta Grata Honoria; Leontia 1; Aemilia Materna Thermantia; Aelia Verina; Aelia Zenonis; cf. Lact. *DMP* 50.6.

interfere with the easy abandonment of a disaffected queen. In this paper I hope to examine how four late antique empresses confronted this growing dilemma with a characteristically late antique solution, travel to the Holy Land. There they were able to reconstruct their positions in a sort of utopian environment. In the Holy Land, I will contend, these empresses found the space, both literal and metaphorical, to fashion an ideal place, a place like no other, where imaginary worlds were made real and the real world was re-imagined with consequences that persist even to the present.

Foremost among these refugee empresses was, I would argue, the first empress to travel to the Christian Holy Land, Constantine's mother Helena. Helena was no stranger to the role of outcast. Being a woman of low birth, she had been quickly dropped as the concubine of Constantius I in 293 in favor of the dynastically endowed stepdaughter of Maximianus Herculius.[3] Even so, with the rise of her son to power in 306, Helena's fortunes waxed to the point that, by 324 she had received the title *Augusta* and begun to see her image minted on imperial coins.[4] All did not, of course, remain well. For Crispus, Constantine's son by his first wife Minervina, was put to death by his own father under mysterious circumstances in May 326.[5] The reasons for this execution were as much a cause for speculation in antiquity as they are now. Nevertheless Zosimus' account seems to come closest to the events in reporting that Crispus was condemned on suspicion of adultery with his stepmother Fausta, Constantine's second wife. Some time shortly afterward, Fausta was herself killed, slow-cooked in a deliberately overheated bath chamber.[6] Zosimus' account has problems, not least being its contention that this double murder prompted Constantine to seek penance by turning to the all-forgiving Christian god.[7] The incident is far too late to be linked so closely to Constantine's official conversion, which happened at least 14 years earlier. Zosimus may not, however, be entirely wrong to assert that Constantine's wavering faith quickened in the aftermath of this double family murder. For in 327 his mother Helena set out for the Holy Land where—with the help of her imperial son—she would eventually restructure the Palestinian landscape into an elaborate pilgrimage destination to fit the new Christian

---

[3] *PLRE* I Flavia Iul. Helena 3; Theodora 1. On Helena's low birth and concubinage with Constantius I see Eutr. 10.2; *Exc. Val.* 2; Amb. *De ob. Theod.* 42; Zos. 2.9.2; Zon. 13.1.5; cf. Drijvers 1992a, 15-19.

[4] Drijvers 1992a, 39-54.

[5] Details at Pohlsander 1984.

[6] Zos. 2.29.2-4; 39.2; 40.1; Philost. 2.4a; Zon. 13.2.38-41; cf. Eutr. 10.6.3; *Epit.* 41.11-12; Jer. *Chron.* s.a. 325; Amm. Marc. 14.11.20; Sid. Ap. *Ep.* 5.8.2. Many theories have been advanced to account for the gaps in our sources, cf. Drijvers 1992b; Woods 1998.

[7] Cf. Jul. *Caes.* 336b; Soz. 1.5.1-2.

regime.[8] Reinterpreted by the pagan Zosimus, the efforts thrown into this Holy Land makeover by Constantine and his mother could easily seem to represent the fruits of a penitent conversion to a stronger Christianity.

The question remains, however, was Helena traveling on behalf of Constantine or despite him? Her son had after all just murdered her first grandchild, and several sources indicate that Helena herself had subsequently pushed for the execution of the emperor's wife Fausta, whom she blamed for Crispus' death.[9] Thus the timing of Helena's visit, in the year immediately following the double murder, raises the suspicion that she may have traveled east in part to escape from her recently disaffected son. Once in Palestine, Helena is known to have been the impetus behind the construction of at least two major churches on two of the most holy sites in the life of Christ, the Eleona church on the Mount of Olives and the church at the cave of the Nativity in Bethlehem. Many have pointed out that Eusebius, our best source for Helena's building projects, is quite explicit that Helena alone initiated the work on these churches and was only aided with funds from Constantine after they were well under way.[10] This already points to some initial distance between Constantine and his pilgrim mother. Few, however, have also noticed that she gave a prominent place in her Nativity church to a 64-columned structure designed to house the remains of the innocent children murdered by Herod. Indeed, one of the earliest liturgical celebrations connected with this church commemorated the anniversary of this event on May 18. Could Helena have intended this part of her project as an expiatory reprimand directed at her child-killing son?[11] If so, Helena may have originally journeyed to the Holy Land and begun her reclamation work there despite her son rather than on his behalf. Only when he witnessed the success of her program to re-sacralize these holy sites for Christianity did Constantine fully sign on.[12]

---

[8] See Hunt 1982, 28-49, esp. 31-2 on the date; Drijvers 1992a, 55-72.

[9] Zos. 2.29.3; *Epit.* 41.12; Suda K 2446. Barnes 1981, 220-1 and Hunt 1982, 32-35 also connect the double murder with Helena's journey. Eusebius of course says nothing of tension between Helena and Constantine, but this means little, for he avoided mention of the incident altogether.

[10] Eus. *VC* 3.41.1-43.5, esp. 43.2-4. Suda K 3213 indicates that at least some of the funds for Helena's projects in the Holy Land were her own. On her estates see Eus. *VC* 3.46.1; cf. 47.3. For the archaeological remains at Bethlehem see Taylor 1993, 110-112; Wilkinson 1999, 11-12. For those of the Eleona church see Bloedhorn, 1995; Wilkinson 1999, 12-16; cf. Walker 1990, 199-234.

[11] On the structure see Petrus Diaconus P 1 (*CCSL* 175.97). On the celebration see Devos 1968. Eus. *VC* 3.42.1 states specifically that Helena traveled to the Holy Land to make offerings on behalf of her son and grandchildren.

[12] Evidence for tensions between mother and son would of course have been glossed over after Constantine reconciled with Helena some time before her death in 329, cf. Drijvers 1992a, 73-76. This may help explain why sources began early on to obscure her role in the

Constantine's mother was, at some point c. 327, joined in the Holy Land by his mother-in-law Eutropia. We know of her presence in Palestine from Eusebius and in turn Sozomen, both of whom report that Eutropia offered the initial motivation behind the construction of a basilica at Mamre, where Abraham was said to have received his three divine visitors (Genesis 18:1-33).[13] Eusebius relays a letter of Constantine that describes how Eutropia had made known to him that the site had since been built over with a pagan altar. In the same letter, Constantine ordered his count Acacius to oversee the total destruction of the pagan shrine and its replacement with a Christian church. Here, as in the case of Helena, we see an empress who, after journeying to the Holy Land, teamed up with the emperor to re-appropriate a holy site for the Christian church. In so doing, however, Eutropia may also have been re-stabilizing her own position vis-à-vis an emperor whose wrath she had tasted at first hand. Eutropia had been the wife of the emperor Maximianus Herculius, who had allied himself with Constantine in 307 but was eventually forced by him to commit suicide in 310. Eutropia was also the mother of Constantine's early nemesis Maxentius, whom Constantine defeated in 312 and whose body he then desecrated.[14] After her son's death, Eutropia was said to have denigrated his pedigree—as well as her own reputation—by charging that Maxentius had actually been sired 'by some Syrian'.[15] This blunt charge of bastardy against her own son must have been useful in shielding Eutropia from possible reprisals by Constantine. The dowager would continue to need the protection of such self-effacement with the disappearance of her final link to Constantine, her daughter. This was because Eutropia was also the mother of Constantine's second wife, the ill-fated Fausta whom, we have just seen, Constantine murdered for infidelity in 326.[16] Eutropia

---

project of Holy Land reclamation. Already in 333, the author of the *Itin. Burd.* 594.2; 595.6; 598.7; 599.6 (*CSEL* 175.17-20) reports that the churches of the Anastasis, Eleona, Nativity and Mamre were all constructed *iussu Constantini* without any mention of the empresses Helena or Eutropia, who initiated the last three projects; cf. Eus. *LC* 9.16-19 (a. 335). We should not be misled by such sources—as Drijvers 1992a, 63-65 and Hunt 1997, 416-419—into casting Helena as a mere agent of Constantine—much less of Eusebius, as Walker 1990, 184-188. She was, as Eusebius states, acting on her own initiative until her projects were co-opted by her son. On Helena's legendary role in the discovery of the cross, see Hunt 1982, 37-48; Heid 1989; Drijvers 1992a, 79-180; Cameron and Hall 1999, 273-291.

[13] Eus. *VC* 3.51-3; Soz. 2.4.6-8. On the date see Hunt 1997, 416 n. 51. On the remains of the church see Taylor 1993, 93-95; Wilkinson 1999, 22.

[14] *PLRE* I Eutropia 1; M. Aur. Val. Maxentius 5; M. Aur. Val. Maximinianus signo Herculius 8.

[15] *Exc. Val.* 12; cf. *Epit.* 40.13. The charge was picked up by Constantine's propagandists, *Pan. Lat.* 12[9].3.4; 4.4, no doubt as a counter to Maxentius' own purported disgust at Constantine's questionable parentage, Zos. 2.9.2.

[16] See especially Drijvers 1992b.

thus witnessed the extermination of husband, son and daughter at the hands of her son-in-law. Perhaps by fleeing to the Holy Land and there actively promoting the emperor's new religious program, she found a means to protect herself from a similar fate.

In the fifth century, the Empress Aelia Eudocia, wife of Theodosius II, actually made two journeys to the Holy Land, one in 438–39 and a second in 442.[17] The first, it is likely, was not motivated by any rift with her husband. The previous year Eudocia had welcomed into Constantinople the eminent Roman aristocrat cum Jerusalem ascetic Melania the Younger and conceived through her visit a desire to travel to Palestine.[18] Thus, when the opportunity arose in the spring of 438 to go and receive relics of St. Stephen in Jerusalem and translate them back to Constantinople, Eudocia sprang to fulfill it. While in Jerusalem Eudocia, like her empress predecessors, oversaw the consecration of a new church, this time—naturally enough—a shrine to St. Stephen.[19] By summer 439 she had returned to the capital, but, in the year that followed, Eudocia's relationship with the emperor deteriorated. Theodosius II, who was by all accounts a spineless cipher, allowed his eunuch Chrysaphius to begin maneuvering potential rivals out of position. Chrysaphius succeeded in forcing the removal of Theodosius' brilliant Prefect Cyrus, his fastidious sister Pulcheria, and his talented but vulnerable wife.[20] In a famous incident involving the mistaken exchange of a possible love token—a prodigious, and heavily over-determined apple—Eudocia was accused of a tryst with the handsome young *Magister Officiorum* Paulinus and disgraced.[21] Capitalizing on the connections she had established in Jerusalem three years earlier, Eudocia returned there to live out the rest of her life, 18 more years down to 460.[22] During this period she continued her program of building and beneficence by expanding the circuit of walls around the city, constructing and endowing monasteries, and above all turning her shrine of

---

[17] *PLRE* II Aelia Eudocia (Athenais) 2; Hunt 1982, 221-248; cf. Holum 1982, 112-146; 175-194; 217-224.

[18] Marcell. Com. s.a. 439; *V Mel.* 56; 58; Soc. 7.47.2-3; Evag. *HE* 2.21. On Melania's visit to Constantinople see *V Mel.* 50-57; *V Petr. Iber.* 29-30 (Raabe, pp. 34-35).

[19] *V Petr. Iber.* 33 (Raabe, p. 37); Theod. *De situ terrae sanctae* 8 (*CCSL* 175.118); Anton. Placent. *Itin.* 25 (*CCSL* 175.142); *V Mel.* 58; cf. Clark 1982.

[20] For the date (based on Marcell. Com. s.a. 440) and discussion, see Cameron 1982, 254-270; ctr. Holum 1982, 176-194.

[21] Joh. Mal. 14.8; *Chron. pasch.*, p. 584-585; Theoph. a.m. 5942; cf. Suda K 2776; Nestorius *Bazaar of Heracleides* 2.2.519.

[22] For Eudocia's death date, see Cyr. Scyth. *V Euth.* 35.

St. Stephen into a magnificent ecclesiastical complex.[23] She also continued to widen the rift with her husband: when Theodosius' *Comes Domesticorum* Saturninus executed two ecclesiastics in Eudocia's attendance, she in turn executed Saturninus, provoking her husband to remove the imperial entourage she had formerly retained.[24] Thus although Eudocia had on her first journey sought spiritual fulfillment and the promotion of her husband's religious agenda, by her second she sought refuge in the Holy City and ended up creating her own identity there as an important political figure independent of the court.

Last among the disaffected Empresses to travel to the Holy Land is the granddaughter of Aelia Eudocia, the daughter of the emperor Valentinian III, also named, after her grandmother, Eudocia.[25] Born c. 438, this young lady knew only troubled times. At just four years of age she was betrothed to Huneric, son of the Vandal king Gaiseric, as part of a diplomatic agreement between Ravenna and Carthage.[26] Shortly after her father was assassinated in 455, Eudocia was instead married off to the son of the usurper Petronius Maximus,[27] an arrangement which was quickly dissolved when Gaiseric showed up in Italy to sack Rome and claim his son's bride. Gaiseric carried Eudocia back to Carthage, where she was duly wed to Huneric and soon gave birth to his son, Hilderic.[28] After living with her rebarbative and persecutorial husband for 16 years, always in resentment, Eudocia found an opportunity to flee in 471. Theophanes tells us that she quickly made her way to Jerusalem, and there, 'like her grandmother, she venerated the revered sites and embraced the tomb of her grandmother in the shrine of St. Stephen'.[29] By now a broken woman, she died not long after her arrival, leaving behind none of

---

[23] Cyr. Scyth. *V Euth.* 30; 35; Joh. Ruf. *Pleroph.* 11; 20 (*PO* 8.27; 39-40); *V Petr. Iber.* 33; 123 (Raabe, pp. 37; 115); Soc. 7.47.3; Evag. *HE* 2.21-22; *Anth. Pal.* 1.105; Anton. Placent. *Itin.* 25 (*CCSL* 175.142); Cass. *Exp. in Ps.* 50.20 (*CCSL* 97.468); Joh. Mal. 14.8; *Chron. pasch.*, p. 585; Niceoph. Call. 14.50 (*PG* 146.1240). For the archaeology, see Kenyon 1974, 267-274; cf. Hunt 1982, 237-243.

[24] Marcell. Com. s.a. 444; Theoph. a.m. 5942; cf. Cedrenos, p. 601; Priscus fr. 14 (Blockley). After her husband's death, Eudocia allied herself with Monophysites in order to continue to maintain distance from Constantinople and particularly her sister-in-law Pulcheria, see Holum 1982, 222-224.

[25] *PLRE* II Eudocia 1.

[26] Merobaud. *Carm.* 1.17-18; 2.13-14; *Pan.* 2.23-29; Priscus fr. 38.1 (Blockley); cf. Clover 1971, 23-28; 52-54.

[27] Hyd. 162; cf. Zon. 13.25.

[28] Hyd. 167; Priscus fr. 38.1; 39.1 (Blockley); Marcell. Com. s.a. 455; Cyr. Scyth. *V Euth.* 30; Theoph. a.m. 5947; Zon. 13.25.

[29] Theoph. a.m. 5964; Zon. 13.25.

the architectural traces characteristic of her predecessors. Even so, she too found escape and a—brief—new life in the utopian world of the Holy Land.

In the instances of four late Roman empresses, then, the Christian Holy Land seems to have offered a new opportunity for facing the crisis of imperial estrangement through travel.[30] Earlier in Roman history, independent travel had not been so easily reconciled to the ideals associated with the empress. Where an empress was expected to reflect a sort of iconic abstraction of imperial power, sexual virtue and religious devotion, independent, long-distance travel apart from their husbands had, for earlier empresses, been eschewed to avoid pointing up female weakness, threatening female virtue and providing an incentive to female superstition.[31] It is thus to the credit of these late Roman empresses that they invented ways to circumvent these threats to their ideal status and thus embark on these journeys as free agents. As we continue, then, let us look briefly at how all four empresses re-inscribed themselves onto the landscape of imperial power, virtue and religion using travel to the Holy Land as their medium.

In as far as the empress was a personification of *imperium*, the women we have examined demonstrate that they could as easily be the targets as the symbols of imperial power. Thus all of our traveling empresses were nearly overwhelmed by the power that they were supposed to personify, and all felt compelled to flee that power for the utopian safety of Palestine. Yet in their journeys, they sought not just distance from the source of their power, but also an opportunity to rebuild that power using tools well tested by their male counterparts. Helena and Eudocia in particular employed the ceremonies of imperial adventus—with its elaborate processions, its distributions of largesse, and its public oratory—to strengthen their image before the urban populations of the east.[32] Eusebius reports that Helena, 'as she visited the whole east in the magnificence of her imperial authority, showered countless gifts upon the citizens of every city'.[33] So too, the

---

[30] We know of several other women with imperial connections who visited or had contact with the Holy Land. Poemenia, a relative of Theodosius I, visited c. 392 and financed the church of the Imbomon on the Mount of Olives, *V Petr. Iber.* 30 (Raabe, p. 35) with Devos 1969. The wife of Theodosius' regent Rufinus fled to the Holy Land with her daughter in the aftermath of her husband's demise in 396, Zos. 5.8.2; Marcell. Com. s.a. 396. There she would have met her sister, Silvia of Aquitaine, who first went to Palestine c. 392, cf. Hunt 1972. In the sixth century, Maurice's sister Damiana and his niece also went to Jerusalem, Moschus *Prat. sp.* 127 (*PG* 87.2988-2989). See also the report at Anton. Plac. *Itin.* 18 (*CSEL* 175.138) that the *ornamenta* of an unnamed empress could be found hanging from the monument of the Holy Sepulcher.

[31] Earlier empresses traveled, but always in the company of their husbands, cf. Halfmann 1986, 90-92. For the religious element in most long-distance leisure travel in antiquity, see Casson 1994, 262-291.

[32] On imperial *adventus*, see MacCormack 1981, 17-89; Halfmann 1986, 146-154.

[33] Eus. *VC* 3.44.1-45.1, trans. Cameron and Hall 1999, 138; cf. Soz. 2.2.3. Compare Eudocia's largesse in Antioch, Joh. Mal. 14.8; *Chron. pasch.*, p. 585. For elements of *adventus* in Helena's journey, see Holum 1990, 74-76.

Life of Melania tells us that some Jerusalemites journeyed as far as Sidon to greet the arrival of Eudocia's entourage in 438–9, and Evagrius even describes how Eudocia addressed the Antiochenes in a learned speech before their assembly during one of her journeys.[34] These empresses thus used travel as it had been used for centuries by their male counterparts, to promote the larger project of empire at the same time they were promoting their own claims to legitimate imperial power.

An empress' sexual virtue was another part of her iconic status which was very much at issue in the four cases discussed here. Helena's wrangling over her daughter-in-law's sexual indiscretions, Eutropia's own disavowal of her son's legitimate conception, Eudocia's alleged marital infidelities, and her granddaughter's virtual sexual slavery all make clear that, for an empress, sexuality was a prime barometer of success or failure. It is thus all the more curious that these empresses chose independent travel as their springboard back to legitimacy, for travel had always been regarded as compromising to modesty.[35] Gregory of Nyssa understood this when he questioned the wisdom of consecrated virgins making pilgrimages by pointing out:

> The constraints of the journey are always disrupting the scrupulous observance of virtue. For it is impossible for a woman to undertake a journey unless she has someone to protect her and, on account of her physical weakness, to help her up onto her mount and to dismount and to support her across rough terrain. But ... whether she is supporting herself on a stranger or on a friend, she is not observing the law of chastity.[36]

Apart from curiously reinforcing the fundamentalist preacher's loaded lament, 'the problem of sex has been mounting for years', Gregory's comment points up what must have been a central concern for an empress journeying to the Holy Land. Yet here too our empresses, like other female contemporaries, stage-managed the issue of sexual virtue to their own advantage. Helena, who was at any rate beyond the age for sexual escapades, nevertheless chose to associate with a coterie of virgins while in Jerusalem.[37] More to the point, Eudocia seems to have made a deliberate effort to stay with ascetics along her way and to cultivate their

---

[34] *V Mel.* 58; Evag. *HE* 1.20; cf. John. Mal. 14.8; *Chron. pasch.*, p. 585. Whitby 2000, 48 n. 172 points out that we cannot know whether this speech was given on her first or second journey. On Eudocia's literary ambitions, see Cameron 1982, 270-289.

[35] Then, as now, travelers were regularly plied with the sex trade, cf. Casson 1994, 204-218.

[36] Greg. Nys. *Ep.* 2.6, trans. Lee 2000, 284; cf. Jer. *Ep.* 58.4.4 and Bitton-Ashkelony 1999.

[37] Ruf. *HE* 10.8; Soc. 1.17.12; Soz. 2.2.2; Theod. 1.18.8; Suda E 3213. Concerns of chastity certainly factored in the widespread establishment of *xenodocheia* for Christian travelers, cf. Casson 1994, 319-324.

attentions in Jerusalem.[38] John of Nikiu even reports that, on her first journey, her husband ordered Cyril of Alexandria to accompany the empress as a chaperon.[39] Cyril and the ascetics who helped these empresses in their journeys were people whose studied abstinence posed no threat to the virtue of their guests. Using them as guides and hosts, the empresses—and those women who followed their example[40]—were able to redefine the modes and destinations of travel and lodging so as to enhance rather than detract from their reputation for chastity.[41]

Lastly, these royal women also redefined the nature of imperial travel so as to enhance the final ideal they were expected to represent, religious devotion. Here more than elsewhere, our itinerant empresses succeeded in rewriting themselves back into the narrative of power using a religious space that had been largely ignored by their Christian predecessors. Though Jews continued to revere holy sites in Judaea long after the destruction of the Temple, it seems to have occurred to very few Christians to do the same prior to the 330s.[42] By traveling to, rediscovering, reclaiming and rebuilding the Christian holy sites, Helena, Eutropia and Eudocia were thus (re)inventing a sacred landscape which would simultaneously transform Christianity and repave their path to power. These empresses were in this sense powerful impresarios in the transformation of the profane landscape of post-Temple Judaea into a sacred stage for the reenactment of Christian religion. The new religious phenomenon they pioneered exerted an impact both locally in Judaea and world-wide across the Mediterranean basin.[43]

Helena's reclamation of the holy sites of Bethlehem and Eleona together with her son's constructions at Golgotha[44] opened the gates for a sea-change in travel

---

[38] *V Mel.* 58; Evag. *HE* 2.21; *V Petr. Iber.* 123 (Raabe, p. 123-124). Of course, for any empress the dangers of violation were minimized by the presence of guards and the opportunity to use the wagons and posting stations of the *cursus publicus*, Halfmann 1986, 74-78. Even so, time away from the emperor opened windows of opportunity.

[39] Joh. Nik. 86.47; cf. Hunt 1982, 230-231.

[40] Cf. *Itin. Eg.* 5.12; 8.2; 23.3; *V Mel.*51; 56; Cyr. Scyth. *V. Euth.* 30.

[41] Compare Pelagia, the harlot of Antioch, who also used Jerusalem as a refuge from her former life of promiscuity and a place to refashion herself as an ascetic, Brock and Harvey 1987, 40-62. Thanks to Daniel Caner for pointing out this parallel.

[42] The case is stated most forcefully at Taylor 1993. Hunt 1999 offers necessary revision but would still agree that there were very few Christian pilgrims before Constantine.

[43] See Brubaker 1997 on Helena as an archetype for Christian architectural patronage. Wilken 1992, 82-100 says surprisingly little about the role of empresses in the construction of the Christian 'Holy Land'.

[44] Note how these three churches form a triad of the primary pilgrimage destinations at Greg. Nys. *Ep.* 2.13; Jer. *Ep.* 58.3.5; cf. Eus. *LC* 9.17; Paul. Nol. *Ep.* 31.4 (*CSEL* 29.271). On this triad, see Walker 1990, 184-194.

patterns which were reoriented toward Jerusalem, the new Christian center of the world.[45] Not only do we see a more general explosion of evidence for Christian travel to the Holy Land in the aftermath of Helena's visit, we see in particular the rise of independent travel by women.[46] Following these empresses, all people and especially women reinvented the purpose and destination of leisure travel. The opening of the new Holy Land also marked the opening of an ongoing, grandiose, year-round reenactment of Christ's life and passion by the bishop and people in Jerusalem. Using the sites (re)discovered and (re)constructed by Helena, Eutropia and Constantine, Jerusalemites and pilgrims from around the *oikoumene* were able to make the divine word of scripture come to life on a daily basis in the physical space of Jerusalem. With painstaking attention to scriptural detail and elaborately choreographed displays of emotional involvement.[47] Jerusalemites and pilgrims succeeded in removing the worldly Jerusalem, from present time/space and transforming it into a Christian utopia.

The empresses thus established in the Holy Land a utopian world in both senses of the word as it was coined by Thomas More. First, for themselves and for those who followed them, they made Jerusalem into a place of flight and refuge from the real world, a nowhere land of temporal and spiritual salvation. But second, and more importantly, the empresses and Jerusalem Christians alike made of Jerusalem a wonderland, an idealized place which existed in and through their (re)imaginings.[48] Through the reclamation and sacralization of Christian *topoi* and through the rituals which were invented to enliven these *topoi*, the empresses and their Jerusalem followers transformed Judaea into a physical manifestation of the holy. In this sense, these empresses seem not to have been fleeing power so much as redefining its locus. In putting a safe distance between themselves and male-dominated imperial power, they were able to re-form an entire landscape into a never-land of holiness which guaranteed them a greater measure of power than they could ever have hoped for had they remained at the side of an emperor.

---

[45] See Elsner 2000, 190-195; Hunt 1982, 182; 246; Hunt 1997, 419-424; Stoltmann 1999, 281-310.

[46] To catalog but a few female travelers to the Holy Land in the fourth and fifth centuries: Albina (*V Mel.* 35; 41); Egeria (*Itin. Eg.*; cf. Wilkinson 1999); Eustochium (Jer. *Ep.* 108.4; Pall. *Hist. Laus.* 41); Fabiola (Jer. *Ep.* 64.8; 77.7-9); Marana and Cyra (Theod. *HM* 29.7 = *SCh* 257.239); Marthana (*Itin. Eg.* 23.3 = *CSEL* 175.66); Melania the Elder (Pall. *Hist. Laus.* 46); Melania the Younger (*V Mel.* 34-70); Paula (Jer. *Ep.* 108.9-14). Cf. above n. 30 and Athanasius *Second Letter to Virgins* in Brakke 1995, 292-293.

[47] On the use of scripture, see Jer. *Ep.* 109.9; *Itin. Eg.* 36.3; 47.5 (*CCSL* 175.80;89); cf. Stoltman 1999, 294-301. On theatricality see Jer. *Ep.* 108.9-109.2; *Itin. Eg.* 24.10; 34.1; 37.7 (*CCSL* 175.69; 78; 82). More on these elements at Hunt 1982, 107-127; MacCormack 1990; Wilken 1992, 101-125; Wilkinson 1999, 41-83.

[48] For a similar reading of late Roman travel to the Holy Land, see Elsner and Rubiés 1999, 1-20; Elsner 2000, 194. I would like to thank Jan Willem Drijvers, Elizabeth Key Fowden and Alison Orlebeke for aid with this paper.

Bibliography

Barnes, T. D. (1981), *Constantine and Eusebius*, Cambridge, MA: Harvard University Press.

Bitton-Ashkelony, B. (1999), 'The Attitudes of Church Fathers toward Pilgrimage to Jerusalem in the Fourth and Fifth Centuries', in Levine, L. I. (ed.), *Jerusalem, its Sanctity and Centrality to Judaism, Christianity and Islam*, New York: Continuum, pp. 188-203.

Bloedhorn, H. (1995), 'Die Eleona und das Imbomon in Jerusalem: Eine Doppelkirchenanlage auf dem Ölberg', in *Akten des XII. Internationalen Kongresses für Christliche Archäologie: JAC Ergänzungsband 20*, Münster: Aschendorff, pp. 568-71.

Brakke, D. (1995), *Athanasius and the Politics of Asceticism*, Oxford: Clarendon Press.

Brock, S. P. and S. A. Harvey, trans. (1987), *Holy Women of the Syrian Orient*, Berkeley: University of California Press.

Brubaker, L. (1997), 'Memories of Helena: Patterns in Imperial Female Matronage in the Fourth and Fifth Centuries', in James, L. (ed.), *Women, Men and Eunuchs: Gender in Byzantium*, London and New York: Routledge, pp. 52-75.

Cameron, A. (1982), 'The Empress and the Poet: Paganism and Politics at the Court of Theodosius II', *Yale Classical Studies*, **27**, 217-89.

Cameron, A. and S. G. Hall, trans. and comm. (1999), *Eusebius Life of Constantine*, Oxford: Clarendon Press.

Casson, L. (1994), *Travel in the Ancient World*, Baltimore: Johns Hopkins University Press.

Clark, E. A. (1982), 'Claims on the Bones of Saint Stephen: The Partisans of Melania and Eudocia', *Church History*, **51**, 141-56.

Clover, F. M. (1971), *Flavius Merobaudes: A Translation and Historical Commentary: Transactions of the American Philosophical Society* **61** (1), Philadelphia: The American Philosophical Society.

Devos, P. (1969), 'La "Servante de Dieu" Poemenia d'après Pallade: la tradition copte et Jean Rufus', *Analecta Bollandiana*, **87**, 189-212.

———(1968), 'Égérie a Bethléem: le 40ᵉ jour après paques a Jérusalem, en 383', *Analecta Bollandiana*, **86**, 87-108.

Drijvers, J. W. (1992a), *Helena Augusta: The Mother of Constantine the Great and the Legend of her Finding of the True Cross*, Leiden: Brill.

———(1992b), 'Flavia Maxima Fausta: Some Remarks', *Historia* **41**, 500-506.

Elsner, J. (2000), 'The *Itinerarium Burdigalense*: Politics and Salvation in the Geography of Constantine's Empire', *Journal of Roman Studies*, 90, 181-95.

Elsner, J. and J.-P. Rubiés (1999), *Voyages and Visions: Towards a Cultural History of Travel*, London: Reaktion Books.

Halfmann, H. (1986), *Itinera principum: Geschichte und Typologie der Kaiserreisen im Römischen Reich*, Stuttgart: Franz Steiner Verlag.

Heid, S. (1989), 'Der Ursprung der Helenalegende im Pilgerbetrieb Jerusalems', *Jahrbuch für Antike und Christentum*, **32**, 41-71.

Holum, K.G. (1982), *Theodosian Empresses: Women and Imperial Dominion in Late Antiquity*, Berkeley: University of California Press.

———(1990), 'Hadrian and St. Helena: Imperial Travel and the Origins of Christian Holy Land Pilgrimage', in Ousterhout, R. (ed.), *The Blessings of Pilgrimage*, Urbana, IL: University of Illinois Press, pp. 66-81.

Hunt, E. D. (1972), 'St. Silvia of Aquitaine: The Role of a Theodosian Pilgrim in the Society of East and West', *Journal of Theological Studies*, **23**, 351-73.

————(1982), *Holy Land Pilgrimage in the Later Roman Empire, AD 312-460*, Oxford: Clarendon Press.

————(1997), 'Constantine and Jerusalem', *Journal of Ecclesiastical History*, **48**, 405-24.

————(1999), 'Were there Christian Pilgrims before Constantine?', in Stopford, J. (ed.), *Pilgrimage Explored*, York: York Medieval Press, pp. 25-40.

Kenyon, K. (1974), *Digging up Jerusalem*. New York: Praeger.

Lee, A. D. (2000), *Pagans and Christians in Late Antiquity: A Sourcebook*, London: Routledge.

MacCormack, S. (1981), *Art and Ceremony in Late Antiquity*, Berkeley: University of California Press.

————(1990), '*Loca Sancta*: The Organization of Sacred Topography in Late Antiquity', in Ousterhout, R. (ed.), *The Blessings of Pilgrimage*, Urbana, IL: University of Illinois Press, pp. 7-40.

Pohlsander, H. (1984), 'Crispus: Brilliant Career and Tragic End', *Historia*, **33**, 79-106.

Raabe, R., ed. and trans. (1895), *Petrus Der Iberer*, Leipzig: Hinrichs'she Buchhandlung.

Stoltmann, D. (1999), *Jerusalem – Mutter – Stadt: Zur Theologiegeschichte der Heiligen Stadt*, Altenberge: Oros Verlag.

Taylor, J. E. (1993), *Christians and the Holy Places: The Myth of Jewish-Christian Origins*, Oxford: Clarendon Press.

Walker, P. W. L. (1990), *Holy City, Holy Places? Christian Attitudes to Jerusalem and the Holy Land in the Fourth Century*, Oxford: Clarendon Press.

Whitby, M., trans. (2000), *The Ecclesiastical History of Evagrius Scholasticus: Translated Texts for Historians 33*, Liverpool: Liverpool University Press.

Wilken, R. L. (1992), *The Land Called Holy: Palestine in Christian History and Thought*, New Haven, CT: Yale University Press.

Wilkinson, J., trans. (1999), *Egeria's Travels*, 3rd ed., Warminster: Aris and Phillips.

Woods, D. (1998), 'On the Death of the Empress Fausta', *Greece and Rome*, **45**, 70-86.

Chapter 10

Itinerant Spirituality and the Late Antique Origins of Christian Pilgrimage

Maribel Dietz

In a letter to Oceanus, Jerome describes the travels of a Roman widow named Fabiola. 'Rome was not large enough for her compassionate kindness. She went from island to island, and travelled round the Etruscan Sea, and through the Volscian province ... where bands of monks have taken up their home, bestowing her bounty either in person or by the agency of holy men of faith'.[1] Eventually, and I believe predictably, she sailed to Jerusalem. Though Jerome urged her to stay in the East, she instead wanted to resume her travels. Jerome described her as living out of her 'travelling baggage ... a stranger (*peregrina*) in every city'.[2] Fabiola was living a religious life of wandering; she was living as an exile. She had not taken Jerome's advice, but followed another path, one that others before her, including other women, had also followed. She resumed her travels and left Jerusalem, eventually returning to her home in Rome. Once again we are told that she wanted to escape—she felt confined, and this time, against the advice of her Roman friends, she departed, going to Ostia with a wealthy widower and setting up a xenodocium—a hostel for travellers—which quickly became popular and, according to Jerome, attracted huge crowds. This short account of Fabiola's travels, her patronage of monks and her foundation of a xenodocium opens a window for us onto the activity of monastic wandering. Fabiola was not alone in combining travel and monastic life into a particularly late antique form of spiritual expression. My intention here is to explore the origins of Christian religious travel in the West through a consideration of the intimate connections between monasticism and the development of pilgrimage. I would like to suggest that pilgrimage was the offspring of a peculiar form of a monasticism based explicitly on ascetic travel and wandering.

---

[1] '*Angusta misericordiae eius Roma fuit. Peragrabat ergo insulas, et totum Etruscum mare, Volscorumque provinciam ... in quibus Monachorum consistunt chori, vel proprio corpore, vel transmissa per viros sanctos ac fideles munificentia circumibat*'. *Ep.* 77, 6, Jerome, *Epistulae*, ed. I. Hilberg, 3 vols *CSEL* 54-56; English translation in F. A. Wright, ed., *Select Letters of St. Jerome, The Loeb Classical Library*, Cambridge, Massachusetts: Harvard University Press, 1991 (1st edition, 1933).

[2] '*Illa, quae tota in sarcinis erat, et in omni urbe peregrina ...*' Jerome, *Ep.* 77, 8.

Scholars often assume that pilgrimage has always existed within Christianity, that it was a vestige of the apostolic movement, but the actual historical origins of religious travel in the complex world of the late antique Mediterranean basin remain largely unknown. Pilgrim and pilgrimage become labels given to any person going to or passing through Jerusalem. Many travellers who are usually labelled pilgrims, perhaps were actually exhibiting monastic behavior. The word *peregrinus* is frequently translated as pilgrim—with all of its English connotations—rather than traveller or stranger. In his *Etymologies,* Isidore of Seville defines *peregrinus* as someone far from home, a stranger in a strange land. We should re-examine how the word is used in late antique sources. By pilgrimage here I am not referring to travel to local shrines or holy people, an activity that was important in late antique society, but instead long-distance travel where the traveling or wandering itself is the focus, rather than arriving at a specific place for a well-defined reason or performing a specific ritual. The image of a Chaucer-esque religious journey toward a particular place can bring with it a host of misleading assumptions. Similarly, projecting Benedictine monasticism, with its emphasis on stability and enclosure, onto too early a period distorts our image of the monastic diversity of the late antique West, a diversity well described in a recent book by Marilyn Dunn.[3] We must look beyond these anachronistic images and try to uncover the integrity of the late antique practice of ascetic travel.

At the core of this late antique spiritual itinerary was the expression of Christian exile and homelessness. Ascetic wandering provided a way of separating from the world by leaving home and stability, and embarking on a life of travel. Such a life, based on *instabilitas* rather than Benedictine-style *stabilitas*, resonated with the culture of movement in the late antique Mediterranean basin, as has been convincingly demonstrated by the papers in this volume. Early monastic wandering did not necessarily involve going to a particular place, though travel to the Holy Land did have a role to play, but instead stressed a particular state of mind and body—homelessness.

This monastic activity appealed to a variety of people—both male and female. Women religious travellers are far more likely to be labelled pilgrims than are men. Egeria and Orosius, for example, took similar voyages only a generation apart, yet Egeria is thought of as the quintessential pilgrim while Orosius, who even brought back relics, is never called a 'pilgrim'. He is always referred to as a messenger of Augustine, or a participant in a church council. Yet Egeria's writings clearly show that she was not on a 'place and time' delimited pilgrimage, but was instead travelling as a spiritual expression. She may very well be placing the reasons for her journey in the mouth of the bishop of Edessa when she quotes him saying, 'My daughter, I see that you have taken on yourself, because of your piety [*gratia religionis*], the great task of journeying from very distant lands to

---

[3] Marilyn Dunn, *The Emergence of Monasticism*, London: Blackwell, 2000.

these places'.[4] Orosius likewise used his departure from Spain to emphasize his life of Christian wandering. Nowhere is this more evident than when he writes of the manner in which a Christian can travel wherever he or she wants and expect to receive hospitality: 'when I flee at the first disturbance of whatever commotion, since it is a question of a secure place of refuge, everywhere there is native land, everywhere my law and my religion. Now Africa has received me as kindly as I confidently approached her ...'.[5]

It is perhaps the life of another fifth century Spaniard, Bachiarius, that best exemplifies late antique spiritual wandering. Gennadius of Marseilles described Bachiarius as 'a Christian philosopher' who 'chose travel as a means of preserving the integrity of his purpose'; his purpose being to 'devote his time to God'.[6] Gennadius writes that Bachiarius defended himself 'against those who complained and misrepresented his travel, and asserting that he undertook his travel not through fear of men but for the sake of God, that going forth from his land and kindred he might become a co-heir with Abraham the patriarch'.[7] In fact, Bachiarius uses many examples for the Old Testament, including Abraham, in his own work.[8]

In the chaotic world of Late Antiquity, flight from barbarians and actual exile could be transformed into religious wandering. Leander of Seville, in a work dedicated to his sister, characterizes their own mother's exile as a sort of Christian wandering and homelessness. Their mother, a physical exile, became a model for

---

[4] '*Quoniam video te, filia, gratia religionis tam magnum laborem tibi imposuisse, ut de extremis porro terris venires ad haec loca*', Egeria, *Itinerarium*, 19, 5, ed. P. Geyer and O. Cuntz, *Itineraria et alia geographica*, CCSL 175, 37-90; English translation by John Wilkinson, *Egeria's Travels*, 3rd edition, Warminster: Aris and Phillips Ltd, 1999.

[5] '*Mihi autem prima qualiscumque motus perturbatione fudienti, quia de confugiendi statione securo, ubique patria, ubique lex et religio mea est. Nunc me Africa tam libenter excepit quam confidenter accessi*', 5, 2, Orosius, *Historiarum adversum paganos libri VII*, ed. Casimiro Torres Rodriguez, *Paulo Orosio su vida y sus obras*, Galicia Historica, Santiago: Milladoiro, 1985, pp. 87-721; English translation by Roy J. Deferrari, ed., *Paulus Orosius: The Seven Books of History Against the Pagans*, Washington, D.C.: Catholic University Press, 1964.

[6] '*Bachiarius vir Christianae philosophiae, nudus et expeditus vacare Deo disponens, etiam peregrinationem propter conservandam vitae integritatem elegit*', Gennadius of Marseilles, *Liber de viris inlustribus*, 24, *PL* 58, 1053; English translation by Ernest Cushing Richardson, ed., 'Jerome and Gennadius: Lives of Illustrious Men', *A Select Library of Nicene and Post-Nicene Fathers of the Christian Church*, Grand Rapids, Michigan: Eerdmans, 1979, pp. 349-402.

[7] '*Satisfacit pontifici Urbis adversum querulos et infamatores peregrinationis suae, indicans se non timore hominum, sed Dei causa peregrinatione suscepisse, ut exiens de terra sua et cognatione sua cohaeres fieret Abrahae patriarchae*', Gennadius of Marseilles, *Liber de viris inlustribus*, 24.

[8] Bachiarius, *Libellus de Fide* and *De reparatione lapsi ad Januarium*, *PL* 20, 1019-63.

spiritual exile. Leander writes that he repeatedly asked his mother whether she ever wished to return to her home and that,

> she knew that she had been removed for her own safety by the will of God, and she used to swear a solemn oath that she never wanted to see and never would see her country again and with many tears she would add: 'My sojourn [*peregrinatio*] has given me to know God; I shall die a sojourner [*peregrina*], and I shall have my tomb where I found the knowledge of God'.[9]

In Ireland we see a form of itinerant spirituality in the characterization of monastic life as a *peregrinatio*, which consists of actual travel.[10] I wish here to distinguish this from penitential pilgrimage, which appears to be a specifically Irish creation and, though related, is quite different from monastic wandering. Penitential pilgrimage appears to consist of a confined timeframe, with defined purpose, the cleansing sins.[11] Adomnan's *Life of Columba* provides evidence for both of these types of *peregrinatio*—each itself different from site-specific pilgrimage. Columba is repeatedly described as embarking of a 'life of *peregrinatio*' and spends much of his life travelling.[12] The monk Cormac, mentioned a few times in

---

[9] '... *nosse cupiens si vellet reverti ad atriam, illa autem, quae se noverat Dei voluntate causa inde salutis exiisse, sub divina obtestatione dicebat nec velle se videre nec unquam visuram patriam illam esse*; *et cum magnis dicebat fletibus: "Peregrinatio me Deum fecit agnoscere, peregrina moriar; et ibi sepulturam habeam, ubi Domini cognitionem accepi"'*. Leander of Seville, *De institutione virginum et contemptu mundi*, 31.3, Jaime Velazquez, ed., *De la Instruccion de las virgenes y desprecio del mundo*, Madrid: Fundacion Universitaria Española, 1979; English translation in Claude W. Barlow, ed., *Iberian Fathers, volume 1: Martin of Braga, Paschasius of Dumium, Leander of Seville*, Washington, D.C.: Catholic University Press, 1969.

[10] For monastic travel and pilgrimage in Ireland see Lisa M. Bitel, *Isle of the Saints: Monastic Settlement and Christian Community in Early Ireland*, Ithaca and London: Cornell University Press, 1990; Thomas Charles-Edwards, 'The Social Background of Irish Peregrinatio', *Celtica* 11 (1976), pp. 43-59; Kathleen Hughes, 'The Changing Theory and Practice of Irish Pilgrimage' and 'On an Irish Litany of Pilgrim Saints', in David Dumville (ed.), *Church and Society in Ireland A.D. 400-1200*, London: Variorum Reprints, 1987, pp. 143-51, 302-31.

[11] On penitential pilgrimage in Ireland see Ludwig Bieler, ed., *The Irish Penitentials*, *Scriptores Latini Hiberniae, vol. 5*, Dublin: Institute for Advanced Studies, 1963.

[12] Adomnan, *Life of Columba*, about the monk Fintenus, '*ut nostrum sanctum Columbam Heuerniam deserens perigrinaturus adiret*', bk. 1:2 'life of pilgrimage'; bk. 1:13 '*Hic namque de patria cum aliis duobus fratribus effugatus ad sanctum in Britanniam perigrinantem exsul venit*', and '*sum sanctus in sua conversaretur perigrinatione*', bk. 2:10 in Alan Orr Anderson and Marjorie Ogilvie Anderson, eds., *Adomnán's Life of Columba*, *Oxford Medieval Texts*, Oxford: Clarendon Press, 1991. English translation by Richard Sharpe, trans., *Adomnán of Iona, Life of St Columba*, London: Penguin, 1995.

the life, is another example of someone seeking a monastic life by wandering—Adomnan describes him and his companions as men who 'seek a place of retreat in the sea'—the word here is *eremos*, looking for the desert in the ocean, in other words a monastic life through sea travel.[13]

As late as the eighth century we find the monastic language of itinerant spirituality expressed by the monk, and later bishop of Eichstätt, Willibald. Huneberc, his hagiographer, believed that he sought monastic perfection through travel. She writes, 'He began also to devise means of setting out on a journey [*peregrinatio*] and traveling to foreign countries that were unknown to him'.[14] It was not necessarily travel to the holy city of Jerusalem that accomplished this perfection, though he did eventually visit the city three times; it was the travel itself, and meeting other holy people and getting to know their lives. The central point of her account was his yearning for a stricter life, a life in which he gave up his homeland and family for almost constant travel.

If the religious meaning of travel for these monks was to be found not in their destination but in the experience of travel itself—what did that experience consist of? What did they do during their travels? Perhaps the most important part of wandering was meeting holy people. Monastic wanderers, men and women alike, sought out holy people wherever they went, collecting stories and acquaintances—creating, in a sense, monastic travel networks. Visiting monks was Egeria's main objective in her travels. Many have noted that Egeria refers to Old Testament figures as 'sancti', such as *sanctus Moyses, sanctus Abraam, sancta Rebecca*. Egeria uses the same word in describing the various monks, *sancti monachi*, she meets during her travels, and the usage is significant.[15] In Egeria's estimation, the holy places she visits are not inherently holy, they are holy due to the continuity of holy people there. It is the *sancti monachi* on Mount

---

[13] Adomnan, *Life of Columba*, bk. 1:20 *'cum ceteris in mari herimum quaesiturus'* and *'qui ad quaerendum in ociano desertum'*. For another account of Cormac looking for a retreat in the ocean, *'etiam secunda vice conatus est herimum in ociano quaerere'*, bk. 2:42.

[14] *'Cumque ista sedule intus intra mentis volubilitate volvans tractare cepit, qualiter ista cogitatio depromeri proferrique poterit in effectum, ut caduca cuncta cosmi istius contemnere sive derelinquere quearet et non solum temporales terrenarum divitias, set et patriam et parentes atque propinquos deserere peregrinationisque temptare telluram et ignotas externarum requirere ruras'*. Huneberc of Heidenheim, *Vita Willibaldi Episcopi Eichstetensis*, 89.29-33, ed. O. Holder-Egger, *MGH* 15, Hanover: Hahnsche Buchhandlung, 1887, pp. 86-106; English translation by C. H. Talbot, ed., 'The *Hodoeporicon* of St Willibald by Huneberc of Heidenheim', in *The Anglo-Saxon Missionaries in Germany*, London and New York: Sheed and Ward, 1954, pp. 153-177; Revised and reprinted in Thomas Head and Thomas F. X. Noble, eds., *Soldiers of Christ: Saints and Saints' Lives from Late Antiquity and the Early Middle Ages*, University Park, Pennsylvania: Pennsylvania State University Press, 1995, pp. 141-164.

[15] For some examples of monks referred to as '*sancti monachi*,' see Egeria, *Itin.* 3, 6; 11, 3; 12, 3; 16, 5; 19, 4; 20, 6; 20, 11; and 20, 13.

Sinai who tell her where *sanctus Moyses* spoke with the burning bush.[16] A similar emphasis on visiting monks and virgins, rather than places, can be seen in the travels of Paula, the Piacenza pilgrim and even Willibald.[17]

Another activity that these travellers have in common is the gathering of stories and experiences, often to share with others either back home or people met during their travels. Egeria is collecting stories for her community of sisters back home. She even collects manuscripts—as she did on her visit to Edessa, where she receives copies of the King Abgar letters from the bishop.[18] Orosius, too, brought manuscripts and relics with him on his return journey—he left the Holy Land with the relics of St Stephen the protomartyr and a copy of a Latin translation of the account of their discovery.[19] Perhaps the most prolific collector of stories was Palladius, who had left home for the Holy Land and the stability of a monastery on the Mount of Olives, only to then leave and begin a wandering life, visiting monks and virgins. The *Lausiac History* is his attempt to share his knowledge, knowledge of monasticism born by his own wandering and visiting. Palladius began his story with a description of how he obtained his evidence. He wrote that he,

> travelled on foot and looked into every cave and cabin of the monks of the desert with all accuracy and pious motive. I wrote down some of the things I saw, and also some accounts I heard from the holy fathers. It is

---

[16] '*Locus etiam ostenditur ibi iuxta, ubi stetit sanctus Moyses, quando ei dixit Deus: "Solue corrigiam calciamenti tui," et cetera ... et sic, quia sera erat, gustavimus nobis loco in horto ante rubum cum sanctis ipsis*'. Egeria, *Itin.* 4, 8.

[17] For Paula see Jerome, *Ep.* 108, 7 and *Ep.* 108, 10; for Willibald see Huneberc, *Vita Willibaldi*, 93.23, 96.14-15, 97.9, and 99.5; for the Piacenza pilgrim see *Itinerarium Placentini*, 34, P. Geyer and O. Cuntz, eds, *Itineraria et alia geographica*, CCSL 175, 127-174; English translation by John Wilkinson, *Jerusalem Pilgrims before the Crusades* Warminster: Aris and Phillips Ltd, 1977, pp. 79-89.

[18] '*Et licet in patria exemplaria ipsarum haberem, tamen gratius mihi visum est, ut et ibi eas de ipso acciperem, ne quid forsitan minus ad nos in patria pervenisset; nam vere amplius est, quod hic accepi. Unde si Deus noster Iesus iusserit et venero in patria, legitis vos, dominae animae meae*', Egeria, *Itin.* 19, 19.

[19] *Epistula de inventione corporis S. Stephani martyris*, *PL* 41, 805-808. Severus of Minorca, *Epistola Severi Episcopi*, ed. Eusebio Lafuente Hernández, *Edición paleográfica y Transcripción latina seguidas de las versiones castellana y catalana de su texto*, vol. 1, *Documenta Historica Minoricensia*, Menorca: Ediciones Nura, 1981; English translation by Scott Bradbury, *Severus of Minorca: Letter on the Conversion of the Jews*, Oxford: Oxford University Press, 1996. Gennadius states it was Orosius who brought the relics of Stephen to the West, Gennadius of Marseilles, *Liber de viris inlustribus*, 40.

all in this book—the contests of the great men, and of the women, too,
...²⁰

Palladius wanted Lausus to learn from and imitate the *Historia*, but he also urged him to seek out meetings with holy men and women. 'But go near a bright window and seek encounters with holy men and women, in order that by their help you may be able to see clearly also your own heart as it were a closely-written book, being able by comparison to discern your own slackness or neglect'.²¹ In the eighth century, Huneberc stated a similar opinion concerning the benefit of learning by example in her account of Willibald's life and travels. Even though Willibald would eventually become a bishop, Huneberc continued to emphasize his monastic activities and the role his travel played in these activities. Huneberc made this connection in the following passage.

> ... then he was consecrated bishop. Afterwards he began to build a monastery in the place called Eichstätt, and he shortly afterwards practised the monastic life there according to the observance which he had seen at St Benedict's, and not merely there, but also in many other monastic houses, which he had examined with his experienced eye as he travelled through various lands. This observance he taught to others by the example of his own life.²²

To make her case clear, Huneberc compared Willibald to a 'busy bee' who flies from flower to flower bringing back to his hive only the sweetest nectar.²³ His travels, far from threatening his monastic pursuit, actually enhanced his monasticism. Huneberc ended her account of his life by relating how popular his monastic foundation in Bavaria became, especially to those who came from afar.²⁴

---

²⁰ Palladius, *HL*, Prol., 3, W. K. Lowther Clarke, ed. (1918), *The Lausiac History of Palladius*, New York: Macmillan; Also Robert T. Meyer, ed., *Lausiac History*, Westminster, Maryland: Newman Press, pp. 1965.

²¹ Palladius, *HL*, Prol., 15.

²² '... *sacri episcopatus gradum accepit, et in loco que dicitur Eihstat monasterium construere incipiebat atque oceo ibidem sacram monasterialis vitae disciplinam in usum prioris vitae, quod videndo ad Sanctum Benedictum, et non solum ibi, sed in aliis multis monachorum mansionibus, quas ipse solers et sophyrus vaste per ruras rimando explorabat, ast illorum cata normam venerandis vitae conversationem in semet ipso ostendendo exercebat* ...' Huneberc, *Vita Willibaldi*, 105.19-24. The 'cata' in this passage is a transliteration of the Greek.

²³ '*et sic apis prudentissima, que per purpura violarium virecta et per fulvas frondosorum flosculos et per olida holerum florida loetalem liquantes toxicam et suavissimum sorbentes sucum nectaris* ...' Huneberc, *Vita Willibaldi*, 105.26-28.

²⁴ '*statim undique de illis regionum provinciis et nihilominus de aliis longinquum limis ad saluberrimam eius sapientiae dogmam confluere ceperunt.*' Huneberc, *Vita Willibaldi*, 106.5-6.

Gift-giving and gift-receiving were an important part of travel for these wandering ascetics. Exchanges sealed the meeting between travelers and the monastic hosts. Gifts were crucial in legitimizing visits and they functioned to enhance the sanctity of the holy people. The Piacenza pilgrim collected souvenirs of his visits and frequently commented on the collecting of other travelers. Some of his gifts were then bestowed on others. In Jericho he purchased giant dates which, upon his return home, he presented to his patron.[25] Both of the Melanias, grandmother and granddaughter, participated in similar gift collecting and exchanges. When Melania the Younger died, she is buried with a vast collection of items she had collected from the holy people she had visited throughout her life.[26]

Melania the Elder, with her foundation of a women's monastery on the Mount of Olives, introduces another common practice of these travelers: establishing monastic institutions and xenodocia especially for the care of travelers and foreigners.[27] Rather than viewing them as pilgrims themselves, we ought to see these wanderers as promoters or facilitators of travel, pilgrimage and monasticism. In Jerusalem, the Piacenza pilgrim describes a guesthouse run by monks that could accommodate 3000 guests.[28]

Though they were clearly different in essence from later medieval *locus*-centered pilgrimages, many of these journeys did include a visit to the Holy Land. This was the case with the Bordeaux pilgrim, Egeria, Orosius, Piacenza pilgrim, Paula, Melania, Fabiola, Palladius, and, much later on, Willibald. Interestingly it appears that travel to the Holy Land was more prevalent in the earliest monastic travel—the fourth and fifth centuries, though it was this aspect more than any other that was later actualized in the form of pilgrimage. Paula, in a letter, urges Marcella to make the journey to Jerusalem. The letter ends with an emotional

---

[25] '*Ibi nascitur dactalum de libra, ex quibus mecum adduxi in provincia, ex quibus unum domino Paterio patricio dedi.*' *Itin. Plac.*, 14.

[26] 'She had the tunic of one holy man, the veil of another handmaid of God, a piece of a sleeveless tunic which had belonged to another holy man, the girdle of a third (with which she always girt herself when alive), the cowl of a fourth, and, as a pillow the haircloth cowl of a fifth—from it we made a cushion and placed it beneath her honoured head. It was fitting that she should be buried in the garments of those whose virtues she had acquired in her lifetime.' Gerontius, *Life of Melania*, 69, in Denys Gorce, ed., *Vie de sainte Mélanie*, vol. 90 SC, Paris: Editions du Cerf, 1962; English translation in Joan M. Petersen, ed., *Handmaids of the Lord: Contemporary Descriptions of Feminine Asceticism in the First Six Christian Centuries*, Kalamazoo: Cistercian Publications, 1996, pp. 311-361.

[27] Palladius, *HL* 436, 5.

[28] '*ubi est congregatio nimia monachorum, ubi sunt et xenodochia virorum ac mulierum, susceptio peregrinorum, mensas innumerabiles, lecta aegrotorum amplius tria milia*'. *Itin. Plac.*, 23.

description of how Marcella's arrival would be greeted by 'every band of monks and every troop of virgins shall unite in a song of welcome'.[29]

The letter of Paula to Marcella also reveals the importance of itinerant spirituality for women. Women are promoting it to other women. The only single holy person Egeria meets during her journey whom she actually names is a monastic woman, Marthana, who was also on a journey at the time.[30] It is a woman, Huneberc, who wrote so fondly about the journeys and wandering lifestyle of Willibald. It was women, rather than male, travelers who most often set up monasteries and xenodocia. The patterns of late antique Christian travel defy our assumptions about social and gender roles. Itinerant spirituality held a special appeal to women, perhaps the relatively marginal role of women in late antique society made them ideally suited to its pursuit.

In the increasingly chaotic world of the Mediterranean in the early Middle Ages, monastic wandering came to be viewed as suspect and even dangerous by both the episcopal hierarchy of the church and the secular authorities. Monastic legislators began to deride ascetic wandering and monastic travel as aberrations and threats to ecclesiastical order. The danger of itinerant spirituality lay in its freedom of experience, and reliance on the practitioner's own will. Attacks on monastic wandering took the form of attacks on a lack of *discretio*, being able to discern proper conduct for oneself. The lack of physical stability and the danger to communing with the wrong people also came into play. The *Regula Magistri* provides us with the best evidence of this sort of attack in its long diatribe against the *gyrovague* or 'wandering monk'.[31] One of the most biting attacks occurs in a letter written by Evagrius Ponticus to Melania the Elder. He wrote that she should, 'teach your sisters and your sons not to take a long journey or to travel through deserted lands without examining the matter seriously. For this is misguided and unbecoming to every soul that has retreated from the world … . And I wonder whether a woman roaming about and meeting myriads of people can achieve such a goal'.[32]

---

[29] '*O quando tempus illud adveniet, cum anhelus nuntium viator apportet, Marcellam nostram ad Palaestinae littus appulsam: et toti Monachorum chori, tota virginum agmina concrepabunt? Obviam iam gestimus occurrere: et non expectato vehiculo, concitum pedibus ferre corpus … . Ergo ne erit illa dies, quando nobis liceat speluncam Salvatoris intrare? In sepulcro Domini flere (a) cum sorore, flere cum matre? Crucis deinde lignum lambere, et in Oliveti monte cum ascendente Domino, voto et animo sublevari?*' Paula and Eustochium [Jerome], *Ep.* 46, 12.

[30] '*Nam inveni ibi aliquam amicissimam michi, et cui omnes in oriente testimonium ferebant vitae ipsius, sancta diaconissa nomine Marthana, quam ego aput Ierusolimam noveram, ubi illa gratia orationis ascenderat;*' Egeria, *Itin.* 23, 3.

[31] The attack on the *gyrovague* is in bk. 1, 13-74, *Regula Magistri*, in Adalbert de Vogüé, ed., *La règle du maître*, 3 vols SC 105-107, Paris: Editions du Cerf, 1964; English translation by Luke Eberle, ed., *The Rule of the Master*, Kalamazoo: Cistercian Publications, 1977.

[32] Evagrius Ponticus, *Ep.* 8, quoted in Elm, *Virgins of God*, 278.

Carolingian monastic reform, aided by the efforts of Benedict of Aniane, would mean the tightening and narrowing of legitimate monastic behavior.[33] Charlemagne's promotion of the Benedictine rule gave the secular authorization for this transformation. The later Cluniac movement solidified this process, and Benedictine monasticism became normative in the West. An asceticism of wandering gave way to physical stability as Benedictinization spread in the West. Religious travel was channelled into the creation of long-distance pilgrimage for the laity. The result was the creation of the first truly medieval, long-distance pilgrimage site, that of Santiago de Compostela. As these conventions took hold, the memory of wandering monasticism as a legitimate pursuit was suppressed and the vulgar image of the *gyrovague* was all that remained.

---

[33] On monastic reform see Raffaello Morghen, 'Monastic Reform and Cluniac Spirituality', in Noreen Hunt, ed., *Cluniac Monasticism in the Central Middle Ages*, London: Macmillan, 1971, pp. 11-28; J. M. Wallace-Hadrill, *The Frankish Church*, Oxford: Oxford University Press, 1983, pp. 258-303; Rosamond McKitterick, *The Frankish Church and the Carolingian Reforms, 789-895*, London: Royal Historical Society, 1977; John Van Engen, (1986), 'The "Crisis of Cenobitism" reconsidered: Benedictine monasticism in the years 1050-1150', *Speculum* 61, 2 (1975), pp. 269-304.

Chapter 11

Sinai Pilgrimage and Ascetic Romance: Pseudo-Nilus' *Narrationes* in Context

Daniel Caner

This paper explores the special attractions and challenges that Mount Sinai's Old Testament associations presented to Christian imaginations in Late Antiquity. Compared to other late antique holy land sites, Mount Sinai has received little attention either as an early pilgrimage destination or as the background for an evolving hagiographic tradition.[1] Perhaps the most interesting testament to both is the *Narrationes*, traditionally ascribed to the monk Nilus of Ancyra († c.430).[2] This first-person narrative purports to be an autobiographical account of a father who travels with his son, Theodoulos, to the Sinai in search of tranquility with monks living below God's Mountain. They find mayhem instead: a week after Epiphany, 'barbarian' nomads raid the settlement, kill many monks, and take Theodoulos captive, to be sacrificed to their own god, the Morning Star, at dawn. The father escapes, but his experience makes him question God's failure to act, question divine Providence, and question the point of pursuing righteousness at all. The rest of the narrative tells how father and son reunite. Having slept past the time for sacrifice, Theodoulos's nomadic captors turn north to sell him in the settled regions of the Negev. Failing to attract a buyer in a village called Sobata, they sell him as a slave to the bishop of the city of Elusa. Here his father eventually finds him. The story ends as the two set off to fulfill vows of ascetic

---

[1] An exception is R. Solzbacher, *Mönche, Pilger und Sarazenen. Studien zum Frühchristentum auf der südlichen Sinaihalbinsel*, Altenberge: Telos, 1989; see also P. Maraval, *Lieux saints et pèlerinages d'Orient*, Paris: Cerf, 1985, pp. 119-20. The literary sources are few and (like the *Narrationes*) problematic. See, besides Solzbacher (1989), R. Devreesse, 'Le christianisme dans la péninsule sinaïtique, des origines à l'arrivée des Musulmans', *Revue biblique* 49, (1940), pp. 205-23; and P.-L. Gatier, 'Les traditions et l'histoire du Sinaï du IVe au VIIe siècle', in T. Fahd (ed.), *L'Arabie préislamique et son environnement historique et culturel*, Leiden: Brill, 1989, pp. 499-523.

[2] Ps.-Nilus, *Narrationes* (Διηγήματα), ed. F. Conca, *Nilus Ancyranus: Narratio*, Leipzig: Teubner, 1983a. For a detailed epitome see P. Mayerson, 'Observations on the "Nilus" *Narrationes*: Evidence for an Unknown Christian Sect?', *Journal of the American Research Center in Egypt* 12, (1975), pp. 58-71.

servitude (*douleia*) that each had made to God to obtain salvation. Both, we are told, lived 'more happily' after.

Rich in geographical and ethnographic detail, this narrative has been mined for factual information concerning pilgrimage, monasticism, and non-Christian religion in both the Sinai and Negev regions in pre-Islamic times. Yet its date, provenance, and historical value have remained controversial ever since Karl Heussi declared it to be neither a work by Nilus of Ancyra, nor an actual autobiography, but a fiction in the tradition of Hellenistic romance. Heussi noted that many features of its plot (including *narratio in medias res*, ethnographic excursuses, human sacrifice, and the separation and reunification of loved ones in exotic lands) were typical of that genre.[3] Heussi's influence is apparent in two recent studies: one judges the *Narrationes* to be a composite of three sources joined together in the early fifth century,[4] while the other regards it as a 'theological romance' written by a learned monk of Mount Sinai in the sixth.[5] Neither gives it much credit as testimony to the actual experience or concerns of early Christians who visited, settled, or lived in the Sinai and Negev regions.

There is no question that the *Narrationes* displays conventions of ancient romance. However, Heussi's judgments can be accepted without diminishing the historical importance of this narrative.[6] To begin with, Heussi's suggestion that the *Narrationes* was written in Elusa—where the story ends—has never been adequately developed.[7] There are reasons for doing so that should raise confidence in the author as a witness to late antique circumstances in both the Sinai and Negev regions. Yet this author obviously meant to offer readers something more than historical testimony or entertainment. His very use of romance conventions would have alerted them that his central concern was the question of human endurance against what seemed outrageous Fortune.[8] In fact his *Narrationes* addresses serious doubts and presumptions about divine Providence that seem to have been raised by actual experience on the Sinai Peninsula. Rather than treat his work

---

[3] K. Heussi, *Untersuchungen zu Nilus dem Asketen*, Leipzig: Hinrichs, 1917, pp. 123-59; F. Conca, 'Le *Narrationes* di Nilo e il romanzo greco', *Atti del IV Congresso Nazionale di Studi Bizantini*, Galatina: Codego, 1983b, pp. 343-54.

[4] Solzbacher (1989), pp. 200-51.

[5] Gatier (1989), p. 518; cf. Devreesse (1940), pp. 220-22.

[6] Already argued by V. Christides, 'Once Again the "Narrations" of Nilus Sinaiticus' *Byzantion* 43, (1973), pp. 39-54; see however C. Rapp, 'Storytelling as Spiritual Communication in Early Greek Hagiography: The Use of *Diegesis*', *Journal of Early Christian Studies* 6, (1998), pp. 431-48.

[7] Heussi (1917), pp. 145, n. 2, and 152, n. 1, followed by Solzbacher (1989), pp. 246-48.

[8] For the conventional role of Providence in ancient romance see G. Van Steen, 'Destined to Be? Tyche in Chariton's *Chaereas and Callirhoe* in the Byzantine Romance of *Kallimachos and Chrysorroi*', *L'Antiquité classique* 67, (1998), pp. 203-11.

merely as a source for late antique experience on the Sinai, we must use other late antique testimony for that Sinai experience to appreciate what this author sought to communicate to his readers. As we shall see, he recasts late antique assumptions about how the God of Mount Sinai operates in the world, and did so to affirm not only divine Providence, but also the purpose that brought many Christians to Mount Sinai in Late Antiquity: ascetic *douleia*. But first, like most late antique travelers to the Sinai, we must begin in Elusa.

In caput deserti qui vadit ad Sina: Elusa

Heussi proposed that the *Narrationes* was written in Elusa (modern Halusa) not merely because it ends there, but because its author obviously considered himself well informed about the cult of the Morning Star goddess, and because we know there was indeed a major temple at Elusa where festivals continued to be held for Aphrodite (that is, al-'Uzza) in the late fourth century. 'They worship her', explained Jerome c. 390, 'because of Lucifer, to whose cult the Saracen race is devoted. In fact the town itself is almost half barbarian, because of its location'.[9] An author in Elusa would therefore have been well placed to write about the Morning Star cult and other 'barbarian' (that is, nomadic) customs described in the *Narrationes*.

That, however, is not the only reason to place the origins of the *Narrationes* at Elusa. Its author gives accurate details about distances and topographical features between Elusa, Sobata, and the Sinai oasis town of Pharan,[10] as an inhabitant of Elusa might: for Elusa was a crossroads city, located at the juncture of the Gaza and Jerusalem highways with the desert roads heading south. It therefore became the administrative hub and gateway to southern Palestine, a region that boomed in Late Antiquity with increased caravan traffic and viticulture.[11] It was no cultural backwater either, despite what Jerome might imply. Papyri found at Nessana, a military outpost farther south in the Negev desert, show that Greek-speaking inhabitants were still trying to read the *Aeneid* there late into the sixth century.[12] At Elusa itself excavators have found a small theater or odeion with honorary seats built around a *cavea* that was re-paved for further use in the middle of the fifth

---

[9] Jerome, *Vita Hilarionis* 25 (PL 23.41): *colunt autem illam ob Luciferam cuius cultui Saracenorum natio dedita est. Sed et ipsum oppidum ex magna parte semibarbarum est propter loci situm.* See also Epiphanius, *Panarion* 51.22.11.

[10] P. Mayerson, 'The Desert of Southern Palestine according to Byzantine Sources', *Proceedings of the American Philosophical Society* 107, (1963), pp. 162-67.

[11] K. Gutwein, *Third Palestine: A Regional Study in Byzantine Urbanization*, Washington, D.C.: University Press of America, 1981, pp. 13-14.

[12] L. Casson and E.L. Hettich, *Excavations at Nessana, Volume 2: Literary Papyri* Princeton: Princeton University Press, 1950, pp. 7-78.

century.[13] But the most important evidence for Elusa's cultural aspirations comes from that master of late Hellenism, Libanius. From him we learn not only that Elusa in the fourth century had its own rhetorical school with resident sophist on imperial stipend, but that Elusa had even produced none other than his own teacher, Zenobius.[14]

Thus Elusa could easily have also produced our author, whose baroque style and familiarity with romance literature show all the signs of a writer who had been overly trained in the second sophistic.[15] In fact, no other provenance for the *Narrationes* is so plausible.[16] It should be prized as the sole literary effort to have survived for us from the school of Elusa, and as precious testimony to the creative vitality of late antique Hellenism in southern Palestine.[17] This, of course, was Hellenism exercised in the service of Christianity at a crossroads.[18] The location that made Elusa 'half-barbarian' also linked it to the Sinai frontier. As one pilgrim put it, the city lay 'at the head of the desert that leads to the Sinai'. Since it was the terminus for the two shortest routes to Sinai in Late Antiquity, it also became the main staging post for pilgrims headed for the holy mountain and back.[19] The experience of Sinai pilgrims was therefore an obvious topic for a Christian writing in late antique Elusa. But why did he also make 'barbarian' cult and ascetic servitude so central to his narrative? We must consider both the Christian expectations and the pagan realities that met on the Sinai in Late Antiquity.

---

[13] A. Negev, 'Survey and Trial Excavations at Haluza (Elusa), 1973', *Israel Exploration Journal* 26, (1976), pp. 92-93; id., *Greek Inscriptions from the Negev*, Jerusalem: Hebrew University, 1981, pp. 73-76.

[14] P. Mayerson (1983), 'The City of Elusa in the Literary Sources of the Fourth-Sixth Centuries', *Israel Exploration Journal* 33, (1983), p. 249.

[15] For the author's literary style see Mayerson (1975) and Conca (1983b).

[16] Gatier (1989) and others argue for sixth-century provenance in the Mount Sinai Monastery, but the *Narrationes* is unparalleled by other known Sinai literature; Conca (1983b) and others defend the Nilus of Ancyra attribution on stylistic grounds, but such similarities more likely reflect similar training in second sophistic Greek.

[17] The author may be considered the successor to a number of Arab sophists: G.W. Bowersock, *Roman Arabia*, Cambridge, Mass.: Harvard University Press, 1983, p. 135.

[18] Elusa's main church was built adjacent to the ancient odeion in the early fifth century: the two seem meant to function together. The odeion's restorer was 'Abraamius son of Zenobius': perhaps a descendant of Libanius' teacher, converted to Christianity. See A. Negev (1975), 'Elusa (Haluza)', *Revue biblique* 85, (1975), pp. 109-13, and Mayerson (1983), p. 250.

[19] Piacenza Pilgrim, *Itinerarium* 34, ed. P. Greyer, *Itineraria et alia geographica*, Turnhout: Brepols, 1965, p. 145; P. Mayerson, 'The Pilgrim Routes to Mount Sinai and the Armenians', *Israel Exploration Journal* 32, (1982), pp. 44-57.

Sinai Pilgrimage in Late Antiquity

Mount Sinai (Gebel Musa) differed from other Christian Holy Land sites in its physical setting and in its scriptural associations, and therefore in its imaginative possibilities and problems as well. This was, above all, 'the Holy Place of the Almighty',[20] the domain of God in His Old Testament aspect: for here Yahweh was believed to have revealed Himself to Moses, the Israelites, and Elijah in all His raw glory (Ex 3:16; 19:18-25; 24:16, 33:13-23; 1 Kings 19:11-12). For that reason, and not for any direct New Testament affiliation, Mount Sinai fired Christian imaginations, to become a major monastic center and pilgrimage destination from the fourth century onward.[21]

It was also most distant of all Holy Land destinations from ordinary civilization. Procopius of Caesarea imagined it to be an 'utterly wild mountain' at the end of a vast, waterless terrain, inhabited by monks who lived 'a kind of careful rehearsal of death'.[22] To see such hardened ascetics and actually experience their dedication first-hand was one reason people went there in Late Antiquity.[23] Hagiography also indicates that arrival at the Sinai summit might mark either the beginning or end of a pilgrim's own ascetic dedication to God.[24] The Piacenza Pilgrim reports that 'many' in the sixth century (including himself) cut their hair and beard on the Sinai summit *pro devotione*: 'as a pious act' or 'for the sake of a vow'.[25] By the seventh century such summit tonsuring was part of monastic initiation at Sinai.[26] The Piacenza Pilgrim, however, seems to refer here to a

---

[20] *Ammonii Monachi Relatio*, Christian Palestinian Aramaic version, fol.58a, trans. A. Smith Lewis, *The Forty Martyrs of the Sinai Desert and the Story of Eulogius from a Palestinian Syriac and Arabic Palimpsest*, Cambridge: Cambridge University Press, 1911, p. 1.

[21] B. Flusin, 'Ermitages et monastére. Le monachisme au mont Sinaï à la période protobyzantine', in Ch. Bonnet and D. Valbelle, eds., *Le Sinaï durant l'antiquité et le moyen âge: 4000 ans d'histoire pour un désert*, Paris: Éditions errance, 1998, pp. 133-38.

[22] *De Aedificiis* V.viii.1-4; trans. H. Dewing, *Procopius: Buildings*, Cambridge, MA: Harvard University Press, 1954, pp. 354-55.

[23] Maraval (1985), p. 120. Egeria was pleased to discover that the priest on the Sinai summit was an *ascitis et ... qualis dignus est esse in eo loco*: *Itinerarium* III.4, ed. A. Franceschini and R. Weber (1965), *Itineraria et alia geographica*, Turnhout: Brepols, p. 40. In general see G. Frank, *The Memory of the Eyes: Pilgrims to Living Saints in Christian Late Antiquity*, Berkeley and Los Angeles: University of California Press, 2000.

[24] Maraval (1985), pp. 123-24; John Moschos, *Pratum spirituale* 100.

[25] *Itin.* 37: *in quo loco multi pro devotione tondent capillos suos et barbas. Nam et ego ibi tetigi barbam meam*, ed. Greyer (1965), p. 171.

[26] F. Nau (1902), 'Le texte grec des récits du moine Anastase sur les saints pères du Sinaï', *Oriens Christianus* 2, p. 80, no. 34.

devotional act being performed more generally by Christian pilgrims who had reached their Sinai destination. The practice may reflect an Arab custom of cutting hair to mark the end of a journey.[27] But in this setting it might be better explained by reference to Sinai's association with the Old Testament Nazarite vow (instituted on Mount Sinai, Num 6:5-10) initiating a special period of abstinence that similarly ended with cutting one's hair.[28]

Why else did early pilgrims go to Mount Sinai? Adoration of God and pursuit of tranquility are the motives explicitly ascribed to them;[29] while Sinai rock inscriptions record formulaic prayers for salvation, mercy, and release from sins.[30] Can we say more? At Sinai Moses and Elijah, both considered prototypes for Christian monks, received their revelations. Some late antique authorities interpreted Moses' ascent of the mountain as the Old Testament type for the spiritual ascent of a Christian that culminates in a mystical experience of God.[31] Gregory of Nyssa warned that such ascent and theophany were not for the multitude,[32] but pilgrims traveling to Sinai may have felt otherwise. Despite theologians' denial that God was located or circumscribed in any physical place,[33] the Spanish pilgrim Egeria observes that it was customary to say a prayer when first you saw God's Mountain,[34] and many prayer niches along Sinai ascent routes enabled those who used them to focus on its peak.[35] That peak was every pilgrim's goal. One fourth-century ascetic is said to have prostrated himself 'at the very spot

---

[27] B. Kötting, *Peregrinatio Religiosa. Wallfahrten in der Antike und das Pilgerwesen in der alten Kirche*, Münster: Stenderhoff, 1980, p. 75 n. 381.

[28] Julian Saba went to Sinai 'in the heavy toils of naziriteship': Philoxenus of Mabbug, *Letter to Patricius* 51; ed. R. Lavenant (PO 30.5), p. 108. In Syrian tradition, severe penitential asceticism, emphasizing servitude, was called *nzirutâ*: A. Palmer, *Monk and Mason on the Tigris Frontier*, Cambridge: Cambridge University Press, 1990, p. 85. Jewish tradition recognized travel (especially to the Jerusalem temple) as a way of fulfilling the nazirite vow: Kötting (1980), p. 326.

[29] Theodoret, *Hist. rel.* VI.8; Moschos, *Prat. spirit.* 100, citing the motives commonly given for pilgrimage to other sites: Maraval (1985), pp. 137-38 and Kötting (1980), pp. 322-27. Pursuit of tranquility (*hesychia*) is the motive cited in the *Narrationes*.

[30] A. Negev, *The Inscriptions of Wadi Haggag, Sinai*, Jerusalem: Hebrew University, 1977, p. 84.

[31] For example, Gregory of Nyssa, *Vita Moysis* I.46, II.154-166; Ps.-Dionysius, *De mystica theologia* I. 3.

[32] *V. Moysis* II.160; see Frank (2000), pp. 84, 88-90.

[33] For example, Gregory of Nyssa, *Ep.* II; Theodoret, *Hist. rel.* VI.8; cf. John 4:24.

[34] *Itin.* I.2.

[35] I. Finkelstein, 'Byzantine Prayer Niches in Southern Sinai', *Israel Exploration Journal* 31, (1981), p. 86.

where Moses was accounted worthy to see God', till he 'heard a divine voice announcing to him his Master's favor'.[36]

Such anecdotes suggest that at least some pilgrims went to Sinai in Late Antiquity in the belief that on God's Mountain they might come closest to His actual presence. Not until the eighth century did that belief receive theological confirmation, when John of Damascus put Mount Sinai first in his list of sites and relics deemed worthy of veneration as physical 'receptacles of divine energy'.[37] By that time the emperor Justinian had already built his fortified church and monastic complex to accommodate a large number of pilgrims below the Sinai summit.[38] Rising above the Burning Bush, its magnificent church apse mosaic reflects why they came: here they saw Jesus transfigured in shimmering radiance, flanked by Moses and Elijah, his Old Testament Sinai forebears. When viewed below Mount Sinai, this rendering of Matthew 17:2 had special significance.[39] Not only did it represent the consummate moment of New Testament theophany, but also the one that subsumed the Old Testament theophanies experienced by Moses and Elijah on the Sinai. This depiction of Jesus' transfiguration in the Sinai church apse may have been viewed, like other Christian monuments on Mount Sinai,[40] as a step toward the 'Christianization' of this Old Testament setting. But the image also affirmed contemporary expectations that God's 'energy' was still active on the Sinai and could be experienced there by Christians as it had previously been by Moses and Elijah.

Such expectations are in fact attested in numerous sources. Procopius, for example, imagined that no one could pass a night on the Sinai summit because the 'constant thunder and other divine manifestations heard at night' would 'shock both mind and body'.[41] Seventh-century anecdotes record that the summit's chapel

---

[36] Theodoret, *Historia religiosa* VI.12, trans. R. Price, *A History of the Monks of Syria*, Kalamazoo: Cistercian Publications, 1985, p. 67. Cf. Egeria, *Itin.* III.2.

[37] *Contra imaginum calumniatores* III.34: θείας ἐνεργείας εἰσὶ δοχεῖα, ed. B. Kotter, *Die Schriften des Johannes von Damaskos* 3, Berlin: De Gruyter, 1975, p. 139. See Maraval (1985), pp. 146-47, on this statement's relevance to pilgrimage.

[38] G. Forsyth, 'The Monastery of St. Catherine at Mount Sinai: The Church and Fortress of Justinian', in J. Galey, *Sinai and the Monastery of St. Catherine*, Cairo: American University in Cairo Press, 1985, p. 51.

[39] For date (550–51 or 565–66) and possible significance to Sinai pilgrims see J. Elsner, *Art and the Roman Viewer: The Transformation of Art from the Pagan World to Christianity*, Cambridge: Cambridge University Press, 1995, pp. 99-124.

[40] Ephraim developed the notion of Christianizing Mount Sinai in his fourth-century hymns celebrating Julian Saba's construction of a summit chapel: see Solzbacher (1989), pp. 114-19 and U. Dahari, 'Les constructions de Justinien au Gebel Mousa', in Ch. Bonnet and D. Valbelle, eds., *Le Sinaï durant l'antiquité et le moyen âge: 4000 ans d'histoire pour un désert*, Paris, Éditions errance, 1998, p. 152.

[41] *Aed.* V.viii.7; ed. and trans. Dewing, p. 356.

would glow at night and frighten off intruders with sudden bursts of flame.[42] Egeria does not record such dramatic miracles during her fourth-century visit. Yet her own account noticeably emphasizes not only the sublimity of the place where, she repeatedly reminds us, 'God's Majesty descended',[43] but also the gradual alterations in physical perception that occurred to her as she approached the Sinai summit. She notes that, although God's Mountain looked like a single mass from afar, it broke into several peaks as she drew near; that she had never seen peaks so high, but all seemed like hilltops when looked down upon from the peak 'where God's Majesty descended'; and that this peak, though higher than the rest, could not itself be seen until you passed by the others, and suddenly 'it was right in front of you'.[44] Such effects she describes as *admirabile*, ascribing the last to the *gratia* or 'plan' of God.[45] Thus Egeria confirms her late antique readers' expectations that 'God's Majesty' could be experienced on His mountain. No doubt such expectations were both heightened and safeguarded by a custom (or rule) that no one could spend a night on the Sinai summit.[46]

Sinai Pilgrimage and Pagan Menace

In reality, however, Mount Sinai was not just 'the Holy Place of the Almighty'. The same sources attest the competing presence and active menace of pagan nomads as well. As Egeria remarks, this was 'Saracen country'.[47] Procopius claims that monks enjoyed solitude on Sinai without fear, but clearly that was not the case: bedouin raids in the fourth century created a local martyr tradition,[48] and prompted Justinian to fortify Sinai's church and monastery in the sixth.[49] Still the

---

[42] Nau (1902), nos 1-3, 16, 22, 36-38.

[43] *Itin.* II.5-7; III.2.

[44] *Itin.* II.5-6.

[45] *Itin.* II.7: *sine Dei gratia ... illud non esse*, ed. Franceschini-Weber, p. 39.

[46] Egeria, *Itin.* III.5; Piacenza Pilgrim, *Itin.* 37; Nau (1902), p. 83 (no. 39); also see Dahari (1998), p. 152.

[47] Egeria, *Itin.* VII.6: *terras Saracenorum*, ed. Franceschini-Weber, p. 48; cf. *Narrationes* III.1. For the description see I. Shahîd, *Byzantium and the Arabs in the Fourth Century*, Washington, D.C.: Dumbarton Oaks, 1984, pp. 295-329.

[48] Solzbacher (1989), pp. 200-50; P. Mayerson, 'An Inscription in the Monastery of St. Catherine and the Martyr Tradition in Sinai', *Dumbarton Oaks Papers* 30, (1976), pp. 375-79.

[49] P. Mayerson, 'Procopius or Eutychius on the Construction of the Monastery at Mount Sinai: Which is the More Reliable Version?', *Bulletin of the American Schools of Oriental Research* 230, (1978), pp. 33-38.

attacks continued, and Sinai pilgrimage routes only seem to have been free of danger when Saracen festivals were under way.[50] The Piacenza Pilgrim even reports that Sinai Saracens in the sixth century kept an impressive idol on the slopes of Mount Horeb.[51] Thus hostile pagan nomads remained a clear and present danger below the holy mountain, right at the place where God's Majesty was imagined to be still manifest and active.

Sinai Experience and Ascetic Romance

The incongruity of such a pagan menace below the 'Holy Place of the Almighty' was not lost on the author of the *Narrationes*. He contrasts the 'impious' customs of barbarian nomads with the 'God-pleasing' customs of Sinai monks immediately before describing those same monks' slaughter.[52] Justinian's fortification was the historical response to that barbarian challenge: the *Narrationes* represents an earlier response on the imaginative and theological level. As earlier novelists had done, its author employed the romance framework to highlight his chaste heroes' perseverance against inscrutable fortune.[53] In this romance, however, the Old Testament Sinai tradition was both the backdrop and the central problem. Its author's primary concern was to reconcile Christian expectations about the power and Providence of their God of Mount Sinai with pagan violence being successfully perpetrated against 'those who blamelessly serve (*douleuontes*) Him'.[54]

The *Narrationes* is indeed unusual, either as a Christian romance or martyr narrative. As others have observed, it makes no reference to 'Jesus' or 'Christ', uses the word 'Christian' only once, and only once alludes to New Testament scriptures, otherwise drawing all its citations and examples from the Old.[55] We must not dismiss the possibility that this reflects an Old Testament sense of

---

[50] Evagrius, *Historia ecclesiastica* V.6; Piacenza pilgrim, *Itin.* 39; Gatier (1989), p. 509 n. 34. For the threat, B. Isaac, 'Bandits in Judaea and Arabia', *Harvard Studies in Classical Philology* 88, (1984), pp. 197-203 and T.S. Parker, 'Peasants, Pastoralists, and Pax Romana: A Different View', *Bulletin of the American Schools of Oriental Research* 265, (1987), pp. 35-51.

[51] *Itin.* 38.

[52] *Narrationes* III.1-IV.1, ed. Conca, pp. 12-20.

[53] See *Narrationes* VI.24, with Van Steen (1998) and W. Robins, 'Romance and Renunciation at the Turn of the Fifth Century', *Journal of Early Christian Studies* 8, (2000), pp. 531-57.

[54] *Narrationes* II.7: πῶς οἱ δουλεύοντες ἀμέμπτως θεῷ παρεδόθησαν τοῖς ἀσεβέσιν εἰς ἀπώλειαν, παίγνιον βαρβαρικῆς γενόμενοι χειρός, καὶ ἤργησε τῆς προνοίας ἡ δύναμις . . ., ed. Conca, pp. 7,24-8,2.

[55] Mayerson (1975), pp. 55-57.

identity or orientation, if not Jewish influence, among early Christians in southern Palestine: Old Testament names predominate in the region's inscriptions, and one from Sobata preserves a list of Old Testament heroes paired with virtues in a paratactic manner that resembles the *Narrationes'* pairing of Moses and Elijah with the virtues of fortitude and endurance.[56] However, this seemingly 'un-Christian' aspect of the work may simply have been intended to focus a Christian reader's attention on God in His Old Testament aspect. That this God was supposed to respond to transgressors in the fourth and fifth centuries as in Old Testament times is illustrated by contemporary explanations for Julian the Apostate's failure to rebuild the Jerusalem Temple: the project had to be abandoned because 'terrifying balls of flame kept bursting forth' from the Temple foundations and scorched the workmen.[57] Additional late antique accounts of pagan attacks on the Sinai display similar expectations: in one, Saracens are scattered by flame and smoke that descend from the Sinai summit; in the other, a saint's sudden intervention saves the day.[58] In the *Narrationes*, however, it is the very absence of such miracles that causes astonishment: Why, asks the narrator, had 'divine Providence' let 'lawless hands' fall on 'holy bodies'? Why had the 'terrifying marvels of Mount Sinai' not appeared? Why had the 'avenging power' not acted as Scripture says it had, so dramatically, in the past?[59]

What follows is instruction on how the God of Mount Sinai operates in the world. It begins with a dying monk's allusion to 1 Corinthians 2:9—'no eye has seen nor ear heard nor heart conceived what God has prepared for those who love him'. In the *Narrationes*, however, that passage has been significantly altered. Instead of 'those who love him' (*tois agapôsin auton*) the author has written 'those who struggle on his behalf' (*tois huper autou agônismenois*): these are the ones for whom God has prepared 'prizes for piety...surpassing thought and perception'.[60] The author does not seem to refer here to just any martyr who endures persecution

---

[56] *Narrationes* III.18, ed. Conca, p. 19,16-17. Mayerson's (1975) suggestion that the text reflects the Old Testament sensibilities of an early sect below Mount Sinai has been rejected, but it is notable that one Christian inscription found in the Negev lists only Old Testament figures as exemplars of virtue; see Negev (1981), pp. 63-64.

[57] Ammianus Marcellinus, *Res gestae* XXIII.i.3, trans. J.C. Rolfe, *Ammianus Marcellinus*, vol. 2, Cambridge, MA: Harvard University Press, 1986, p. 311. The church historians Socrates, III.20; Philostorgius, VII.9; Sozomen, V.22; and Theodoret, III.15 each add a new element of divine power.

[58] *Ammonii monachi relatio*, Syriac version, fol. 27a, trans. Smith Lewis, p. 2, and Nilus, *Ep.* IV.62. For the relation of these accounts to the *Narrationes* see Solzbacher (1989), pp. 214-15, 228-35 and Gatier (1989), pp. 512-20.

[59] *Narrationes* IV.7-8 (cf. II.7-10): κατέλιπεν ὑμᾶς . . . ἡ θεία πρόνοια. . . πῶς δὲ ἡσύχασαν οἱ τοῦ Σιναίου ὄρους τετρατώδεις φοβερισμοί . . ., ed. Conca, pp. 23,18-24,4; referring to Gen 19:10-11; Ex 14:27-28; Josh 10:11-14; numerous references to 1 and 2 Kings.

[60] *Narrationes* IV.12, ed. Conca, p. 25,23-26.

and death, for he otherwise uses the words *agon* and *agonizomenoi* solely to describe the ascetic struggles of monks who 'blamelessly serve (*douleuontes*) God' below Mount Sinai.[61] The ascetic focus of the narrative becomes most clear in the resolution with which it ends. Father and son are miraculously reunited 'by the grace (*charis*) of God', but only after both vow to assume the 'harsh servitude (or slavery, *douleia*) of continence and other mortifications'.[62] As Theodoulos explains, to perform such toils in fulfilment of a vow is to store up recompense with God, who rewards them doubly and in advance with *charis*.[63]

In this way the author of the *Narrationes* shifts the burden of divine action from the Mount Sinai God onto the ascetic toils of his subjects below. He entertains Christian readers with the sober point that divine Providence is not made manifest through thunderbolts, but through their own affirmation of the 'struggle'.

The *Narrationes* in Context

Though couched in romance, this message was meant to be taken seriously. The *Narrationes* was probably written in the early fifth century.[64] This was a time of 'barbarian' devastation not only for the Roman Empire but for the monastic world as well. Nomadic raids on desert settlements in Egypt and Palestine as well as the Sinai Peninsula stimulated reflection on theodicy and Providence.[65] John Cassian, for example, wrote his sixth Conference in response to the 'Saracen' slaughter of holy men at Thekua (modern Tekoa, south of Bethlehem) sometime in the early fifth century:

> We wondered why men of such great worthiness and so many virtues
> would be slain by bandits and why the Lord had permitted such a crime
> to be perpetrated on his servants, that he would give men who were
> remarkable in every respect over into the hands of the impious.[66]

---

[61] For example, *Narrationes* II.2; III.12-13; IV.7, 12; VII.4; VII.18.

[62] *Narrationes* VII.13 (cf. VII.5): δουλείαν ἐγκρατείας καὶ τῆς ἄλλης κακοπαθείας . . . σκληράν, ed. Conca, p. 50,18-19. This δουλεία motif may owe something to Gal 4:24: εἰσιν δύο διαθῆκαι, μία μὲν ἀπὸ ὄρους Σινᾶ εἰς δουλείαν γεννῶσα, one of the few references to Mt. Sinai in the New Testament; cf. generally Lev 25:42 and Rom 6:16-23.

[63] *Narrationes* VII.14-15, ed. Conca, p. 50,24-51,16.

[64] On this matter I follow Solzbacher (1989), pp. 240-42.

[65] D. Chitty, *The Desert a City* (1966), Oxford: Basil Blackwell, pp. 60-77; Jerome, *Ep.* CXXVI.2, Philostorgius, *Historia ecclesiastica* XI.8.

[66] *Collatio* VI.i.2; trans. B. Ramsey, *John Cassian: The Conferences*, New York: Paulist Press, 1997, p. 217.

Cassian urges stoic acceptance and patient endurance, reminding his readers that what seemed to be afflictions were no more than God's methods of testing, cleansing, or warning about sins.[67]

Writing about the same time, some 50 miles south of Thekua, the author of the *Narrationes* was responding to similar questions, but within the shadow of Mount Sinai itself. Heussi interpreted his work as a representation of Christian triumph over the Morning Star cult at Elusa.[68] That, however, seems an overstatement, given the lack of evidence for Christianity's triumph in the narrative or in the central Negev at this time. As the provincial capital, Elusa seems to have received its first bishop and church early in the fifth century. Yet for nearly a century more Elusa remained a 'small island in a sea of paganism'; even here, Christian inscriptions do not become common until the early sixth century.[69] In fact, it may be that the only Christians our author would have known at Elusa would have been the pilgrims headed for Sinai, the numerous ascetics living in the surrounding desert, and the first attested bishop of Elusa, known from records of the first Council of Ephesus (431) as none other than Abdalla, 'Slave of God', or in Greek, Theodoulos.[70]

Whether our author's story about the perseverance of God's faithful slave Theodoulos was meant to eulogize this early bishop of Elusa must remain an open question: 'Slave of God' was a common name among Arabs in the Negev and Sinai regions before the advent of Christianity.[71] It is nonetheless clear that the author of the *Narrationes* meant to eulogize Christians who persevered to serve their God in these regions despite the potentially hostile pagan menace that surrounded them. Like Cassian, this author considered stoic resignation a possible response to their attacks.[72] Yet he ultimately resolves his tale through an act of divine *charis* that is generated by the affirmation of ascetic vows. In this way he affirms the role of Christian ascetic *douleia* in activating God's 'energy' and grace: indeed, he specifically defines a Sinai monk as an 'instrument of grace in action'.[73] This would have been an encouraging conclusion, not only for Christian

---

[67] *Collatio* VI.xi.1.

[68] Solzbacher (1989), p. 247.

[69] A. Negev, 'Christen und Christentum in der Wüste Negev', *Antike Welte* 13, (1982), pp. 2-33; quotation from Mayerson (1963), p. 167.

[70] Mayerson (1963), p. 168; Jerome, *V. Hilarionis* 25.

[71] For the name see Gatier (1989), p. 521 n. 70; Mayerson (1963), pp. 168-69.

[72] *Narrationes* II.11-15; cf.IV.9-10.

[73] *Narrationes* III.9: ὄργανον τῆς ἐνεργούσης χάριτος, ed. Conca, p. 15,26-27. It is possible that ὄργανον should be translated 'tool' (*instrumentum*), which would strengthen the metaphor of asceticism as *douleia* (servitude or slavery to God).

ascetics living permanently beneath Mount Sinai's shadow, but also for the pilgrims who passed through Elusa to leave their hair on its peak.

Chapter 12

Pilgrims and Foreigners:
Augustine on Travelling Home[1]

Gillian Clark

In the later fourth century Christians were developing a tradition of travel to places of spiritual significance.[2] *Peregrinatio*, the Latin word for travel or residence abroad, came to mean specifically this kind of travel, so translators of late antique Christian texts often render the word as 'pilgrimage', and interpreters often assume without argument that if a journey is late antique and Christian, it must be a pilgrimage.[3] Images of the *Pilgrim's Progress* and the pilgrim church still have a powerful appeal that reinforces this assumption: 'through the night of doubt and sorrow onward goes the pilgrim band, singing songs of expectation, marching to the promised land'. [4] But Augustine's use of *peregrinatio* presents a challenge to the familiar interpretation. For Augustine, classical education and Platonist philosophy combine with Scripture to give *peregrinatio* the dominant sense of being away from where one wants to be. A *peregrinus* is not a pilgrim, a purposeful traveller in search of enlightenment, but is someone who feels foreign and wants to go home.

One of the most famous passages of Augustine's *Confessions* is about going home.

> *Non enim pedibus aut spatiis locorum itur abs te aut reditur ad te, aut vero filius ille tuus minor equos vel currus vel naves quaesivit aut avolavit pinna visibili aut moto poplite iter egit, ut in longinqua regione vivens prodige dissiparet quod dederas proficiscenti, dulcis pater...* (1.18.28)

---

[1] I am indebted especially to Philip Burton, Jas Elsner, Karla Pollmann, Danuta Shanzer and Dennis Trout.

[2] See the pioneering study of Hunt, 1982; recent bibliography in Elsner, 2000.

[3] See, for instance, the careful work of Claussen, 1991. For further discussion see the paper by Maribel Dietz in this collection.

[4] B.S. Ingemann (1789–1862), tr. S. Baring-Gould.

> One does not go far away from you or return to you by walking or by any
> movement through space. The younger son in the Gospel did not look for
> horse or carriages or ships; he did not fly on any visible wing, nor did he
> travel along the way by moving his legs when he went to live in a far
> country and prodigally dissipated what you, his gentle father, had given
> him on setting out ... (tr. Chadwick, 1991.)

A reader who knows the New Testament responds at once to the story of the
Prodigal Son (Luke 15: 11-32), but for some of Augustine's implied readers the
phrasing and the emphasis on modes of travel also evoked Plotinus.

> 'Let us fly to our dear country.' What then is our way of escape, and how
> are we to find it? We shall put out to sea, as Odysseus did, from the witch
> Circe or Calypso - as the poet says (I think with a hidden meaning) - and
> was not content to stay though he had delights of the eyes and lived
> among much beauty of sense. Our country from which we came is there,
> our Father is there. How shall we travel to it, where is our way of escape?
> We cannot get there on foot, for our feet only carry us everywhere in this
> world, from one country to another. You must not get ready a carriage,
> either, or a boat. Let all these things go, and do not look. Shut your eyes,
> and change to and wake another kind of seeing, which everyone has but
> few use. (*Ennead* 1.6.8, tr. Armstrong, 1960.)

Plotinus contrasts the stillness and introspection of a spiritual going home with the
familiar activities of travellers booking their transport, covering ground, and
enjoying new scenery and experiences. He makes the travel plans less prosaic by
evoking the archetypal travels of Odysseus to his 'dear homeland' and the
allegorical interpretation of Homer as concerned with the journey of the soul
through spiritual dangers.[5] He also uses some consciously literary language. Land
transport is a 'chariot of horses', *hippon ochema*,[6] sea transport is *thalattion ti*,
'something marine'. This passage made an impression on Ambrose, who used its
imagery in *Isaac* 8.78-9, listing feet and ships and carriages and horses. Augustine
may have heard that sermon, or read the passage of Plotinus in a Latin translation,
or even made his own translation (O'Donnell, 1992, II pp. 413-24). In *Confessions*
1.18.28 he develops the theme of movement in space, also using consciously
literary language. He adds the 'visible wing', *pinna visibilis*, perhaps as an
allusion to the flight of Daedalus and Icarus described by Virgil (*Aeneid* 6.14-20).[7]
Translators find various solutions for the odd phrase 'making his journey with
moved thigh', *moto poplite*,[8] but all emphasize the sheer physicality of movement

---

[5] See on this tradition Lamberton, 1986.

[6] Danuta Shanzer suggests a contrast with the soul-vehicle, *ochema* (for which see
Finamore, 1985).

[7] Courcelle, 1944, pp. 67-9, offers parallels.

[8] Philip Burton notes that *poplite moto* could be part of a hexameter.

that it suggests. Thus a recent translation (Burton, 2001) has 'he did not grow wings and fly off in view of all, or go striding on his way'.

In *Confessions* 8, as Augustine struggles to commit himself to God, a much briefer allusion to modes of travel is enough to evoke Plotinus:

> But to reach that destination one does not use ships or chariots or feet. It was not even necessary to go the distance I had come from the house to where we were sitting. (8.8.19, tr. Chadwick, 1991.)[9]

'The saying of Plotinus', *illud Plotini*, remained part of Augustine's mental furniture. In *City of God*, he assumes that his readers know it, and cites it probably from memory:

> *ubi est illud Plotini, ubi ait fugiendum est igitur ad carissimam patriam, et ibi pater, et ibi omnia. Quae igitur, inquit, classis aut fuga? Similem deo fieri.* (9.17)[10]

> Where now is that saying of Plotinus, where he says that we must flee to our dear homeland, and our Father is there, and everything is there? What expedition or flight, he asks, is this? To become like God. (tr. Dyson, 1998.)

Plotinus and Augustine use imagery of travel to convey different understandings of God's relation to humanity. In *Confessions* 1.18.28, the going home of the Plotinian soul and of the Prodigal Son express the contrast between Platonist self-reliance and Christian humility that is so prominent a theme of *Confessions*. The prodigal in Jesus' story is clearly to blame for taking his inheritance and dissipating it in a foreign land. But he need only make the decision to go home, recognizing that he does not deserve to be accepted as a son: as soon as he comes in sight, his father rushes out with open arms to reinstate him. Plotinus considered, but did not decide, the question whether our absence from our spiritual home is our own fault: that is, whether the soul has wilfully chosen to leave the heavens and become involved with the body, dissipating its resources on the material world (Clark, 2000, pp. 134-5). His student Porphyry also leaves it open, but is clear that we need to work hard to be taken back.

> We are like those who, whether intentionally or unintentionally, have gone away to a foreign people, and not only are excluded from what is their own, but have been filled by the foreign land with alien passions and habits and customs, and have acquired an inclination towards them. Someone who is preparing to return from there to his homeland is not only eager to be on the journey, but also, in order to be accepted,

---

[9] 'ships or chariots or feet' translates *navibus aut quadrigis aut pedibus*; *quadriga* for *currus* avoids a clumsy sequence of three ablatives ending in -*ibus*.

[10] *Classis aut fuga* is a literal translation of *stolos kai phuge* in the passage of Plotinus.

> practises putting aside everything foreign that he has acquired, and reminds himself of what he once had but has forgotten, and without which he cannot be accepted among his own people. (*Abst* 1.30, tr. Clark, 2000.)

There may be personal experience at work here, as well as philosophical principle. The sense that our true home is elsewhere, 'there', goes back to Plato (*Theaetetus* 176b). For people who believed this, it may have been easy to leave their earthly homes in pursuit of wisdom and to find a new community of shared commitment. From the archaic sages Solon and Pythagoras to the 'spiritual tourists'[11] of Late Antiquity, travel abroad   (Greek *apodemia*, being away from one's people) enhanced the authority of a philosopher. It showed that he was more concerned to acquire wisdom than to pursue property and status, and that, like Odysseus, he had learned the thought-patterns of many people. Thus Philostratus, writing in the early third century, described Apollonius of Tyana moving effortlessly around the eastern Mediterranean, the Near East and India, debating with Egyptian priests and Indian Brahmans.[12]

Plotinus and Porphyry both travelled abroad in search of wisdom and of teachers. Plotinus left the Egyptian town he would never discuss (Lycopolis, apparently) to find a teacher in Alexandria. He may have gone with the Roman army into Persia; even if this is a legend, it reveals expectations about late antique philosophers and eastern wisdom. He eventually settled in Rome, attracting a group of students who had come from Egypt and Arabia and Palestine and Phoenicia to practise their professions, or to make money, or to study.[13] Porphyry left his home city of Tyre to work with Longinus in Athens, then with Plotinus in Rome. Neither his extant works, nor the brief biography by Eunapius (*Lives of the Philosophers*), mention any return to Tyre. He represents the students of Plotinus as sharing the cultural identity of Hellenism and the awareness that they had a spiritual homeland.[14] But Plotinus and Porphyry did not write about travel as if they were explorers, mapping spiritual journeys for others to follow. The much-travelled Plotinus told his much-travelled students that covering ground is not the point: inward contemplation is better than seeing the sights. (He may have had in mind that Greek *theoria* can be used for both these forms of seeing.) For both Plotinus and Porphyry, being away from home means being abroad, in foreign parts where you do not belong, and where you risk losing your true identity.

Did Porphyry himself go home with a changed accent and speech-patterns, or with foreign habits, that made him not entirely welcome? Did he also continue to

---

[11] I owe the phrase to Polymnia Athanassiadi.

[12] See further Elsner, 1997, on the travels of Apollonius; Montiglio, 2000, on other wandering philosophers.

[13] Porphyry, *Life of Plotinus*, with full discussion in Brisson, 1982 and 1992, and in Edwards, 2000, especially pp. xxxviii-xxix on the journey to Persia.

[14] Clark, 1999; 2000, pp. 4-5.

feel like a foreigner in Italy, despite years of residence? He never admits to knowing Latin, though that may be Greek cultural snobbery.[15] Augustine certainly knew about feeling foreign, and about having a noticeable accent and belonging to an identifiable regional group.[16] Plotinus' saying, *illud Plotini*, had an immediate resonance for him in Milan, the furthest he had ever been from home. He was not legally *peregrinus*, an alien, for he shared Roman citizenship and Latin language with the Milanese and all other residents in the empire. But living in Milan was *peregrinatio* in the sense of travel or residence away from home, and Augustine began to love Ambrose simply because Ambrose, as befits a bishop, showed paternal kindness to someone in this position: *suscepit me paterne ille homo dei et peregrinationem meum satis episcopaliter dilexit (Conf.* 5.13 23).

This use of *peregrinatio* could be translated 'pilgrimage', for Augustine came to see his journey to Milan as also a spiritual journey to Christian commitment. Thus Maria Boulding (1997) has 'This man of God welcomed me with fatherly kindness and showed the charitable concern for my pilgrimage that befitted a bishop'. But Book 1 of *Christian Teaching (de doctrina Christiana)*, probably written close in time to *Confessions*, supports the Plotinian interpretation of *peregrinatio*.

> Suppose we were travellers [*peregrini*] who could live happily [*beate vivere*] only in our homeland, and because our absence [*peregrinatio*] made us unhappy [*miseri*] we wished to put an end to our misery and return there: we would need transport by land or sea which we could use to travel to our homeland, the object of our enjoyment. But if we were fascinated by the delights of the journey [*amoenitates itineris*] and the actual travelling [*ipsa gestatio vehiculorum*], we would be perversely enjoying things that we should be using; and we would be reluctant to finish our journey quickly, being ensnared in the wrong kind of pleasure and estranged from the homeland whose pleasures can make us happy. So in this mortal life we are like travellers away from our Lord [*peregrinantes a domino*]; if we wish to return to the homeland where we can be happy we must use this world, not enjoy it. (1.4.4, tr. Green, 1995.)

Augustine here contrasts use and enjoyment, *uti* and *frui*. If we are travelling in order to reach our homeland, *pervenire ad patriam*, we ought not to be diverted by sightseeing (*amoenitates itineris*) or by the physical experience of travel, the movement of land and sea transport (*ipsa gestatio vehiculorum*) that doctors prescribed as a form of passive exercise. But 'travel' and 'absence' understate the force of *peregrinus* and its cognates, just as 'live happily' understates the force of *beate vivere*. These *peregrini* are not just unhappy but objectively wretched, *miseri,* in their *peregrinatio*. They cannot live a blessed life, that is a good life,

---

[15] Clark, 1999; see further Swain, 1996.

[16] African accent: *de doctrina Christiana* 4.65 (Augustine does not say that he himself had one). African networks in Milan: *Confessions* 8.6.14. See also *City of God* 19.7: 'a man would rather be with his own dog than with a foreign [*alienus*] man'.

away from their homeland. Augustine here links Plotinus with the Bible, as he did in *Confessions*. The 'travellers away from our Lord', *peregrinantes a domino*, derive from a passage in the second letter of Paul to the Corinthians (2 Corinthians 5.6-9) that Augustine often used in preaching.[17] Paul, most famous of Christian travellers, played on the related Greek words for 'being resident' and 'being away', *endemein* in the body and *ekdemein* from the Lord, and concluded that while we are in the body we are away from God. It would therefore be better to be away from the body: in Latin, *peregrinari a corpore*.

Peregrinatio in this passage of *Christian Teaching* is plainly not pilgrimage. That is, it is not a purposive journey in search of holiness or to a promised land, but the opposite: it is being away from where you belong. Travelling home is not *peregrinatio*. But when Augustine is preaching, he does sometimes add to *peregrinari* the encouraging sense of a journey home. Thus in *Enarrationes in Psalmos* 37.15 he cites, from the same passage of Paul, *quamdiu enim sumus in corpore, peregrinamur a Domino* ('so long as we are in the body, we are away from the Lord'), and adds 'these are the words of *peregrinantes* who are not yet established in their homeland'. Similarly, in *Enarrationes* 123.2 he glosses Paul's *peregrinamur* with 'he who *peregrinatur* and walks in faith is not yet in his homeland, but is on the road'.[18] The concluding prayer of *Confessions* 9 may also invoke 'pilgrimage' as well as estrangement. Augustine prays that his readers will remember those who are dear to him: [*meminerint*] *civium meorum in aeterna Hierusalem, cui suspirat peregrinatio populi tui ab exitu usque ad reditum* (9.13.37). Chadwick translates '... my fellow citizens in the eternal Jerusalem. For this city your pilgrim people yearn, from their leaving it to their return'. This *peregrinatio*, clearly, will end in a return to home.

The Bible passage underlying Augustine's prayer is Hebrews 11.13-16, which begins by saying that the patriarchs who died in faith acknowledged themselves to be 'strangers and sojourners on earth': *xenoi kai parepidemoi* in Greek, *peregrini et hospites* in Latin. The author of Hebrews interprets this as showing that they were in search of their homeland, and could have turned back if they meant the homeland they had left, 'but they want better, the homeland in heaven'. Here *peregrini* are foreigners who are also travellers with a purpose. But in Ephesians 2.11-12 *peregrinus* can only mean 'foreigner', as it does in Roman legal contexts. The Latin version is *eratis illo tempore sine Christo, alienati a societate Israel et peregrini testamentorum*, translated by the Jerusalem Bible (1966) as 'you had no Christ and were excluded from membership of Israel, aliens with no part in the covenants'.

The Latin Bible, then, offered Augustine both *peregrinus* as foreigner and *peregrinus* as traveller.[19] But the fullest study of Augustine as traveller concludes that he always used *peregrinatio* to mean 'travel away from home', not in the purposive sense of 'pilgrimage', and moreover that his representation of travel

---

[17] See for instance *En.Ps*. 37.15, 41.6, 123.2.

[18] Cf. Markus, 1970, p.186.

[19] See Burton, 2000 for the methods of Latin translators.

was always negative, focussing on hardship, delay and isolation.[20] As a bishop, he accepted the need to travel in order to preach or attend councils, but he did not advocate pilgrimage for his clergy or his congregation. There is a notable silence in a letter, addressed to his congregation in Hippo, about one journey that he did demand, and that could easily be classed as a pilgrimage.[21] Augustine, unable to decide between the conflicting stories of the priest Bonifatius and another cleric, required them to take an oath at the shrine of St Felix of Nola. This is unexpected, for Augustine was generally cautious about any claim that the relics or burial-places of saints had special sanctity.[22] But his letter explains that although an oath is equally serious wherever it is taken, and although Africa itself has many relics of saints, nevertheless saints apparently have different gifts, just as living people have different gifts. The shrine of St Felix is known to have unmasked falsehood, and that is why the journey is to be made. Augustine's (epistolary) friend Paulinus had established Nola as a pilgrimage centre, but Augustine does not mention this. He uses *peregrinatio* only once, to make the point that Bonifatius, as an act of humility, was not taking letters on his *peregrinatio* to ensure respect for his clerical status (*Ep* 78.3-4)

Was Augustine consciously resisting a new meaning for *peregrinatio*?[23] Further work will be needed to show whether the meaning 'pilgrimage' was yet established in Latin of the late fourth and early fifth centuries; it is not clear that Paulinus himself used *peregrinatio* in this way. [24] But there is at least good reason to hesitate before translating *peregrinus* and its cognates as 'pilgrim', in Augustine and perhaps in other Latin patristic authors. Classical education, philosophy and the Latin Bible reinforced its meaning of alien, foreigner, someone away from home.[25]

Yet the 'pilgrim church' remains especially appealing as an interpretation of the *peregrina civitas regis Christi*, the community proclaimed in the opening sentence of *City of God*: *gloriosissimam civitatem Dei sive in hoc temporum cursu, cum inter impios peregrinatur ex fide vivens* ... The most recent translation (Dyson, 1998) renders *peregrinus* consistently as 'pilgrim', and has 'Most glorious is the City of God: whether in this passing age, where she dwells by faith as a pilgrim among the ungodly ... .' The widely used translation by Bettenson

---

[20] Perler, 1969, pp. 45-7; see also Brown, 1967, p. 323 (developing an earlier article by Perler).

[21] *Ep.* 78 (*CSEL* 34.2, pp. 334-7): see Trout, 1999, pp. 235-8.

[22] Relevant passages in O'Donnell, 1992, III pp. 112-3.

[23] I owe this suggestion to Dennis Trout.

[24] C. Conybeare (pers.comm.): see further Conybeare, 2000.

[25] Jerome *Ep.* 108.1, to Eustochium, is an interesting comparison: her mother Paula chose Bethlehem in preference to Rome, but wept all her life for the *peregrinatio* of her soul away from God (Psalm 119.5). Paula's journey to Bethlehem is not presented as a pilgrimage.

(1972) has here 'a stranger among the ungodly', and elsewhere 'pilgrim', 'foreign' and 'alien' in a single chapter (19.17). It is quite possible that Augustine, and his implied readers, remained aware of all the resonances of *peregrinus*, especially if he was writing nominally for questioning pagans but in practice for the converted whose language-use included 'pilgrimage'.[26] But in *City of God*, a strongly Ciceronian work, the classical sense of *peregrinus* predominates to the extent that 'pilgrim' is never a necessary translation.[27]

For classically trained readers, *civitas peregrina* is a contradiction in terms: a *civitas* consists of citizens and *peregrini* are precisely those who are not *cives*. But Cicero supplied exactly the paradoxical sense of *peregrinus* that Augustine wanted. In his *Academics* Cicero praised the *Antiquities* of Varro, which supply much material for Books 1-5 of *City of God*.[28] 'We [Romans] were *peregrinantes* in our own city, wandering around like visitors, *hospites*, until your books showed us the way home and allowed us to see who and where we were' (*Acad.* 1.3.9). In his *Tusculans*, Cicero observed 'as for exile, if you consider the fact not the disgrace of the name, how far does it differ from permanent *peregrinatio*?' (5.107). His purpose was to show that exile is no more terrible than *peregrinatio* in its familiar sense of travel away from home; but for Augustine, Cicero converges with Plotinus and the Bible to make *peregrinatio* exile, or at least the rootless residence of strangers and sojourners. Augustine wrote *City of God* in response to the challenge of Romans who were *peregrini* in just the same sense as he had been in Milan (O'Donnell, 1979). As refugees in Carthage from the Gothic sack of Rome, they lived among people who accepted or even welcomed their presence, spoke their language and shared their values; but they wanted their *peregrinatio* to end, and to go home where they belonged.

Augustine recognized that words have multiple meanings and that many interpretations are compatible with truth. In his lifetime, *peregrinatio* was acquiring the meaning of 'pilgrimage', but if we interpret his use of *peregrinatio* as 'pilgrimage' we imply that he saw a different relationship of the church to late antique society. Augustine's point was not that the *civitas peregrina* was a church in transit, travelling hopefully to the heavenly Jerusalem, but that its citizens did not quite belong. They shared language and customs and political status with the citizens of the earthly city, to the point of being indistinguishable. But they knew they were *peregrini*, resident aliens, living away from home.

---

[26] O'Daly, 1999, pp. 36-7. For 'language communities' interpreting words in a special sense, see Augustine, *Christian Teaching*, especially Book 2.

[27] O'Daly, 1999, p. 63 confirms that *peregrinus* in *City of God* almost always means 'alien', but (p. 193) suggests 18.51, *ab ipso Abel ... usque in huius saeculi finem inter persecutiones mundi et consolationes Dei peregrinando procurrit ecclesia*, as an example of 'pilgrimage'.

[28] O'Daly, 1999, pp. 236-40; see further, for Cicero, Testard, 1958.

References

Armstrong, A.H. (1960-88), *Plotinus*, 7 vols, London: Heinemann (Loeb Classical Library).

Brisson, L., (1982 and 1992), ed. *Porphyre: Vie de Plotin*, 2 vols, Paris: Vrin.

Brown, P.R.L. (1967, revised 2000), *Augustine of Hippo*, Faber, London.

Burton, P. (2000), *The Old Latin Gospels*, Oxford University Press, Oxford.

Clark, G. (1999), 'Translate into Greek: Porphyry of Tyre on the new barbarians', in Miles, R. (ed) *Constructing Identities in Late Antiquity*, London: Routledge, pp. 112-32.

—— (2000), *Porphyry: On Abstinence from Killing Animals*, Duckworth, London.

Claussen, M.A. (1991), '*Peregrinatio* and *peregrini* in Augustine's *City of God*', *Traditio*, **46**, pp. 33-75.

Conybeare, C. (2000), *Paulinus Noster: self and symbols in the letters of Paulinus of Nola*, Oxford University Press, Oxford.

Courcelle, P. (1944), 'Quelques symboles funéraires du néo-platonisme latin', *Revue des Etudes Anciennes*, **46**, pp. 65-93.

Edwards, M. (2000), *Neoplatonic Saints: the lives of Plotinus and Proclus by their students*, Liverpool University Press, Liverpool.

Elsner, J. (1997), 'Hagiographic geography: travel and allegory in the *Life of Apollonius of Tyana*', *Journal of Hellenic Studies*, **117**, pp. 22-37.

—— (2000), 'The *Itinerarium Burdigalense*: Politics and Salvation in the geography of Constantine's empire', *Journal of Roman Studies*, **90**, pp. 181-95.

Finamore, J. (1985), *Iamblichus and the theory of the vehicle of the soul*, Scholars Press, Chico.

Hunt, E.D. (1982), *Holy Land Pilgrimage in the Later Roman Empire, AD 312–460*, Clarendon Press, Oxford.

Lamberton, R. (1986), *Homer the Theologian: Neoplatonist allegorical reading and the growth of the epic tradition*, University of California Press, Berkeley.

Markus, R. (1970, rev. 1988), *Saeculum: history and society in the theology of St Augustine*, Cambridge University Press, Cambridge.

Montiglio, S. (2000), 'Wandering philosophers in Classical Greece', *Journal of Hellenic Studies*, **120**, pp. 86-105.

O'Daly, G. (1999), *Augustine's City of God: a reader's guide*, Oxford University Press, Oxford.

O'Donnell, J.J. (1979), 'The inspiration for Augustine's *De Civitate Dei*', *Augustinian Studies*, **10**, pp. 75-9

—— (1992), *Augustine: Confessions*, 3 vols, Oxford University Press, Oxford; also at www.stoa.org.

Perler, O. (1969), *Les voyages de Saint Augustin*, Institut des Etudes Augustiniennes, Paris.

Swain, S. (1996), *Hellenism and Empire*, Oxford University Press, Oxford.

Testard, M. (1958), *St Augustin et Cicéron*, 2 vols, Institut des Etudes Augustiniennes, Paris.

Trout, D. (1999), *Paulinus of Nola: Life, Letters and Poems*, University of California Press, Berkeley.

Translations of Augustine

Bettenson, H. (1972), *St Augustine: City of God*, Penguin Classics, Harmondsworth.

Boulding, M. (1997), *The Confessions: St Augustine*, New York City Press, New York.

Burton, P. (2001), *Augustine: The Confessions*, Everyman, London.

Chadwick, H. (1991), *Saint Augustine: Confessions*, Oxford University Press, Oxford.

Dyson, R. (1998), *Augustine: The City of God against the Pagans*, Cambridge University Press, Cambridge.

Green, R. (1995), *Saint Augustine: On Christian Teaching*, Oxford World's Classics, Oxford University Press, Oxford.

Index of Persons

Index of Geographical Names